The Myth of Separation

What is the correct relationship between Church and State?

An examination of the Supreme Court's own decisions

by
David Barton

WallBuilder Press
P.O. Box 397
Aledo, Texas 76008

Nehemiah 2:17: "You see the distress that we are in...come, let us build the walls that we may no longer be a reproach."

Published by WallBuilder Press
P.O. Box 397
Aledo, Texas 76008

Printed in the United States of America
ISBN 0-925279-04-8

Acknowledgements

While there were many special and hard-working individuals who participated in the formation of this book, some should be individually honored. The first who is worthy of mention is my wife Cheryl, who patiently withstood months of my sixteen and eighteen hour workdays while I was compiling and writing; she generously and consistently offered to me support and encouragement. Second, Kit Marshall spent hours, literally days, in the basement of the law library diligently searching through dusty storage boxes of old Court cases in search of evidence from across the decades that might reveal the position of the Court on religion in government. Third, my parents, Grady and Rose, had a significant impact in this work through the habits and attitudes they instilled within me, both through their instruction and example. There were numerous others involved in typing, running errands, compiling materials, and editing text, etc., without whom this work might have taken years instead of months. A grateful thanks to them all!

There is one other group of individuals worthy of special honor. This group includes men like Steven McDowell of the Providence Foundation, Steve Dawson of the Plymouth Rock Foundation, Dr. Tim LaHaye, and many others who are faithfully presenting to the nation the portions of America's history which have been deliberately censored in recent years.

David Barton

Contents

Preface

This book will examine the doctrine of the separation of church and state. The phrase "separation of church and state" is a phrase well-known by the citizens of the nation. In recent years, studies show that up to two-thirds of the nation believe that this phrase is actually found in the Constitution.

The Courts' use of separation of church and state has enabled it to alter many aspects of the nation's public affairs. Things that had been part of American life for generations are now banned. There is probably no other single phrase used by the Courts that has created as many widespread and revolutionary changes in our culture.

Few know the origin of this phrase, how it was originally applied, nor when it was introduced into contemporary American life. This book will examine the history of the doctrine of the separation of church and state.

In search of the truth about the separation of church and state, this book will offer information and statements from George Washington, John Jay, Alexander Hamilton, Benjamin Franklin, James Madison, Samuel Adams, John Adams, Roger Sherman, John Quincy Adams, Thomas Jefferson, Patrick Henry, and many, many other Founders. In addition, excerpts from Court rulings during the first 160 years under the Constitution will be offered. Many of these decisions were made by Justices who had signed either the Declaration of Independence or the Constitution. These men were experts on the form of government we now have. Their rulings in these cases will show how the legal system originally viewed and applied the doctrine of separation of church and state.

Hundreds of Court cases were researched for this book, cases both from the past and from the present. The majority of the cases examined were from the United States Supreme Court, but also included cases from State Supreme Courts, Federal Courts of Appeal, and State District Courts. Over fifty of those cases have been excerpted in this book which represent a broad and accurate view of the separation of church and state. While not every excerpt is from the Supreme Court, the excerpts used are taken from cases where final decisions had been rendered--cases where a higher Court or the Supreme Court refused to consider or overturn the decision of the lower Court. The quotes given represent the "final word" of the Courts.

The Appendix at the end of this book contains a copy of the words

8

of the Constitution of the United States. The reader is encouraged to read it in its entirety and to refer to it when it is referenced or quoted in this book.

Foreword

We are a truth-conscious nation. Telling the truth is a virtue we impress on our children and a requirement we demand in our courts of law. Truth is so important that oaths are extracted from witnesses, binding them to tell the "truth, the whole truth, and nothing but the truth," even threatening them with criminal penalties for perjury if they do not declare the truth.

There is much to be said in regard to knowing the truth about a subject. Truth has a very liberating effect--it brings a type of freedom. As Jesus once declared to his followers, "You will know the truth, and the truth will set you free" (John 8:32). Despite the popular axiom, ignorance is **not** bliss! Hosea 4:6 says that people are destroyed for a lack of knowledge. Therefore, it is important for us to know the truth about the roots and foundations of this nation. We need to know what our Founders said and taught, and what earlier Courts ruled. This book will help us know our nation's roots.

The prophet Malachi spoke of a "book of remembrance." That "book of remembrance" was important to the people and provided them three benefits. First, as they looked back into former years, they received a better perspective on the present. After looking back, they were then able to return to the present and clearly distinguish between the right and the wrong at a time when the two were often confused and even reversed. Second, because they had read the "book of remembrance" and could now identify the difference between right and wrong, they were motivated to rise up and trample down the wrong. The third result of the "book of remembrance" was that it caused the hearts of the children to be turned toward their fathers.

This book is also a "book of remembrance" and can provide the same three benefits to the people of this nation. First, as people look back into the earlier years of the Supreme Court and the nation, they will understand and recognize the difference between right and wrong in the Courts' conduct at a time when the two have been reversed. What was previously unconstitutional for the Court is now its standard practice; what was previously practiced by the Court is now completely rejected by it. Second, after seeing how right and wrong have been reversed, the people will be able to rise up and trample down the wrong. Lastly, through this "book of remembrance," the hearts of the nation will again be turned back toward their fathers--their Founding Fathers.

10

~1~
The Way It Is

The First Amendment has erected a wall between church and state. That wall must be kept high and impregnable. We could not approve the slightest breach.

This Supreme Court announcement, from the 1947 case *Everson v. Board of Education,* was the first occasion on which the Court declared there to be a separation of church and state in the First Amendment. Since it began ruling by that new 1947 standard, the Court has reversed long-standing national traditions and has unraveled part of the fabric of American life. Notice what the contemporary Courts have now decreed:

☐ A verbal prayer offered in a school is unconstitutional, even if it is both denominationally neutral and voluntarily participated in. *Engel v. Vitale, 1962; Abington v. Schempp, 1963; Commissioner of Ed. v. School Committee of Leyden, 1971*

☐ Freedom of speech and press is guaranteed to students unless the topic is religious, at which time such speech becomes unconstitutional. *Stein v. Oshinsky, 1965; Collins v. Chandler Unified School Dist., 1981*

☐ If a student prays over his lunch, it is unconstitutional for him to pray aloud. *Reed v. van Hoven, 1965*

☐ It is unconstitutional for kindergarten students to say: "We thank you for the flowers so sweet; We thank you for the food we eat; We thank you for the birds that sing; We thank you for everything." Even though the word "God" is not contained in it, someone might think it is a prayer. *DeSpain v. DeKalb County Community School Dist.,1967*

☐ It is unconstitutional for a war memorial to be erected in the shape of a cross. *Lowe v. City of Eugene, 1969*

☐ It is unconstitutional for students to arrive at school early to hear a student volunteer read prayers which had been offered by the chaplains in the chambers of the United States House of Representatives and Senate, even though those prayers are contained in the public *Congressional Record* published by the U.S. government. *State Bd. of Ed. v. Board of Ed. of Netcong, 1970*

☐ It is unconstitutional for a Board of Education to use or refer to the word "God" in any of its official writings. *State v. Whisner, 1976*

☐ It is unconstitutional for a kindergarten class to ask during a school assembly whose birthday is celebrated by Christmas. *Florey v. Sioux Falls School Dist., 1979*

☐ It is unconstitutional for the Ten Commandments to hang on the walls of a classroom since it might lead the students to read them, meditate upon them, respect them, or obey them. *Stone v. Graham, 1980; Ring v. Grand Forks Public School Dist., 1980; Lanner v. Wimmer,1981*

☐ A bill becomes unconstitutional, even though the wording may be constitutionally acceptable, if the legislator who introduced the bill had a religious activity in his mind when he authored it. *Wallace v. Jaffree, 1984*

☐ It is unconstitutional for a kindergarten class to recite: "God is great, God is good, let us thank Him for our food." *Wallace v. Jaffree, 1984.*

☐ It is unconstitutional for a school graduation ceremony to contain an opening or closing prayer. *Graham v. Central Community School Dist., 1985; Disselbrett v. Douglas School Dist., 1986*

Numerous other accounts have arisen as a result of these types of Court rulings:

In the Alaska public schools [in 1987], students were told that they could not use the word "Christmas" in school because it had the word "Christ" in it. They were told that they could not have the word in their notebooks, or exchange Christmas cards or presents, or display anything with the word "Christmas" on it. In Virginia, a federal court has ruled that a homosexual newspaper may be distributed on a high school campus, but religious newspapers may not. 1

Recently public schools were barred from showing a film about the settlement of Jamestown, because the film depicted the erection of a cross at the settlement [despite the truth that] according to historical facts, a cross *was* erected at the Jamestown settlement...2

This year [1987], a 185-year-old symbol of a Nevada city had to be changed because of its "religious significance"... [and] a fire station was forced to remove a cross, a Christian symbol in remembrance of a fellow fireman who lost his life in the line of duty. 3

In December 1988, an elementary school principal in Denver removed the Bible from the school library and an elementary school music teacher in Colorado Springs stopped teaching Christmas carols because of alleged violations of the separation of church and state. 4

In Omaha, Nebraska, 10-year-old James Gierke was prohibited from reading his Bible silently during free time...the boy was forbidden by his teacher to open his Bible at school and was told doing so was against the law. 5

Why were these activities never declared unconstitutional prior to 1947? The Constitution is still the same; yet, somehow, its meaning now appears to be different! This is because the 1947 *Everson* Court used an unprecedented legal maneuver--a maneuver no previous Court had ever dared to make: it took the Fourteenth Amendment as a tool to apply the First Amendment *against* the states. Never before had the Fourteenth Amendment been used to forbid religious practices from the public affairs and public institutions of the individual states. This action by the 1947 Court was without precedent.

The Fourteenth Amendment was ratified in 1868, after the Civil War, to guarantee that recently emancipated slaves would have civil rights in all states.   It is a strange interpretation that takes an Amendment providing citizenship to former slaves and uses it to prohibit religious activity in the schools or public affairs of any state. It is no small wonder that previous Courts had never applied the Fourteenth Amendment as the 1947 Court had done!

In *Walz v. Tax Commission, 1970,* the Court, in reviewing its use of the Fourteenth Amendment, admitted that by using it in such a manner, they had created an American revolution, a revolution that:

...involved the imposition of new and far-reaching constitutional restraints on the States. Nationalization of many civil liberties has been the consequence of the Fourteenth Amendment, reversing the historic position that the foundations of those liberties rested largely in state law. And so the revolution occasioned by the Fourteenth Amendment has progressed as Article after Article in the Bill of Rights has been incorporated in it and made applicable to the States.

The Court has now given titles to the two religious portions of the First Amendment. The first portion, which it says contains the separation of church and state, it calls "The Establishment Clause." The second portion it titles "The Free Exercise Clause." The Court purports the doctrine of separation to be a great American belief, present since the nation's birth. However, in *Walz v. Tax Commission, 1970,* the Court conceded that the separation doctrine is of recent origin, having been introduced into widespread legal use only through the revolution spawned by the Court's unprecedented use of the Fourteenth Amendment:

> ...The Establishment Clause [of the First Amendment] was not incorporated in the Fourteenth Amendment until *Everson v. Board of Education* was decided in 1947...the meaning of the Establishment Clause and the Free Exercise Clause [has been] made applicable to the States for only a few decades at best.

Although the Court announced its doctrine of separation in 1947, it was 15 years before it was applied widely in the Court's decisions, as evidenced by this statement from *Walz v. Tax Commission, 1970:*

> It was, for example, not until 1962 that...prayers were held to violate the Establishment Clause...

That 1962 case *(Engel v. Vitale)* which declared voluntary non-denominational prayer in schools to be unconstitutional, was the first sweeping prohibition ever made by the Court in terms of separating religion from education. Notice this comment on that case from the World Book Encyclopedia's *1963 Yearbook:*

> The significance of the decision regarding this [school] prayer was enormous, for the whole thorny problem of religion in public education was thus inevitably raised.

Even though the doctrine of separation had first been introduced in 1947, it had never been "raised" as an issue affecting education until the 1962 decision! Imagine! Prior to 1962, there had been over 340 years of recorded history in this country concerning schools--175 of those years had occurred under the First Amendment of the Constitution! What schools and students were doing through those years had *never* been ruled unconstitutional!

The First Amendment, which the Court now uses to prohibit religious activities in public, simply states in reference to religion that:

Congress shall make no law respecting the establishment of religion or prohibiting the free exercise thereof...

Neither the phrase "separation of church and state" nor the words "church" or "separation" are contained therein. The public's understanding (actually, misunderstanding) of this Amendment has been molded by the Court's oft-repeated usage of the phrase "separation of church and state."

Only 11 years after their 1947 announcement, the Court had already said so much so often about separation of church and state that it appeared some Justices were already tired of hearing the phrase, as evidenced by this comment in *Baer v. Kolmorgen, 1958:*

Much has been written in recent years concerning Thomas Jefferson's reference in 1802 to "a wall of separation between church and State."...Jefferson's figure of speech has received so much attention that one would almost think at times that it is to be found somewhere in our Constitution.

Were there no controversies over religion before 1947? Is the Court's current use of the separation doctrine finally correcting a constitutional violation that should have been corrected decades earlier? Or did previous Courts rule differently on the same issues?

These questions can be answered by examining Supreme Court records from earlier years and comparing them with current Court decisions. The Framers of the Constitution also had much to say about the proper relationship between church and state. Their writings and statements will be examined as well as numerous Court decisions, some dating from as early as 1795. Using the standards applied by the Constitution's Framers, it can be easily determined if the application of the First Amendment by current Courts is proper.

It is important to know the intent of the Framers concerning the First Amendment. They had specific reasons for doing what they did and doing it the way they did. Only by following the plan upon which our government was founded can we hope to attain the results our Founders intended for us to enjoy.   As President Woodrow Wilson stated:

> A nation which does not remember what it was yesterday, does not know what it is today, nor what it is trying to do. We are trying to do a futile thing if we do not know where we came from or what we have been about. 6

It is significant that the 1947 *Everson* case, which introduced the phrase "separation of church and state," had to do with education. In fact, ten of the twelve case excerpts mentioned at the beginning of this chapter involved education. Education has become so important to the Court that the Court felt it worthwhile to review phrases that five-year-olds recite at school *(Wallace v. Jaffree, 1984).* It is not by accident that education has become the focus of the separation of church and state.   Abraham Lincoln expressed the principle so well understood by the current Court when he declared:

> The philosophy of the school room in one generation will be the philosophy of government in the next. 7

In recent years, numerous cases similar to *Trietley v. Board of Ed., 1978,* and *Brandon v. Board of Ed., 1980,* have occurred. In the *Trietley* case, students were forbidden to form, on their own initiative, Bible clubs of voluntary membership in public high schools. In the *Brandon* case, members of a group called "Students for Voluntary Prayer" were prohibited from arriving early for prayer before the beginning of the school day. From the Courts' rulings in these types of cases, it became obvious that there was no way, form, or fashion in which the Courts were going to allow the second half of the First Amendment's statement on religion (...nor prohibit the free exercise thereof...) to occur in schools or public affairs, no matter how voluntary the activity, how widely supported it was by the community, nor how non-denominational it might be.

Such unilateral and consistent prohibitions by the Court caused public outcries. It was argued that if students *wanted* to participate voluntarily in prayer or Bible reading before school, they should be allowed to do so.   After all, schools permitted Rodeo clubs, Homemaking clubs, Journalism clubs, Athletic clubs, and other types of clubs to meet before and after school--why couldn't students form their own Bible clubs? Observers noted an obvious dichotomy in the Court's decisions:

THE WAY IT IS   17

In many schools, baccalaureate or commencement speakers are free to expound on an endless variety of ideas, but are sometimes barred from speaking about religious subjects. In other schools teachers are free to use occult symbols such as witches and goblins at Halloween, but are prohibited from using Christian symbols at Christmas. Students are taught evolution but are not allowed to hear the evidence for special creation...teachers are free to force unwilling students to read semi-pornographic books but are sometimes prevented from sharing books about Jesus Christ. Taxpayer-funded student newspapers publish all sorts of materials, even if they contain foul language or anti-religious messages, but have been stopped from printing pro-religious material...The religious person has *less* freedom than the secular-minded person to publicly discuss and promulgate ideas that are important to him. 8

Even to casual, disinterested observers, this was obvious religious discrimination by the Court. Following nationwide criticism of such inequities, Congress acted to guarantee to religious groups the same access to school facilities that was extended to others. The result was the passing of the Equal Access Bill of 1984. In an address delivered in December of 1984, President Reagan described the enactment of that bill:

In 1962, the Supreme Court in the New York prayer case banned the...saying of prayers. In 1963, the Court banned the reading of the Bible in our public schools. From that point on, the courts pushed the meaning of the ruling ever outward, so that now our children are not allowed voluntary prayer. We even had to pass a law--pass a special law in the Congress just a few weeks ago--to allow student prayer groups the same access to school rooms after classes that a Young Marxist Society, for example, would already enjoy with no opposition. 9

With the Equal Access Bill thus providing a legitimate legal basis, student groups began to petition their schools for the right to use rooms before or after school. To their surprise, many of their requests were denied, despite the new law. Unable to reach agreements with their schools, several students pursued their desire to pray and have Bible clubs in school through legal challenges based on this new law.

Cases were filed against school districts, requesting the Courts to instruct the schools to allow the access that had been provided through the Equal Access Law. Up through the first part of 1988, a dozen cases had been decided. In an insult to the form of government established by the Constitution, the Courts refused to rule in favor of the students under the new law. The score so far? The Courts--12; students wanting to use a classroom--0.

The Court's rulings under the separation doctrine have even caused a censoring of history and social studies textbooks. Dr. Paul C. Vitz, conducting a study through the Department of Education, scrutinized the nation's most commonly used history and social studies books in all grade levels to see how they had dealt with religious events in history. One would expect there to be no deviation from factual written history. Even the Court, in the first two cases in which the separation doctrine was used to overturn long-standing school policies, had declared:

"...religion has been closely identified with our history and government," *Abington School District, 1963,* and that "[t]he history of man is inseparable from the history of religion." *Engel v. Vitale, 1962.* (quoted from *Stone v. Gramm, 1980*).

With even the Supreme Court acknowledging that American history is inseparable from religion, what did Dr. Vitz discover?

In the first part of the project a total of sixty representative social studies textbooks were carefully evaluated...None of the books...contain one word referring to any religious activity in contemporary American life... 10

...not one of the...ten thousand pages had one text reference to a primary religious activity occurring in representative contemporary American life. 11

An excellent illustration of the censorship of textbooks was provided through Vitz's description of an incident between the author of a short story and the textbook publisher who wanted to reprint it:

The issue centered on a children's story of hers [Barbara Cohen's] called "Molly's Pilgrim."...A major textbook publisher (Harcourt Brace Jovanovich) wanted to reprint part of the story for their third grade reader. But like most such stories, the publishers wanted to shorten it greatly and to rewrite parts to make it more acceptable. They phoned Ms. Cohen and asked for her permission to reprint their modified version. But her story wasn't just modified, it was maimed...So Barbara Cohen refused to give them permission. They called back dismayed and tried to convince her to let them go ahead with the heavily censored version. They argued, "Try to understand. We have a lot of problems. If we mention God, some atheist will object. If we mention the Bible, someone will want to know why we don't give equal time to the Koran. Every time that happens, we lose sales." "But the Pilgrims *did* read the Bible," Barbara Cohen answered. "Yes, you know that and we know that, but we can't have anything in it that people object to," was the reply!...God and the Bible were "eternally unacceptable" and they had to go. The publisher claimed, "We'll get into terrible trouble if we mentioned the Bible." 12

Textbooks form the basis for what students learn about the history of the nation. It is important that texts reflect historically accurate information. The story mentioned above dealt with Pilgrims--the Pilgrims *were* a religious group. The Mayflower Compact that they signed before they landed, and their history recorded in *Of Plymouth Plantation,* both affirm that the Pilgrims maintained a predominantly Christian focus in their activities. These facts about the Pilgrims are history, not religion! There is no reason to exclude this information from textbooks. Dr. Vitz revealed how important textbook content is for students:

It is common in these books to treat Thanksgiving without explaining to whom the Pilgrims gave thanks...the Pilgrims are described *entirely* without any reference to religion; thus at the end of their first year they "wanted to give thanks for all they had" so they had the first Thanksgiving. But no mention is made of the fact that it was God they were thanking...One mother wrote me that her first grade son was told by his teacher that at Thanksgiving the Pilgrims gave thanks to the Indians! When she complained to the principal that Thanksgiving was a feast to thank God...the principal said that "they could only teach what was contained in the history books." 13

While education has obviously been a target of the Supreme Court, other areas have not been exempt. President Reagan made an interesting observation on the repercussions of the widespread application of the separation doctrine to public policy:

The 1962 decision opened the way to a flood of similar suits. Once religion had been made vulnerable, a series of assaults were made in one court after another, on one issue after another. Cases were started to argue against tax-exempt status for churches. Suits were brought to abolish the words "Under God" from the Pledge of Allegiance, and to remove "In God We Trust" from public documents and from our currency...14

Others made similar observations:

...I heard of almost no attacks on churches over religious freedom issues. Gradually that began to change; in the mid '70s a total of eighty-four such intrusions into religious matters were reported. Today, one of the organizations in Washington, D.C. that keeps track of such issues had tabulated 10,000 current cases. 15

The Courts have restructured the traditions and habits that had formed part of American life since our nation's founding by their use of the First Amendment. Has the First Amendment always been understood as it is now? What is its history? When and how was it written, and under what circumstances?

~2~
The Way It Was--
Building the Constitution and
the First Amendment

The First Amendment has become the center of a controversy that focuses on the "separation of church and state," which the Supreme Court says is contained in the Amendment's intent. This controversy has resulted in the recent restructuring of many of the traditions and habits that long formed part of American life. Since this Amendment is at the center of the controversy, it would be good to review its history. When and how was it written, and under what circumstances?

Detailed records answering these questions have been carefully preserved. These accounts, revealing the proceedings surrounding the construction and wording of this Amendment, were officially recorded both by the individuals and by the Congress responsible for its framing.

Before considering the construction of the First Amendment, the process by which the Constitution itself was constructed should be noted. Those who attended the Constitutional Convention in Philadelphia in 1787 comprised a first-class team of statesmen, patriots, and thinkers. Professor Bradford, in his book *A Worthy Company,* provides an insightful mini-biography of each of the participants of the original Constitutional Convention. These biographies detail not only their distinguished political careers, but also the highlights of their private and educational backgrounds. Bradford described the public experience of the collective group with these words:

> ...there was no anomaly in the selection of this particular group to serve as delegates in Philadelphia. Thirty-six of the fifty-five had been members of the Continental Congress. Most of them had been or were to be called upon repeatedly by their neighbors and peers to fill other offices of trust. Twenty were at one time governors of states; twenty were United States Senators. Eight were Federal judges and thirteen were members of the United States House of Representatives. Washington and Madison were President of the United States, and Elbridge Gerry Vice-President. Several served as diplomats in representing the Republic overseas. Others held cabinet posts. Their total political experience at

the state and national level is so great as to suggest that as a company they are a dependable barometer of American attitudes and beliefs at the close of the eighteenth century...[1]

Until the time of the Constitutional Convention, the states had never actually functioned as a nation in the true sense of the word. They had always been individual states. Although joined together in a singular purpose for the War, they had not been required to relinquish any rights as individual states. The states were more like a confederation of several small, independent, neighboring nations on the same continent than a single, unified nation.

The states' first attempts at national government (the Articles of Association, followed by the Articles of Confederation) reflected their lack of commitment to any centralization of power that might divest them of their own rights. The words "association" and "confederation" accurately described their relationship to the central government--a loose-knit voluntary gathering of states under a non-binding agreement.

Each of these forms of government had placed severe limitations on the central government. Decisions were not based on majority votes of the member states--votes had to be unanimous. A single state could block the action of the entire central government. It was difficult for the government to accomplish much, but the restrictions accurately portrayed the strength of the states' resolve about their own rights and sovereignty.

It was against this background that delegates were selected and sent to the Constitutional Convention. As a result of the War, the states recognized the need for a central government to perform functions they individually were not able to perform: for example, national defense. Even though they were still individual states, they had become, by reason of common belief and common geography,. united states (although the emphasis was still more on the "states" than on the "united"). These delegates were intensely committed both to states' rights and to forming a workable national government. The difficulty facing them was to create a form of government to which the states would be committed, but which would not threaten their sovereignty.

There was obviously a sense of the profound as the states contemplated whom they would send to represent them in the effort to form a better national government. The men chosen as delegates were not random selections. There were clearly written laws within each state prescribing the qualifications of those who would serve in public affairs. Every delegate who attended the Constitutional Convention did so in a legal manner--he fulfilled the requirements mandated by his own state's constitution.

These written constitutional qualifications for holding public office were not obscure statements that had been developed decades earlier and were now lost to public awareness. Most of the state constitutions were less than a decade old; in many cases, those who went as delegates to the Convention had participated in the writing of their own state's constitution. Therefore, they were not only cognizant of the stipulations for public office in their states, but in several instances they had helped to formulate them--they were intimately aware of these requirements. What were some of the requirements? Consider those found in the constitution of Delaware:

> Article 22. Every person who shall be chosen a member of either house, or appointed to any office or place of trust...shall...make and subscribe the following declaration, to wit: "I,_____, do profess faith in God the Father, and in Jesus Christ His only Son, and in the Holy Ghost, one God, blessed for evermore; and I do acknowledge the holy scriptures of the Old and New Testament to be given by divine inspiration." 2

These qualifications were not denominational qualifications [i.e., he must be a Baptist, a Lutheran, a Congregationalist, etc.]--they were simply general Christian qualifications, beliefs common to any orthodox Christian denomination. The delegates sent from Delaware to the Constitutional Convention had fulfilled these requirements. Notice the diversity of denominations from which they came: John Dickinson (Quaker/Episcopalian), George Read (Episcopalian), Richard Bassett (Methodist), Gunning Bedford (Presbyterian), and Jacob Broom (Lutheran). 3

The Pennsylvania constitution contained similar requirements:

> Frame of Government, Section 10. ...And each member [of the legislature], before he takes his seat, shall make and subscribe the following declaration, viz: "I do believe in one God, the creator and governor of the universe, the rewarder to the good and the punisher of the wicked. And I do acknowledge the Scriptures of the Old and New Testament to be given by Divine inspiration."

Again, the qualifications included any who embraced the tenets of general Christianity. The Pennsylvania delegates also represented many denominations: Benjamin Franklin (Deist), Robert Morris (Episcopalian), James Wilson (Episcopalian/Deist), Gouverneur Morris (Episcopalian), Thomas Mifflin (Quaker/Lutheran), George Clymer (Quaker/Episcopalian), Thomas FitzSimmons (Roman Catholic), and Jared Ingersoll (Presbyterian). Each of these delegates had fulfilled the state's requirements and was eligible to serve his state at the Convention.

Notice the similar requirements in the Massachusetts constitution:

> Chapter VI, Article I. [All persons elected to State office or to the Legislature must] make and subscribe the following declaration, viz.: "I, _____, do declare, that I believe the Christian religion, and have firm persuasion of its truth..."

And the North Carolina provisions:

> Article XXXII. ...no person who shall deny the being of God or the truth of the Protestant religion or the divine authority either of the Old or New Testaments, or who shall hold religious principles incompatible with the freedom and safety of the State, shall be capable of holding any office or place of trust or profit in the civil department within this State.

And those of Maryland:

> Article XXXV. That no other test or qualification ought to be required...than such oath of support and fidelity to this State...and a declaration of a belief in the Christian religion.

Similar requirements from the other states' constitutions could also be noted. It becomes obvious that the delegates were not selected merely because they were good politicians; they were selected because they were good *Christian* politicians. Considering what was required for service in public office, it would be unreasonable to imagine that these men went to the Constitutional Convention with the design of separating church and state. After all, the delegates had not only voluntarily subscribed themselves to their state's stipulations, many of them had helped write the requirements. This group of statesmen and delegates was far from being religiously inactive:

...with no more than five exceptions (and perhaps no more than three), they were orthodox members of one of the established Christian communions: approximately twenty-nine Anglicans, sixteen to eighteen Calvinists, two Methodists, two Lutherans, two Roman Catholics, one lapsed Quaker and sometime Anglican, and one open Deist--Dr. Franklin, who attended every kind of Christian worship, called for public prayer, and contributed to all denominations. 4

The requirements for public service and the strong Christian commitment of those who attended the Convention were common knowledge to the people of that day, as well as to historians for the next 150 years. It has only been since the middle of this century that history books have ceased to carry any mention of the faith of our Founders. Nonetheless, this was such common knowledge during the Constitutional founding era, that statements like the following from Patrick Henry summarize what was already well known:

It cannot be emphasized too strongly or too often that this great nation was founded, not by religionists, but by Christians, not on religions but on the gospel of Jesus Christ! For this very reason peoples of other faiths have been afforded asylum, prosperity, and freedom of worship here. 5

While the Convention did produce a document that successfully created a new federal government, it ended on a divisive tone. Some prominent delegates refused to sign the new document because they strongly felt that not enough protection had been given to the rights of individuals or states. They feared that unless specific stipulations were placed on what the federal government could *not* do, it might give itself more and more unlimited power and swallow-up the rights of individuals and states.

Those who did sign felt that the power of the states was so obvious that it would be impossible for the federal government to usurp it. They further argued that if they began to list the specific rights retained by the states, they might inadvertently omit some, and thus they would not be protected. Despite this conflict, most of the delegates did sign the Constitution. It was then sent to the states for ratification.

The ratifying process among the states uncovered the same opposition that had been raised at the Convention. Massachusetts, South Carolina, New Hampshire, Virginia, and New York gave conditional approval to the Constitution, stipulating that some type of limitations be added to it to protect the states and citizens from the unlimited power that might someday be assumed by a central government. North Carolina flatly refused to ratify it until some express restrictions were included.

George Washington, in his inaugural address, urged Congress to move quickly to form some type of declaration of the rights of states and individuals to be added to the Constitution. James Madison, at that time a member of the U.S. House of Representatives, submitted nine articles to the Congress that expressed protection for fundamental rights. Madison's articles were passed on to the Committee of Eleven, a select committee in the House that included one member from each of the eleven states. The committee reviewed his nine articles and referred them to the House for full consideration. In the House, additions were made that resulted in seventeen total articles. Those seventeen were passed to the Senate which, after consideration, reduced the number to twelve.

A conference committee of the two houses convened to work out the differences in the two lists. James Madison led the House delegation and Oliver Ellsworth the Senate delegation. This committee agreed on final wording for twelve amendments and returned them to the full Congress for final approval. These twelve were first accepted by the House on September 24, 1789, and then by the Senate on September 25, 1789. They were then submitted to the states for ratification.

Of the twelve proposed Amendments, the states approved only ten. On December 15, 1791, Virginia became the last state to ratify them. These ten articles were added as Amendments to the Constitution and are now known as the Bill of Rights--*a declaration of what the federal government could **not** do!* Thus, Congress had provided for the states the promise of state sovereignty and individual protection in at least ten specific Amendments.

The states had already stipulated that Christians were the ones who would serve in public office, and the federal Constitution had made no change in that. Had it attempted to violate or reverse the provisions of the states' constitutions, it would have been defeated by the delegates or rejected by the states.

The historical records of the drafting of the First Amendment show a strong reliance by the delegates on provisions from their own state constitutions. Notice the various proposals that led to the final House version of the First Amendment:

JUNE 7 [1789]. Initial proposals of James Madison. "The Civil Rights of none shall be abridged on account of religious belief or worship, nor shall any national religion be established, nor shall the full and equal rights of conscience be in any manner, nor on any pretext infringed."

JULY 28. House Select Committee. "No religion shall be established by law, nor shall the equal rights of conscience be infringed."

AUGUST 15. Full day of debate with many alterations and additions, with some question, still, whether any such amendment was necessary. Following the suggestion of his own state's ratifying convention, Samuel Livermore of New Hampshire proposed: "Congress shall make no laws touching religion, or infringing the rights of conscience."

AUGUST 20. Fisher Ames (Massachusetts) moved that the following language be adopted by the House, and it was agreed: "Congress shall make no law establishing religion, or to prevent the free exercise thereof, or to infringe the rights of conscience."

This last version was sent to the Senate, which began its own work on the wording:

SEPTEMBER 3. Several versions proposed in quick succession.

"Congress shall not make any law infringing the rights of conscience, or establishing any religious sect or society."

"Congress shall make no law establishing any particular denomination of religion in preference to another, or prohibiting the free exercise thereof, nor shall the rights of conscience be infringed."

"Congress shall make no law establishing one religious society in preference to others, or to infringe on the rights of conscience."

Passed at the end of the day: "Congress shall make no law establishing religion, or prohibiting the free exercise thereof."

SEPTEMBER 9. "Congress shall make no law establishing articles of faith or a mode of worship, or prohibiting the free exercise of religion."

This version was sent back to the House where a Conference

Committee convened to work out the differences in wording. This committee agreed that the final wording should be:

"Congress shall make no law respecting an establishment of religion, or prohibiting the free exercise thereof."

It was then returned to the full House and Senate, where it was approved as recommended by the Conference Committee. 6

As evident from these records, the word "religion" was used interchangeably with "religious sect," "religious society," and "particular denomination." Today we would best understand the actual context of the First Amendment by saying, "Congress shall make no law establishing one Christian denomination as the national denomination."

Today when the First Amendment is discussed, there seems to be a general consensus that it was something unique and original for the time--a very progressive act by the members of Congress. This was not the case; recall the House records from August 15:

AUGUST 15. Full day of debate with many alterations and additions, with some question, still, whether any such amendment was necessary. *Following the suggestion of his own state's ratifying convention,* Samuel Livermore of New Hampshire proposed: "Congress shall make no laws touching religion, or infringing the rights of conscience."

The members of Congress relied on their own state's wording when composing the First Amendment. The following excerpts from state constitutions not only reveal wording very similar to that proposed and used by Congress, they also reveal the spirit behind the First Amendment:

MASSACHUSETTS, 1780. First Part, Article II. It is the right as well as the duty of all men in society, publicly, and at stated seasons, to worship the Supreme Being, the great Creator and Preserver of the universe. And no subject shall be hurt, molested, or restrained, in his person, liberty, or estate, for worshiping God in the manner and season most agreeable to the dictates of his own conscience.
Article III. *And every denomination of Christians, demeaning themselves peaceably, and as good subjects of the common-*

wealth, shall be equally under the protection of the law; and no subordination of any one sect or denomination to another shall ever be established by law.
NEW HAMPSHIRE, 1784. Part One, Article I, Section 5. Every individual has a natural and unalienable right to worship God according to the dictates of his own conscience, and reason...
Article I, Section 6. *And every denomination of Christians demeaning themselves quietly, and as good subjects of the state, shall be equally under the protection of the laws: and no subordination of any one sect or denomination to another, shall ever be established by law.*
SOUTH CAROLINA, 1778. Article XXXVIII. That all persons and religious societies who acknowledge that there is one God, and a future state of rewards and punishments, and that God is publicly to be worshipped, shall be freely tolerated. *That all denominations of Christians...in this State, demeaning themselves peaceably and faithfully, shall enjoy equal religious and civil privileges...*

There are similar provisions in the other state constitutions, but these are sufficient to show the primary intent of the First Amendment. The states themselves did not allow one denomination of Christianity to be the official denomination; it is certain they would not allow the federal government to do something they prohibited.

The intent of the First Amendment was not to separate Christianity and state--had that been the intent, it would never have been ratified. Even when the state constitutions stated that their citizens had a right to worship God according to their conscience, a statement immediately followed stipulating that it be within Christian standards. In other words, as long as someone was pursuing some form of orthodox Christianity, he was protected in his freedom of worship and conscience. The constitutions did not guarantee that freedom outside of traditional Christianity.

In today's application of the First Amendment, the Court states that since the First Amendment declares "Congress shall make no law respecting an establishment of religion..." that any group maintaining any type of religious belief, whether Christian or non-Christian, is protected under the First Amendment. Even atheism and secular humanism have been declared religions by the Court, and are therefore entitled (so says the Court), to the protection of the First Amendment. But how can atheism be a religion? According to the Court, the religious practice of atheists is the practice of *no* religious practice. That is, atheists religiously believe that there is no God and no religious duty; therefore, since they "religiously" believe these things, they are a "religion" and are entitled to constitutional protection. The legal usage of the word "religion" has now become so broad that the Court demands that atheism and secular humanism be co-equal with Christianity.

Such an interpretation defies the spirit and intent underlying the First Amendment. Additional evidence that the First Amendment did not provide protection to atheism or secular humanism is provided by the meaning of the word "religion." The original Webster's 1828 dictionary provides an insight into the meaning of the word as used in the First Amendment:

> RELIGION. Includes a belief in the being and perfections of God, in the revelation of his will to man, and in man's obligation to obey his commands, in a state of reward and punishment, and in man's accountableness to God; and also true godliness or piety of life, with the practice of all moral duties...the practice of moral duties without a belief in a divine lawgiver, and without reference to his will or commands, is not religion. [7]

This is the definition of religion that was commonly understood and used during the time the Constitution was being written. Notice the requirements to be a religion and to receive the protection of the First Amendment:

(1) Belief in the being and perfections of God;
(2) Belief in His revealed will to man;
(3) Belief in man's obligation to obey God's commands;
(4) Belief in accountability to God, with rewards and punishments;
(5) Belief in godliness, piety of life, and practice of moral duties.

Whatever is not a religion is not protected:

> The practice of moral duties without a belief in a divine lawgiver and without reference to his will or his commands *is not religion.*

Neither atheism, secular humanism, nor other groups who have been granted the status of "religion" by the Courts qualify for protection under the First Amendment. Further reinforcement that this was the common application of the word comes from Congressional investigations that occurred in the mid-1850's:

In the Senate of the United States, January 19, 1853, Mr. Badger made the following report:--
The [First Amendment] clause speaks of "an establishment of religion." What is meant by that expression? It referred, without doubt, to that establishment which existed in the mother-country...endowment at the public expense, peculiar privileges to its members, or disadvantages or penalties upon those who should reject its doctrines or belong to other communions,--such law would be a "law respecting an establishment of religion"...They intended, by this amendment, to prohibit "an establishment of religion: such as the English Church presented, or any thing like it. But they had no fear or jealousy of religion itself, nor did they wish to see us an irreligious people...they did not intend to spread over all the public authorities and the whole public action of the nation the dead and revolting spectacle of atheistic apathy. Not so had the battles of the Revolution been fought and the deliberations of the Revolutionary Congress been conducted.

March 27, 1854. Mr. Meacham, from the [House] Committee on the Judiciary, made the following report:
...What is an establishment of religion? It must have a creed, defining what a man must believe; it must have rites and ordinances, which believers must observe; it must have ministers of defined qualifications, to teach the doctrines and administer the rites; it must have tests for the submissive and penalties for the non-conformist. There never was an established religion without all these.
...Had the people during the Revolution had a suspicion of any attempt to war against Christianity, that Revolution would have been strangled in its cradle. At the time of the adoption of the Constitution and the amendments, the universal sentiment was that Christianity should be encouraged, not any one sect [denomination]. Any attempt to level and discard all religion would have been viewed with universal indignation. 8

32   THE MYTH OF SEPARATION

The Founders understood that allowing and encouraging religious practice was not the same as establishing a religion. Because a man prayed, or an individual read the Scriptures, that did not establish a religion. An establishment of religion required the ingredients delineated in the reports: a defined creed, ordinances which believers must observe, official ministers to teach these doctrines, and penalties for those who do not conform. As the report said, "there never was an established religion without all these."

Yet today, the Court has ruled that allowing voluntary prayer establishes a national religion; allowing a manger scene to be viewed at Christmas establishes a national religion; allowing students to pray aloud over their lunch establishes a national religion; permitting them to read the Ten Commandments establishes a national religion; etc. This viewpoint holds that religious exercise is equal to establishing a national religion, and thus is used to prevent any form of Christian activity.

This stand is exactly opposite to those taken by the first Supreme Court Justices, many of whom were members of the Constitutional Convention and of the state ratifying conventions.   The following comments are from Justice Joseph Story, appointed by James Madison (which is probably an ample endorsement of Story's Constitutional understanding):

...We are not to attribute this prohibition of a national religious establishment to an indifference to religion in general, and especially to Christianity which none could hold in more reverence than the framers of the Constitution...Probably at the time of the adoption of the Constitution and of the Amendments to it, the general, if not universal, sentiment in America was that Christianity ought to receive encouragement from the State...An attempt to level all religions, and to make it a matter of state policy to hold all in utter indifference, would have created universal disapprobation, if not universal indignation. 9

Similar comments from several more Supreme Court Justices appointed by George Washington, John Adams, James Madison, etc., are presented in Chapter 4.

Another interesting comment on the widespread support of general Christianity in America's politics comes from Alexis de Tocqueville, a French historian who traveled extensively in America:

For Americans, the ideas of Christianity and liberty are so completely mingled that it is almost impossible to get them to conceive of the one without the other...[10] In the United States, if a politician attacks a sect [denomination], that is no reason why the supporters of that very sect should not support him; but if he attacks all sects together [Christianity], everyone shuns him, and he remains alone. [11]

The consensus of recorded history requires that the Constitution and the First Amendment be interpreted within the understanding of Christianity. However, Article VI of the Constitution states:

...no religious test shall ever be required as a qualification to any office or public trust under the United States.

Does Christianity then become a religious test of the type prohibited by Article VI of the Constitution? Our current understanding of what constitutes a religious test was considerably different from that of early Americans, as demonstrated by this excerpt from the 1796 Tennessee constitution:

Article VIII, Section 2. No person who denies the being of God, or a future state of rewards and punishments, shall hold any office in the civil department of this State.
Article XI, Section 4. That no religious test shall ever be required as a qualification to any office or public trust under this State.

A fixed set of religious beliefs for an office holder is prescribed in Article VIII, and then a religious test is prohibited in Article XI. Obviously, in their view, requiring a belief in God and in future rewards and punishments to hold office was *not* a religious test.
Currently, a religious test is perceived as something as simple as "Are you a Christian or an atheist?" This was not the question for our Founders. As a matter of fact, prescribing a requirement professing "I,_____, do profess faith in God the Father, and in Jesus Christ His only Son, and in the Holy Ghost, one God, blessed for evermore; and I do acknowledge the holy scriptures of the Old and New Testament to be given by divine inspiration [DELAWARE, 1776]" was not considered a religious test; it was merely a qualification for office--a civil requirement. An unacceptable religious test to our Founders would be what we would now call a denominational

test: "You must be an Anglican (Baptist, Presbyterian, Methodist, etc.) to hold office." A religious test did not pertain to the general Christian beliefs, but only to specific denominational requirements. The fact that espousing general Christianity was not considered an unconstitutional religious test is further illustrated by provisions from other state constitutions:

MARYLAND, 1776. Article XXXV. That no other test or qualification ought to be required...than such oath of support and fidelity to this State...and a declaration of a belief in the Christian religion.

VERMONT, 1786. Frame of Government, Section 9. ...And each member [of the legislature], before he takes his seat, shall make and subscribe the following declaration, viz: "I do believe in one God, the Creator and Governor of the universe, the rewarder of the good and punisher of the wicked. And I do acknowledge the scriptures of the old and new testament to be given by divine inspiration, and own and profess the [Christian] religion."

And no further or other religious test shall ever, hereafter, be required of any civil officer or magistrate in this State.

Every individual was protected in his right to worship God according to his own conscience unless his mode of worship directly threatened the state, led to licentiousness, or caused physical injury to another. However, despite the fact that there was religious tolerance for individual citizens, there was a minimum belief that a *political* candidate must hold. The Founders were well aware that there were atheists and agnostics in that day; but they, or any individual with unorthodox Christian beliefs (relating to the inspiration of the Old and New Testaments, future rewards and punishments, and the acknowledgement of the Being of God) could *not* hold office in government. This exclusion was allowable and completely constitutional as evidenced by the fact that *it was part of their constitution.*

That the religious tests to which the constitutions referred were actually denominational tests is reflected in the manner in which Founders like William Penn guided his state's government. This description of Penn appeared in the *Biographical Review* in London in 1819:

...it was his wish that every man who believed in God should partake of the rights of a citizen; and that every man who adored Him as a Christian, of whatever sect he might be, should be a partaker in authority...[12]

While rights for citizens were broad, the right of public service and public exercise of authority was extended only to those who were Christians. The denomination was irrelevant, only that he be a Christian. An incident involving Roger Sherman is another example indicating that our Founders expected Christians to be the ones holding public office. Sherman has a unique and distinguished position among the Founding Fathers. He is the only one who signed the nation's four major founding documents: the Articles of Association in 1774, the Declaration of Independence in 1776, the Articles of Confederation in 1777, and the Constitution in 1787. With his intimate knowledge of our government, what was his view of Christians in government?

...when serving on a congressional committee which wrote instructions for an embassy going to Canada, Sherman included an order that the delegation was "further to declare that we hold sacred the rights of conscience, and may promise to the whole people, solemnly in our name, the free and undisturbed exercise of their religion," but added that...*the right to hold office [was] to be extended to persons of any Christian denomination.* [13]

Another Founder with extensive knowledge of the Constitution was John Jay. Jay had campaigned long and hard in behalf of the Constitution. It was he who, along with James Madison and Alexander Hamilton, authored *The Federalist Papers.* He was probably one of the three men most responsible for the ratification of the Constitution and was selected by George Washington as the first Chief Justice of the Supreme Court. With his Constitutional expertise, what did he say about Christians in office?

Providence has given to our people the choice of their rulers, and it is the duty, as well as the privilege and interest, of a Christian nation to select and prefer Christians for their rulers. [14]

That this was the practice of the nation under the Constitution is underscored in the events surrounding the nation's second Presidential race between John Adams and Thomas Jefferson. The entire

focus of the race was on whether Jefferson was actually a Christian--
if he was not, he would not hold office.

Jefferson was strongly attacked for his religious beliefs when
he ran for President against John Adams in 1800. One of
the most powerful attacks came from Rev. William Linn, a
Dutch Reformed minister in New York City. In the pamphlet
Serious Considerations on the Election of a President, Linn
asked, "Does Jefferson ever go to church? How does he
spend the Lord's day? Is he known to worship with any
denomination of Christians?" Linn continued: "Let the first
magistrate to be a professed infidel, and infidels will
surround him. Let him spend the sabbath...never in going to
church; and to frequent public worship will become unfash-
ionable...universal dissoluteness will follow...

"Will you then, my fellow-citizens, with all this evidence...
vote for Mr. Jefferson?...As to myself, were Mr. Jefferson
connected with me by the nearest ties of blood, and did I owe
him a thousand obligations, I would not, and could not vote
for him. No; sooner than stretch forth my hand to place him
at the head of the nation 'Let mine arms fall from my shoulder
blade, and mine arm be broken from the bone.'"

John Adams, Jefferson's opponent, was much more
orthodox in his Christian faith; Adam's wife, Abigail, joined
the attack, charging that Jefferson was a deist: "Can the
placing at the head of the nation two characters known to be
Deists be productive of order, peace, and happiness?"

But supporters came to Jefferson's defense. Tunis
Wortman wrote the pamphlet *A Solemn Address to the Christians and Patriots upon the Approaching Election of a President of the United States,* in which he declared, "That the
charge of deism...is false, scandalous and malicious--That
there is not a single passage in the *Notes on Virginia,* or any
of Mr. Jefferson's writings, repugnant to Christianity; but on
the contrary, in every respect, favourable to it." Dewitt
Clinton also defended Jefferson by declaring, "we have the
strongest reasons to believe that he is a real Christian."
Clinton said, "I feel persuaded that he is a believer" and "I
feel happy to hail him a Christian." He continued with: "And
let me add...that he has for a long time supported out of his
own private revenues, a worthy minister of the Christian
church--an instance of liberality not to be met with in any of

his rancorous enemies; whose love of religion seems princi-
pally to consist in their unremitted endeavors to degrade it
into a handmaid of faction."
    Two issues pinpointed in the debate deserve special
mention. First, no one questioned the propriety of inquiry
into a presidential candidate's religious beliefs. Second...the
question was whether Jefferson was a deist or a Christian. 15

    A strong declaration that the First Amendment was never intended
to separate Christianity from public affairs came in the form of legislation passed in Congress on the same day that Congress approved
the First Amendment. The legislation, entitled "An Ordinance for the
Government of the Territory of the United States, North-West of the
River Ohio," later shortened to the "Northwest Ordinance," dealt with
the structure of government for the territories. The Constitution of
the United States was already in effect for those states that were part
of the nation. But what of those areas which had not yet become
states? There were literally thousands of Americans in the wilderness and the western territories across the Ohio River; what was to
be their form of government?
    The Northwest Ordinance not only provided frameworks for the
government of these territories (the Congress understandably had
relied heavily on portions of the Constitution in constructing their
requirements for territorial government), it also included the process
for attaining statehood. Article III of the Ordinance addressed the
importance of religion to the territories. To make an interesting
emphasis concerning the thinking of the Congress, one portion of
Article III will be intentionally omitted; consider which word or phrase
the Founders would have used to fill that blank:

    Article III: "Religion, morality, and knowledge being neces-
    sary to good government and the happiness of mankind,
    _____shall forever be encouraged.

    If religion and morality are "necessary to good government and to
the happiness of mankind" and "shall forever be encouraged," what
means would they utilize to encourage religion and morality? What
would be the best and most effective institution for promoting religion
and morality? A clear majority today would emphatically respond:
"The Church!" Such a response indicates the degree to which our
thinking has been distorted by the doctrine of the separation of

church and state.   Notice what our Founders felt should promote religion, morality, and knowledge:

Article III: Religion, morality, and knowledge being necessary to good government and the happiness of mankind, *schools and the means of education* shall forever be encouraged.

The Framers felt schools and educational systems were the proper means to encourage "religion, morality, and knowledge." This was approved by Congress the *same day* that it approved the wording of the First Amendment.   Since both were approved on the same day, it is evident that our Founders did not believe that establishing a frame of government *mandating* that religion, morality, and knowledge be provided through schools was a violation of the First Amendment prohibition on the establishment of religion.

That piece of legislation was not an obscure act in America's history.   In the *United States Code Annotated,* under the heading "The Organic Laws of the United States of America" our most significant governmental instruments are listed: the Articles of Confederation, the Declaration of Independence, the Constitution, and the Northwest Ordinance.   What can be concluded from the records surrounding the Constitutional Convention and the framing of the First Amendment?

The concept of a secular state was virtually non-existent in 1776 as well as in 1787, when the Constitution was written, and no less so when the Bill of Rights was adopted.   To read the Constitution as the charter for a secular state is to misread history, and to misread it radically.   The Constitution was designed to perpetuate a Christian order. [16]

In recent years, those advocating separation of church and state have argued that when the Constitution and First Amendment were ratified, they superseded and invalidated state constitutions and their religious stipulations.   In review, there are three grounds that disprove such an assertion.

First, the records of the Constitutional Convention show that the First Amendment was modeled after many of the states' own provisions regarding "establishment of religion."   From the delegates reliance on their states' documents, it is apparent that they were not attempting to repudiate them.

Second, the Constitutional Convention convened with proponents of, not opponents to, states' sovereignty. The concept of a new national constitution was not only novel, and thus tenuous, it was handled with great deference to the fears and concerns of the states. In order to gain the states' approval, a Bill of Rights, limiting the powers of the federal government and assuring the states that their own power would not be usurped, was added to the Constitution. Had the states perceived an attempt to overthrow or undermine what were already established as fundamental principles of their own self-government, the new Constitution would have had no hope of ratification by the states. The states perceived it as no threat to their own constitutions.

Third, the Constitutional delegates had voluntarily subscribed themselves to the requirements of their own state's constitution regarding public service. These men had with their own lips confessed their belief in God, His Son, Jesus, the Holy Spirit, the Divine inspiration of the Old and New Testaments, and that there existed future rewards and punishments. They would have had to deny their own personal affirmations to allow the First Amendment to reverse the practice common throughout the states.

In order for those delegates to have achieved what the Supreme Court claims requires fantastic imagination, illogical conclusions, and a rejection of the documents existing from the time of the Constitutional Convention. Can our Courts and politicians actually claim that we have a better understanding now of its intent than those who framed it, ratified it, and applied it in their governmental and judicial decisions? We are two centuries removed from its framing. Logic demands that if there is a conflict between the way the First Amendment is now applied and the manner in which our Founders applied it, the current application is the one in error.

The phrase "separation of church and state" is an over-used, misused, and abused phrase. It is a judicial and bureaucratic buzzword now familiar to virtually the entire nation. Everyone knows it, yet few know its history. What is its history? Where did the phrase originate? How has it, in opposition to historical records, become the overriding judicial philosophy of this nation?

~3~

The Origin of the Phrase
"Separation of Church and State"

Most people are surprised when they find that the Constitution does not contain the words "separation of church and state." The common perception is that those words are the heart of the First Amendment and are included in it. Since that phrase does not appear in our Constitution, what is its origin?

At the time of the Constitution, although the states encouraged Christianity, no state allowed an exclusive state-sponsored denomination. However, many citizens did recall accounts from earlier years when one denomination ruled over and oppressed all others. Even though those past abuses were not current history in 1802, the fear of a recurrence still lingered in some minds.

It was in this context that the Danbury Baptist Association wrote to President Jefferson. Although the statesmen and patriots who framed the Constitution had made it clear that no one Christian denomination would become the official denomination, the Danbury Baptists expressed their concern over a rumor that a particular denomination was soon to be recognized as the national denomination. On January 1, 1802, President Jefferson spoke to a gathering of the Danbury Baptists at Danbury, Connecticut. In his remarks to that group, Jefferson addressed their fears, using the now infamous phrase to assure them that the federal government would not establish them, nor any other denomination of Christianity, as the national denomination:

...I contemplate with solemn reverence that act of the whole American people which declared that their legislature should "make no law respecting an establishment of religion, or prohibiting the free exercise thereof," thus building a wall of separation between Church and State.

This phrase was not recorded in the discussions of the Constitutional Convention nor in the records of the subsequent Congress that produced the Bill of Rights--so why did Jefferson select this particular phrase to reassure them?

Recall that he was addressing a group of Baptists, a denomination of which he was not a member. In speaking to them, he sought to establish the common ground necessary between a speaker and the

group he is addressing. By using the phrase "a wall of separation,"
he was actually borrowing the words of one of the Baptist's own
prominent ministers: Roger Williams. Williams' words had been:

> "...when they have opened a gap in the hedge or wall of separation between the garden of the church and the wilderness of the world, God hath ever broke down the wall itself...And that therefore if He will eer please to restore His garden and paradise again, it must of necessity be walled in peculiarly unto Himself from the world..." According to Williams, the "wall of separation" was to protect the "garden of the church" from the "wilderness of the world." Today the metaphor has been stood on its head, and the wall is thought to protect the state from the church. 1

That "wall" was originally introduced as, and understood to be, a
one-directional wall protecting the church from the government. This
was also Jefferson's understanding, as conveyed through statements
he made concerning the First Amendment--statements now ignored
by the Court:

> *Kentucky Resolutions of 1798:* No power over the freedom of religion (is) delegated to the United States by the Constitution...
> *Second Inaugural Address, 1805:* "In matters of religion I have considered that its free exercise is placed by the Constitution independent of the powers of the General (i.e. national) Government."
> *Letter to Samuel Miller, 1808:* "I consider the government of the United States as interdicted [prohibited] by the Constitution from intermeddling with religious institutions, their doctrines, discipline, or exercises. This results not only from the provision that no law shall be made respecting an establishment or free exercise of religion, but from that also which reserves to the states the powers not delegated to the general government (10th Amendment). It must then rest with the states as far as it can be in any human authority..." 2

Such power no longer rests with the states. In 1947, in *Everson v.
Board of Education,* the Court reversed 150 years of established
legal practice under the Constitution and decided that it *did* have the
right to rule on an individual state's decisions regarding religious

practice. Prior to that reversal, the Courts had left the decisions as Jefferson and all other Founders had planned it--"rest[ing] with the states..." State legislatures had been passing laws since the 1600's allowing the free exercise of religious practices in schools and public affairs: voluntary prayer, Bible reading, the use of the Ten Commandments, etc. These laws had been enacted "with the consent of the governed" and through representatives elected "of the people, by the people, and for the people."

Jefferson's words of assurance to the Danbury Baptist Association were soon forgotten since the rumor never became fact. Jefferson's speech remained in obscurity, as is usual with most presidential addresses delivered to specific audiences, until 76 years later, when it appeared in the 1878 case of *Reynolds v. United States.* In that case, a lengthy excerpt from Jefferson's speech was used, and its context clearly presented. In that case, the Court did *not* use Jefferson's speech to attempt to separate church and state, but used it in an opposite manner.

This opportunity for the Court to use Jefferson's speech arose in an 1878 case in which the Mormons claimed the First Amendment's "free exercise of religion" promise and the "separation of church and state" principle should keep the United States government from making laws prohibiting their "religious" exercise of polygamy. Using Jefferson's address, the Court showed that while the government was not free to interfere with opinions on religion, which is what frequently distinguishes denominations from one another, it was still responsible to enforce civil laws according to Christian standards. In other words, separation of church and state pertained to denominations, not to Christian principles. Therefore, and on that basis, the Court ruled that the Mormon practice of polygamy and bigamy was a violation of the Constitution because it was a violation of basic Christian principles.

Nearly 70 years after the *Reynolds* case, in the 1947 *Everson* case, the Court excerpted eight words out of Jefferson's address but did not bother to present the context in which the phrase had originally been used, nor reveal that it had been applied in an opposite manner in the 1878 case. The Court simply found eight words ("a wall of separation between church and state") that it adopted as its battle cry. It announced for the first time the *new* meaning of separation of church and state. Those eight words, when used out of context, concisely articulated the Court's plan to divorce Christianity from public affairs.

After the Court adopted the portion of Jefferson's words with which it agreed and ignored the remainder, it began declaring state laws unconstitutional. It struck down voluntary prayer laws in Maryland, Pennsylvania, Florida, Alabama, New Jersey, and a host of other states. Statutes allowing religious practice in public affairs were overturned in nearly every state in the Union. Laws no longer were being enacted or removed by the people through their elected representatives; it was now occurring through unelected Justices. If as few as five Justices agreed (the majority of the Court), they could overturn the people's will that had been expressed through Constitutionally correct legislative means.

There is probably no other instance in America's history where words spoken by an individual have become the law of the land. Jefferson's remark now carries more weight in judicial circles than does the writing of any other Founder. That Jefferson's speech to the Danbury Baptists should become a national legal policy is absurd when considering:

> Jefferson made the statement in 1802, thirteen years after Congress passed the First Amendment. Jefferson was not a delegate to the 1787 Constitutional Convention, nor was he a member of Congress in 1789 [which framed the First Amendment], nor was he a member of any state legislature or ratifying convention at any time relevant to the passage of the First Amendment; he was serving as U.S. Minister to France throughout this time. [3]

Doesn't it seem unreasonable that the Justices had to bypass all the other Founding Fathers in order to find some words with which they could agree? And even then, they selected someone who was *not* a part of the Constitutional proceedings or even in the nation at the time. And on top of that, they used his words in a manner he never would have approved!

George Washington had much to say about the relationship of Christianity to schools and government. He was President of the Convention that formed the Constitution and then President of the United States when the First Amendment was created and ratified. Why doesn't the Court quote him? Amazingly, the Court seems to have lost the records on George Washington, as well as those on John Adams, Patrick Henry, Samuel Adams, John Jay, and a host of other Founders (Don't worry--we found them and will present them in Chapter 5!). The simple explanation is that the Justices have found in Jefferson's eight words what they want the First Amendment to say, not what our Founders framed it to say, and not even what Jefferson understood it to say.

There is no "wall of separation" in the Constitution, unless it is a wall intended by the Founding Fathers to keep the government out of the church. Jefferson's words have been twisted to mean just the opposite: now the state must be "protected" from the church!

If the American people have ever adopted the principle of complete separation of church and state, we would find the evidence of it in the federal Constitution, in the acts of Congress, or in the constitutions or laws of the several states. There is no such evidence in existence. In its absence, the mere opinion of private individuals or groups that there should be absolute separation of church and state...does not constitute "a great American principle." [4]

As a note of interest, while the phrase "separation of church and state" is not found in the United States Constitution, it is found in another prominent document--The Constitution of the Soviet Union:

Article 124:   In order to ensure to citizens freedom of conscience, the church in the U.S.S.R. is separated from the State, and the school from the church. [5]

It seems that, because of the current Court's rulings, we have more similarities with the Soviet Union than we might have thought; although they seem to have more religious practice in schools under their Constitution than we do under ours:

Who would have believed that the Supreme Court in 1980 would uphold the decision of a Kentucky school board (in *Stone v. Gramm*) that the Ten Commandments, the basis of English law and the most important code of laws ever written, were illegal to display on the walls of the public schools because they represented a religious symbol? Ironically, just a few weeks before the court's decision, some Polish high school students had demonstrated openly against their country's communist authorities for ordering the removal of the Catholic crucifix that still adorned the walls of their public schools--and the government backed down.

Americans cheered the courage of those young people for speaking out against their repressive government. Yet when our atheistically dominated Supreme Court removed the Ten Commandments from our halls, not a whimper was heard...6

William James is considered by many to be the father of modern psychology. He was a strong advocate and early pioneer of the "separation" doctrine. Perhaps a statement credited to him reveals the reason that Jefferson's misapplied phrase has had so much impact on the nation's public policy:

There is nothing so absurd but if you repeat it often enough people will believe it.

The doctrine of separation of church and state is absurd, it has been repeated often, and people have believed it. It is amazing what continually hearing about separation of church and state can do to a nation!

~4~
The Court's Early Rulings--
We Are A _Christian_ Nation

In recent years, the Courts have often declared a need to under-stand the intent of the First Amendment before pronouncing a ruling on a pending case. The legal profession struggles and wrestles with intent because it is now more than two centuries removed from the minds of the Framers.

Is there anything to document the intent of the Founders? It would be logical that any rulings made by the Court in the years immedi-ately following the framing of the Constitution would accurately reflect the Founders' intent. Are there any early accounts available?

Fortunately, there are many legal records from early years. This chapter will examine several of those rulings, some dating back to 1795. In many of these cases, Justices on the Court had personally participated in drafting and ratifying the Constitution. When they ruled on a case, they did not have to struggle with intent--they knew it from first hand experience!

Over the past three decades, the Court has implied in its rulings that the Founders were vehemently opposed _en mass_ to involving Christian principles in schools and government. If that is true, it will be reflected in the rulings of the early Courts--their early decisions and commentaries will verify whether there is any validity to the doctrine of separation of church and state as now enforced by the Court.

Excerpts from fifteen of those cases will be presented. These fifteen, representing hundreds of similar cases, illustrate the spirit and conclusions that pervade them all. This chapter will establish, by records of Court cases, that our Founders would **never** have tolerated the separation of church and state as it now exists. Not even in a nightmare could they have envisioned what the Court is now doing with the First Amendment!

Holy Trinity Church v. United States, 1892

This case provides a good starting point, for it cites several of the earlier cases. This case centered on an 1885 law enacted by the Congress concerning the subject of immigration. The law declared:

> ...it shall be unlawful for any person, company, partnership, or corporation, in any manner whatsoever...to in any way assist

or encourage the importation...of any alien or...foreigners, into the United States...under contract or agreement...to perform labor or service of any kind...

In 1887, the Church of the Holy Trinity in New York employed a clergyman from England as its pastor. That employment was challenged by the United States Attorney General's office as a violation of the law. The case eventually reached the Supreme Court. The first half of the Court's decision dealt with what it termed "absurd" application of laws. The Court was not saying that the legislation was absurd, for in the early years the Court rarely criticized the legislature. "Absurd" referred to cases where an interpretation by the letter of the law and not by the spirit and intent of its framers would lead to absurd results.

The Court examined the Congressional records of the hearings surrounding this legislation and established, from the legislators' own testimony, that the law was enacted solely to preclude an influx of cheap and unskilled labor for work on the railroads. Although the church's alleged violation was certainly within the letter of the law, it was not within its spirit. The Court concluded that only an "absurd" application of the Constitution would allow a restriction on Christianity:

...no purpose of action against religion can be imputed to any legislation, state or national, because this is a religious people...this is a Christian nation.

The Court resolved the legal question within the first half of its written ruling on the case and devoted the remainder to establishing that this nation is indeed Christian and why it would be constitutionally "absurd" and legally impossible to legislate any restrictions on Christianity. Despite the Court's use of only brief historical quotations, its references composed eight of the sixteen pages in the decision. Justice Brewer, who delivered the opinion of the Court, gave the basis for the Court's conclusion:

...this is a religious people. This is historically true. From the discovery of this continent to the present hour, there is a single voice making this affirmation. The commission to Christopher Columbus...recited that "it is hoped that by God's assistance some of the continents and islands in the ocean will be discovered..." The first colonial grant made to Sir Walter Raleigh in 1584...and the grant authorizing him to enact statutes for the government of the proposed colony provided that "they be not against the true Christian faith..." The first charter of Virginia, granted by King James I in 1606 ...commenced the grant in these words: "...in propagating of Christian religion to such people as yet live in darkness..."

Language of similar import may be found in the subsequent charters of that colony...in 1609 and 1611; and the same is true of the various charters granted to the other colonies. In language more or less emphatic is the establishment of the Christian religion declared to be one of the purposes of the grant. The celebrated compact made by the Pilgrims in the Mayflower, 1620, recites: "Having undertaken for the glory of God, and advancement of the Christian faith ...a voyage to plant the first colony in the northern parts of Virginia..."

The fundamental orders of Connecticut, under which a provisional government was instituted in 1638-39, commence with this declaration: "...And well knowing where a people are gathered together the word of God requires that to maintain the peace and union...there should be an orderly and decent government established according to God...to maintain and preserve the liberty and purity of the gospel of our Lord Jesus which we now profess...of the said gospel [which] is now practiced amongst us."

In the charter of privileges granted by William Penn to the province of Pennsylvania, in 1701, it is recited: "...no people can be truly happy, though under the greatest enjoyment of civil liberties, if abridged of...their religious profession and worship..."

Coming nearer to the present time, the Declaration of Independence recognizes the presence of the Divine in human affairs in these words: "We hold these truths to be self-evident, that all men are created equal, that they are endowed by their Creator with certain unalienable Rights..."; "...appealing to the Supreme Judge of the world for the rectitude of our intentions..."; "And for the support of this Declaration, with a firm reliance on the Protection of Divine Providence, we mutually pledge to each other our Lives, our Fortunes, and our sacred Honor."

The Court continued with example after example, citing portions from the forty-four state constitutions (the number of states in 1892), using many of the same excerpts given in this book in earlier chapters. The Court's historical discourse continued for several pages until finally summarizing its findings:

> There is no dissonance in these declarations. There is a universal language pervading them all, having one meaning; they affirm and reaffirm that this is a religious nation. These are not individual sayings, declarations of private persons: they are organic utterances; they speak the voice of the entire people. While because of a general recognition of this truth the question has seldom been presented to the Courts, yet we find that in *Updegraph v. The Commonwealth,* it was decided that, "Christianity, general Christianity, is, and always has been, a part of the common law...not Christianity with an established church...but Christianity with liberty of conscience to all men." And in *The People v. Ruggles,* Chancellor Kent, the great commentator on American law, speaking as Chief Justice of the Supreme Court of New York, said: "The people of this State, in common with the people of this country, profess the general doctrines of Christianity, as the rule of their faith and practice...we are a Christian people, and the morality of the country is deeply engrafted upon Christianity, and not upon the doctrines or worship of those impostors [other religions]." And in the famous case of *Vidal v. Girard's Executors,* this Court... observed: "It is also said, and truly, that the Christian religion is a part of the common law..."
> ...These and many other matters which might be noticed, add a volume of unofficial declarations to the mass of organic utterances that this is a Christian nation...

Quite a convincing argument! And quite broad-based! The Court quoted directly from eighteen sources, alluded to over forty others, and acknowledged "many other" and "a volume" more from which selections could have been made.

In this case, the Court cited *People v. Ruggles, Updegraph v. Commonwealth,* and *Vidal v. Girard's Executors* in establishing its conclusion. The *Ruggles* case was decided by the Supreme Court of New York in 1811, *Updegraph* by the Supreme Court of Pennsylvania in 1826, and *Vidal* by the United States Supreme Court in 1844. Before reviewing these three cases, an observation needs to be made about cases stemming from state Supreme Courts.

With the current federal Supreme Court being so "high profile" and affecting national and private life as it does through its far-reaching decisions, a state's Supreme Court would seem to be a less credible source. However, this was not the attitude of earlier years. For 150 years after the ratification of the Constitution, the states were considered the highest source of authority. Most disputes went no higher than state Courts, and only unusual circumstances would cause a case to go to the federal Supreme Court (i.e., disputes between states, cases involving federal territories not yet states, cases not involving a jury decision, etc.).

Therefore, on items concerning religion and Christianity, the federal Courts were considered *less* of an authority than the state Courts. As the Court itself had noted in the *Holy Trinity* case, it had few occasions in which to decide on issues affecting Christianity:

> While because of a general recognition of this truth [that we are a Christian nation], the question has seldom been presented to the Courts.

When the federal Court did render a decision touching Christianity, it frequently cited the decisions of the state Supreme Courts, as it did in *Holy Trinity*. It is helpful to keep this background information in mind when examining the following cases.

Updegraph v. The Commonwealth, 1824
Supreme Court of Pennsylvania

This was the first case cited in *Holy Trinity*. The following is the description of the grand jury's indictment and the facts of the case:

> Abner Updegraph...on the 12th day of December, 1821...not having the fear of God before his eyes...contriving and intending to scandalize, and bring into disrepute, and vilify the Christian religion and the scriptures of truth, in the presence and hearing of several persons...did unlawfully, wickedly and premeditatively, despitefully and blasphemously say...: "That the Holy Scriptures were a mere fable: that they were a contradiction, and that although they contained a number of good things, yet they contained a

great many lies." To the great dishonor of Almighty God, to the great scandal of the profession of the Christian religion...

Since the indictment was for blasphemy, the Court needed to establish a legal definition of the word. It turned to the writings of Sir William Blackstone:

This offence is thus described by Justice Blackstone: "Blasphemy against the Almighty is denying his being or providence, or uttering contumelious reproaches on our Savior Christ. It is punished at common law by fine and imprisonment, for Christianity is part of the laws of the land."

Blackstone was an oft-quoted authority among lawyers of that day. According to Congressman Robert K. Dornan, in his book *Judicial Supremacy:*

...since colonial America had no regular schools of law, and lawyers educated in England were few, Blackstone's four-volume *Commentaries on the Laws of England (1765-1769)* served as the bible of American lawyers for generations. Indeed, nearly as many copies of Blackstone were sold in the colonies as in England, despite disparity in population. It was from Blackstone that most Americans, including John Marshall, acquired their knowledge of natural law...[1]

Professor John Eidsmoe, in his book *Christianity and the Constitution,* says of Blackstone:

...that his *Commentaries* were in the offices of every lawyer in the land, that candidates for the bar were routinely examined on Blackstone, that he was cited authoritatively in the Courts, and that a quotation from Blackstone settled many a legal argument. [2]

Further evidence of Blackstone's influence in America comes from the findings of two professors of political science. In their ten-year research of 15,000 articles written during the founding era (1760-1805), the two men cited most frequently by our Founders were Baron Charles Montesquieu and Sir William Blackstone. [3] The number of times that our Founders quoted Blackstone testifies to the impact that he had on their thinking and to the respect they paid him.

The Updegraph case went to trial, and the jury found Updegraph guilty. The attorney for the defendant submitted to the Court his reasons that the jury's verdict should be overturned. He pointed out that Updegraph was a member of a debating association which convened weekly and that what he said was uttered in the course of argument on a religious question. Wilkins argued that both the state and federal constitutions protected freedom of speech, and that if any state law against blasphemy did exist, the federal Constitution had done away with it--that Christianity was no longer part of the law.

Undoubtedly, had this case been tried today, the defense would differ little. Arguments for unlimited freedom of speech and against the constitutionality of laws limiting expression have been used since Courts existed. Notice how the Court responded to these arguments:

The jury...finds a malicious intention in the speaker to vilify the Christian religion and the scriptures, and this Court cannot look beyond the record, nor take any notice of the allegation, that the words were uttered by the defendant, a member of a debating association, which convened weekly for discussion and mutual information...That there is an association in which so serious a subject is treated with so much levity, indecency and scurrility...I am sorry to hear, for it would prove a nursery of vice, a school of preparation to qualify young men for the gallows, and young women for the brothel, and there is not a skeptic of decent manners and good morals, who would not consider such debating clubs as a common nuisance and disgrace to the city...it was the out- pouring of an invective, so vulgarly shocking and insulting, that the lowest grade of civil authority ought not to be subject to it, but when spoken in a Christian land, and to a Christian audience, the highest offense *contra bonos mores*; and even if Christianity was not part of the law of the land, it is the popular religion of the country, an insult on which would be indictable...

Having sustained the jury's verdict and the legality of laws on blasphemy, the Court turned its attention to the objections raised by the defense attorney:

The assertion is once more made, that Christianity never was received as part of the common law of this Christian land; and it is added, that if it was, it was virtually repealed by the constitution of the United States, and of this state...If the argument be worth anything, all the laws which have Christianity for their object--all would be carried away at one fell swoop--the act against cursing and swearing, and breach of the Lord's day; the act forbidding incestuous marriages, perjury by taking a false oath upon the book, fornication and adultery--for all these are founded on Christianity--for all these are restraints upon civil liberty...

We will first dispose of what is considered the grand objection--the constitutionality of Christianity--for, in effect, that is the question. Christianity, general Christianity, is and always has been a part of the common law...not Christianity founded on any particular religious tenets; not Christianity with an established church...but Christianity with liberty of conscience to all men.

Thus this wise legislature framed this great body of laws, for a Christian country and Christian people.

This is the Christianity of the common law...and thus, it is irrefragably proved, that the laws and institutions of this state are built on the foundation of reverence for Christianity...In this the constitution of the United States has made no alteration, nor in the great body of the laws which was an incorporation of the common-law doctrine of Christianity...without which no free government can long exist.

To prohibit the open, public and explicit denial of the popular religion of a country is a necessary measure to preserve the tranquillity of a government. Of this, no person in a Christian country can complain...In the Supreme Court of New York it was solemnly determined that Christianity was part of the law of the land and that to revile the Holy Scriptures was an indictable offense. The case assumes, says Chief Justice Kent, that we are a Christian people, and the morality of the country is deeply engrafted on Christianity. *The People v. Ruggles.*

No society can tolerate a wilful and despiteful attempt to subvert its religion, no more than it would to break down its laws--a general, malicious and deliberate intent to overthrow Christianity, general Christianity.

Without these restraints no free government could long exist. It is liberty run mad to declaim against the punishment of these offenses, or to assert that the punishment is hostile to the spirit and genius of our government. They are far from being true friends to liberty who support this doctrine, and the promulgation of such opinions, and general receipt of them among the people, would be the sure forerunners of anarchy, and finally, of despotism.

No free government now exists in the world unless where Christianity is acknowledged, and is the religion of the country ...Its foundations are broad and strong, and deep...it is the purest system of morality, the firmest auxiliary, and only stable support of all human laws.

...Christianity is part of the common law; the act against blasphemy is neither obsolete nor virtually repealed; nor is Christianity inconsistent with our free governments or the genius of the people.

While our own free constitution secures liberty of conscience and freedom of religious worship to all, it is not necessary to maintain that any man should have the right publicly to vilify the religion of his neighbors and of the country; these two privileges are directly opposed.

The People v. Ruggles, 1811
Supreme Court, State of New York

This case was not only cited in the previous case, it was also the second case cited in *Holy Trinity*. The offense and surrounding facts are described from the case:

The defendant was indicted...in December, 1810 for that he did, on the 2nd day of September, 1810...wickedly, maliciously, and blasphemously, utter and with a loud voice publish, in the presence and hearing of divers good and Christian people of and concerning the Christian religion, and of and concerning Jesus Christ, the false, scandalous, malicious, wicked and blasphemous words following: "Jesus Christ was a bastard, and his mother must be a whore," in contempt of the Christian religion...the defendant was tried and found guilty, and was sentenced by the Court to be imprisoned for three months, and to pay a fine of $500.

The attorney for the prisoner presented his defense:

...There are no statutes concerning religion...The constitution allows a free toleration to all religions and all kinds of worship...Judaism and Mahometanism may be preached here, without any legal animadversion...the prisoner may have been a Jew, a Mahometan, or a Socinian: and if so, he had a right, by the constitution, to declare his opinions...

The prosecuting attorney countered:

...While the constitution of the State has saved the rights of conscience, and allowed a free and fair discussion of all points of controversy among religious sects, it has left the principal engrafted on the body of our common law that Christianity is part of the laws of the State, untouched and unimpaired.

The Chief Justice of the New York Supreme Court during this case was Chancellor James Kent. There were few purely American legal precedents or writings in the young nation on which to rely. Therefore, lawyers and judges studied and applied the writing of Sir William Blackstone, an English judge and author of *Blackstone's Commentaries on the Law.* As time progressed and experience accumulated in the young nation, American writings and standards were developed. These were due, in large part, to the four-volume work written by James Kent, *Commentaries on American Law.* Kent's writings, though heavily dependent upon Blackstone, eventually replaced those of Blackstone as the standard in America.

In addition to producing his *Commentaries,* Kent also originated the practice of written decisions in New York. After his years in that state's Supreme Court, he went on to a nine-year term as the head of the Court of Chancery--a specialized Court dealing with complicated and intricate situations that regular Courts were unable to handle. James Kent was much more than an average judge in a northeastern state, he was one of the premier individuals in the history of legal practice in the United States. His words on law carry significant weight and importance. Notice his decision in this case:

Such words uttered with such a disposition were an offense at common law. In *Taylor's* case the defendant was convicted upon information of speaking similar words, and the Court... said that Christianity was parcel of the law, and to cast contumelious reproaches upon it tended to weaken the foundation of moral obligation, and the efficacy of oaths. And in the case of *Rex v. Woolston* on a like conviction, the Court said...that. whatever strikes at the root of Christianity tends manifestly to the dissolution of civil government...The authorities show that blasphemy against God and...profane ridicule of Christ or the Holy Scriptures (which are equally treated as blasphemy), are offenses punishable at common law, whether uttered by words or writings...because it tends to corrupt the morals of the people, and to destroy good order. Such offenses have always been considered independent of any religious establishment or the rights of the church. They are treated as affecting the essential interests of civil society.

...We stand equally in need, now as formerly, of all the moral discipline, and of those principles of virtue, which help to bind society together. The people of this State, in common with the people of this country, profess the general doctrines of Christianity as the rule of their faith and practice; and to scandalize the author of these doctrines is not only... impious, but...is a gross violation of decency and good order. Nothing could be more offensive to the virtuous part of the community, or more injurious to the tender morals of the young, than to declare such profanity lawful.

...The free, equal, and undisturbed enjoyment of religious opinion, whatever it may be, and free and decent discussions on any religious subject, is granted and secured; but to revile...the religion professed by almost the whole community, is an abuse of that right...we are a Christian people, and the morality of the country is deeply engrafted upon Christianity, and not upon the doctrines or worship of those impostors [other religions]...[we are] people whose manners...and whose morals have been elevated and inspired...by means of the Christian religion.

Though the constitution has discarded religious establishments, it does not forbid judicial cognizance of those offenses against religion and morality which have no reference to any such establishment...This [constitutional] declaration (noble and magnanimous as it is, when duly understood) never meant to withdraw religion in general, and with it the best sanctions of moral and social obligation from all consideration and notice of the law....To construe it as breaking down the common law barriers against licentious, wanton, and impious attacks upon Christianity itself, would be an enormous perversion of its meaning.

...Christianity, in its enlarged sense, as a religion revealed and taught in the Bible, is not unknown to our law.

...The Court are accordingly of opinion that the judgment below must be affirmed.   Blasphemy against God, and contumelious reproaches, and profane ridicule of Christ or the Holy Scriptures, are offenses punishable at the common law, whether uttered by words or writings.

These are powerful words, written by one of the fathers of American legal practice! His specific statement concerning Christianity and the Constitution bears repeating:

To construe it [the Constitution] as breaking down the common law barriers against licentious, wanton, and impious attacks upon Christianity itself, would be an enormous perversion of its meaning.

Commonwealth v. Abner Kneeland, 1838
Supreme Court of Massachusetts

This case also involved an attack against God and Christianity, but was different from the previous cases in that these attacks had been published.   Not surprisingly, the publisher claimed "freedom of the press" in his defense.   Specifically, the indictment was for "willfully blaspheming the holy name of God" and for a public disavowal of Christ. The indictment recorded his published statements:

"The Universalists believe in a god which I do not; but believe that their god, with all his moral attributes...is nothing more than a chimera of their own imagination"; "Universalists believe in Christ, which I do not; but believe that the whole story concerning him is...a fable and a fiction..."; etc...this language was used in the sense of a denial of God...so as to bring it within the statute.

An interesting term was used in the indictment, a term unknown to contemporary Courts when used in connection with God:

The defendant admitted the writing and publishing of the libel...

"Libel" is a familiar term when used concerning other persons. It means to intentionally declare things about them that are false and would publicly injure their reputation or expose them to public ridicule. Such attacks on individuals were, and still are, illegal and subject to litigation. Yet, in previous years, attacks on God and Christ fell under the same laws constructed to protect reputations: the laws against libel.

The defendant explained to the Court the reasons his conviction should be overturned. First, he claimed he did not deny a belief in God; he was a pantheist and only denied the belief in *a* God, for he felt that everything was god. Therefore, he asserted no law had been broken. Second, he argued that the law under which he was convicted had been superseded and overturned by the Constitution's guarantee of religious freedom. Lastly, he believed the laws against blasphemy were a violation of the freedom of the press. He felt the Constitution:

> ...guarantees to me the strict right of propagating my sentiments, by way of argument or discussion, on religion or any other subject.

The Court addressed the defendant's first argument, that he had broken no law:

> ...the statute on which the question arises is as follows: "That if any person shall willfully blaspheme the holy name of God, by denying, cursing, or contumeliously reproaching God, his creation, government, or final judging of the world..."
> In general, blasphemy [that is, libel against God] may be described as consisting in speaking evil of the Deity...to alienate the minds of others from the love and reverence of God. It is purposely using words concerning God...to impair and destroy the reverence, respect, and confidence due to him...It is a wilful and malicious attempt to lessen men's reverence of God by denying his existence, or his attributes as an intelligent creator, governor and judge of men, and to prevent their having confidence in him...

The Court reviewed the history of blasphemy laws in America from 1646 until the then current 1782 version of the law. After summarizing the intent of each of those laws and establishing their legal validity, the Chief Justice upheld the jury's verdict finding the defendant guilty of blasphemy and libel. Having disposed of the defendant's first position, the Court addressed the issue of the constitutionality of the law:

> But another ground for arresting the judgment, and one apparently most relied on and urged by the defendant, is, that this statute itself is repugnant to the constitution...and therefore wholly void.
>
> ...[this law] was passed very soon *after* the adoption of the constitution, and no doubt, many members of the convention which framed the constitution, were members of the legislature which passed this law.

The Court showed how the use of laws against blasphemy were compatible with similar provisions in the constitutions of other states and thus were constitutionally valid laws:

> In New Hampshire, the constitution of which State has a similar declaration of [religious] rights, the open denial of the being and existence of God or of the Supreme Being is prohibited by statute and declared to be blasphemy.
>
> In Vermont, with a similar declaration of rights, a statute was passed in 1797, by which it was enacted that if any person shall publicly deny the being and existence of God or the Supreme Being, or shall contumeliously reproach his providence and government, he shall be deemed a disturber of the peace and tranquility of the State, and an offender against the good morals and manners of society, and shall be punishable by fine...
>
> The State of Maine also, having adopted the same constitutional provision with that of Massachusetts in her declaration of rights in respect to religious freedom, immediately after the adoption of the constitution reenacted the Massachusetts statute against blasphemy...
>
> In New York the universal toleration of all religious professions and sentiments is secured in the most ample manner. It is declared in the constitution...that the free exercise and enjoyment of religious worship, without discrimination or preference, shall forever be allowed in this State to all mankind...Notwithstanding this constitutional declaration carrying the doctrine of unlimited toleration as far as the peace and safety of any community will allow, the Courts have decided that blasphemy was a crime at common law and was not abrogated by the constitution. *People v. Ruggles.*

The Court lastly addressed the "freedom of the press" issue raised by the defendant and concluded that much could not be protected by "freedom of the press":

>...According to the argument...every act, however injurious or criminal, which can be committed by the use of language, may be committed...if such language is printed. Not only therefore would the article in question become a general license for scandal, calumny and falsehood against individuals, institutions and governments, in the form of publication...but all incitation to treason, assassination, and all other crimes however atrocious, if conveyed in printed language, would be dispunishable.

Vidal v. Girard's Executors, 1844
United States Supreme Court

This was the third case cited in *Holy Trinity;* it involved the probation of the will of Stephen Girard, a native of France. He arrived in America before the Declaration of Independence was written and settled in the city of Philadelphia, where he lived until his death in 1831. He bequeathed his entire estate and personal property, valued at over $7 million, to the city of Philadelphia. The provisions of his will required the city to construct an orphanage and a college according to his extensive stipulations.

The plaintiffs filed suit claiming that a trust could not be given to a city but only to an individual. The suit centered on who would take possession of the estate: the city or the plaintiffs. The case was eventually decided in favor of Philadelphia. While the issue of who should receive the estate is not pertinent to this study, an ancillary objection was raised that is of interest. It was this objection that received the Court's attention in the *Holy Trinity* case.

Stephen Girard was an adherent to the enlightenment philosophy popular in France. That philosophy decried any relationship between God and government or Christianity and education. It also taught that morality could be attained apart from any religious principles. Girard's restrictions concerning the operation of the college reflected this philosophy:

>I enjoin and require that no ecclesiastic, missionary, or minister of any sect whatsoever, shall ever hold or exercise any station or duty whatever in the said college; nor shall

any such person ever be admitted for any purpose, or as a visitor, within the premises...my desire is, that all the instructors and teachers in the college shall take pains to instill into the minds of the scholars the purest principles of morality...

Such a requirement was unprecedented in America. Though the complaint filed against this provision was only a corollary to the central challenge of the case, the comments of the lawyers for both sides and the statement from the United States Supreme Court deserve special attention. The lawyers for the plaintiffs complained:

...the plan of education proposed is anti-Christian, and therefore repugnant to the law...

The city's attorney said the plaintiffs should not have sued on the issue of the trust; the only thing they should have done was:

...joined with us in asking the state to cut off the obnoxious clause [prohibiting teaching religion]...

How did the Court respond to the stipulation that the students be taught morality separate from Christianity?

The purest principles of morality are to be taught. Where are they found? Whoever searches for them must go to the source from which a Christian man derives his faith--the Bible.

Amazing! All parties involved in the case agreed! The plaintiff's lawyers said separating Christianity from education was "repugnant," the city's lawyers declared it "obnoxious," and the Court said it couldn't be done--moral principles *must* be taught from the Bible!

An interesting footnote to this case is that one of the Justices was Joseph Story--appointed by James Madison, the "Chief Architect of the Constitution"! Certainly Justice Story would know not only the technical aspects of the Constitution, but also its intent.

John M'Creery's Lessee vs. Allender, 1799
Supreme Court of Maryland

This case also centered on a will. Thomas M'Creery, a native of Ireland, had emigrated to the United States. Upon his death, he left the estate he acquired in this nation to his relative, John M'Creery, still of Ireland. It was doubted that an alien could leave an estate in the United States to another alien outside the States. In order to resolve the dispute in M'Creery's favor, it would have to be proven that Thomas M'Creery, who originally acquired the estate, had become a citizen of the United States. A certificate was produced which settled the case by showing that M'Creery had indeed been naturalized before Justice Samuel Chase.

Samuel Chase, like so many of the other men cited in this chapter, was no "lightweight." He was a signer of the Declaration of Independence and was appointed by George Washington to serve as a Justice on the United States Supreme Court. Below is an excerpt from the document Chase executed in the naturalization of M'Creery:

> Thomas M'Creery, in order to become...naturalized according to the Act of Assembly...on the 30th of September, 1795, took the oath...before the Honorable Samuel Chase, Esquire, then being the Chief Judge of the State of Maryland...and did then and there receive from the said Chief Judge, a certificate thereof...: "Maryland; I, Samuel Chase, Chief Judge of the State of Maryland, do hereby certify all whom it may concern, that...personally appeared before me Thomas M'Creery, and did repeat and subscribe a declaration of his belief in the Christian Religion, and take the oath required by the Act of Assembly of this State, entitled, 'An Act for Naturalization.'..."

What was one of the requirements for naturalization of immigrants?

> ...repeat and subscribe a declaration of his belief in the Christian Religion...

Runkel v. Winemiller, 1799
Supreme Court of Maryland

This case involved a conflict between a minister of the German Reformed Christian Church and the church from which he had been dispossessed. In the introduction to the case, the Judge who delivered the ruling noted that it was a decision in which all of the Justices unanimously concurred. What was it upon which they all unanimously concurred?

> Religion is of general and public concern, and on its support depend, in great measure, the peace and good order of

government, the safety and happiness of the people. By our form of government, the Christian religion is the established religion; and all sects and denominations of Christians are placed upon the same equal footing, and are equally entitled to protection in their religious liberty.

Again, the same theme recurs: general Christianity, not denominational Christianity, is part of government in this nation.

The Commonwealth v. Sharpless and others, 1815
Supreme Court of Pennsylvania

This case, and the next two, will deal with issues of morality. Today's oft-repeated contention that "You can't legislate morality!" was not accepted by our Founders. They believed that morality *could* be legislated and had found what they considered to be the perfect example of moral legislation: the Bible. Evidently no one told God He couldn't legislate morality--He had done so; and in the opinion of our Founders, He had done so quite successfully! Consequently, when the Courts had decisions to be made concerning moral values, they relied on Biblical guidelines.

Dr. Sterling Lacy, in his book *Valley of Decision,* concisely describes what is now occurring in the struggle against legislating standards for morality:

"Morality" is defined as the condition of conforming with right principles. It pits right against wrong. To "legislate" means to make a law. Law imposes rules of conduct and enforces them with authority. What law has ever been enacted by any government in the history of man that has not named something wrong and its opposite right? 4

Every law establishes and legislates morality. What today's critics are saying is, "We don't want God to have anything to do with today's morality. We want to determine what is right and wrong without God..."

America has become the battleground between the world's two oldest religions. The first religion to appear in the history of mankind worships God. The second worships man. In America, the first is expressed primarily by Christianity. The second by humanism.

It is not a question of whether morality can or should be legislated. It is a question of which religious guidelines will undergird the legislation: religious guidelines that deify God, or religious guidelines that deify man? 5

The following cases illustrate how the Courts upheld Congress' legislation of moral standards--legislation based on the Bible. The indictment delivered by the grand jury describes the offense in the *Commonwealth v. Sharpless* case:

...Jesse Sharpless, John Haines, George Haines, John Steel, Ephraim Martin, and ---------Mayo...intending to debauch and corrupt the morals of youth as of divers other citizens of this commonwealth, and to raise and create in their minds inordinate and lustful desires...in a certain house there... scandalously did exhibit and show for money...a certain lewd... obscene painting, representing a man in an obscene...and indecent posture with a woman, to the manifest corruption and subversion of youth, and other citizens of this commonwealth...offending...the dignity of the Commonwealth of Pennsylvania.

Here we have a classic description of a porno case, yet this one occurred in 1815! The defense claimed that this was not an indictable offense since it was only a "home viewing," and not a "public porno shop." The Court, with Judge Duncan delivering the opinion, addressed these arguments, stating that many things occurring in private have a public effect and are therefore punishable:

The defendants have been convicted, upon their own confession, of conduct indicative of great moral depravity...This Court is...invested with power to punish not only open violations of decency and morality, but also whatever secretly tends to undermine the principles of society...whatever tends to the destruction of morality, in general, may be punished criminally. Crimes are public offences, not because they are perpetrated publicly, but because their effect is to injure the public. Burglary, though done in secret, is a public offense; and secretly destroying fences is indictable.

Hence, it follows, that an offense may be punishable, if in its nature and by its example, it tends to the corruption of morals; although it be not committed in public.

The defendants are charged with exhibiting and showing... for money, a lewd...and obscene painting. A picture tends to excite lust, as strongly as a writing; and the showing of a picture is as much a publication as the selling of a book...if the privacy of the room was a protection, all the youth of the city might be corrupted, by taking them, one by one, into a chamber, and there inflaming their passions by the exhibition of lascivious pictures. In the eye of the law, this would be a publication, and a most pernicious one.

The Court, by referring to other laws not specifically related to this case, had noted that the laws did not allow lascivious, lewd, or obscene publications--the types of publications that are widely distributed today. This is another example of moral legislation based on Biblical standards. In an act unusual for that period, a second Justice, Judge Yeates, also delivered a statement:

...although every immoral act, such as lying, etc., is not indictable, yet where the offense charged is destructive of morality in general...it is punishable at common law. The destruction of morality renders the power of the government invalid...The corruption of the public mind, in general, and debauching the manners of youth, in particular, by lewd and obscene pictures exhibited to view, must necessarily be attended with the most injurious consequences...No man is permitted to corrupt the morals of the people; secret poison cannot be thus disseminated.

These rulings and opinions clash sharply with those of current Courts who refuse to oppose obscene materials or even to take any stands that would involve having to define "morality." When objective standards for right and wrong are disallowed (i.e., the Bible), the standards for morality become variable and are individually determined. By refusing to sustain standards of morality, the Courts have, by default, installed immorality as the acceptable and prevalent standard.

Davis v. Beason, 1889
United States Supreme Court

In this case, it was argued that what was immoral for one group might be moral for another. To further complicate the case, the alleged immorality was claimed to be part of a religious belief and therefore protected under "the free exercise" portion of the First Amendment. Specifically, this case involved bigamy and polygamy among Mormons in the western territories. Under United States laws, bigamy and polygamy were crimes. The Idaho statute went further and made it illegal for anyone who taught, encouraged, or committed bigamy or polygamy to vote or to hold any public office within the Territory.

Samuel Davis was convicted of bigamy and polygamy and was fined and sentenced to a jail term. Following his conviction, he argued that his imprisonment was solely by virtue of his religious belief. He claimed that the law under which he had been convicted was a violation of the First Amendment, which prohibited laws respecting an establishment of religion or prohibiting their free exercise. He therefore requested that the Court release him. He was freed by a Court order, pending the outcome of the hearing on his arguments.

In arguments before the Supreme Court, his defense attorneys raised three issues. First, they contended that the laws on bigamy and polygamy were a violation of the First Amendment because they interferred with the religious beliefs of Davis and other Mormons. Second, they argued that the laws were a violation of the Fourteenth Amendment, which prohibited the states from making laws that interfered with the rights of their citizens. Third, they claimed the laws violated Article VI of the Constitution, which forbids a religious test as a requirement for office.

Justice Stephen Field, who was appointed to the Supreme Court by President Abraham Lincoln in 1863, and who was also on the Court during the *Holy Trinity* case, delivered the Court's ruling in a very straightforward statement:

Bigamy and polygamy are crimes by the laws of all civilized and Christian countries. They are crimes by the laws of the United States, and they are crimes by the laws of Idaho. They tend to destroy the purity of the marriage relation, to disturb the peace of families, to degrade woman and to debase man...To extend exemption from punishment for such crimes would be to shock the moral judgment of the community. To call their advocacy a tenet of religion is to offend the common sense of mankind.

There have been sects which denied as a part of their relig- ious tenets that there should be any marriage tie, and advocated promiscuous intercourse of the sexes as prompted by the passions of its members...Should a sect of [this] kind ever find its way into this country, swift punishment would follow the carrying into effect of its doctrines, and no heed would be given to the pretence that...their supporters could be protected in their exercise by the Constitution of the United States. Probably never before in the history of this country has it been seriously contended that the whole punitive power of the government for acts, recognized by the general consent of the Christian world...must be suspended in order that the tenets of a religious sect...may be carried out without hindrance.

The constitutions of several States, in providing for religious freedom, have declared expressly that such freedom shall not be construed to excuse acts of licentiousness...the constitution of New York of 1777 provided: "The free exercise and enjoyment of religious profession and worship, without discrimination or preference, shall forever hereafter be allowed, within this State, to all mankind: *Provided:* That the liberty of conscience, hereby granted, shall not be so construed as to excuse acts of licentiousness...The constitutions of California, Colorado, Connecticut, Florida, Georgia, Illinois, Maryland, Minnesota, Mississippi, Missouri, Nevada and South Carolina contain a similar declaration.

The defendant contended that his actions were not licentious, at least in his view. Yet notice the basis for the Supreme Court's rejection of the defendant's argument: they are crimes by the laws of "Christian countries" and the "Christian world." Notice further what the Court said would happen if some group advocating promiscuous intercourse of the sexes should appear in the United States:

...swift punishment would follow the carrying into effect of its doctrines, and no heed would be given to the pretence that...their supporters could be protected in their exercise by the Constitution of the United States.

This was the belief when legislation and judicial rulings were still God-centered and not man-centered. As is obvious from the Court's comments, it never envisioned it would be any other way. Our Founders would be shocked to see what the Court protects today!

Literally hundreds of magazine, film publishers, and other groups "advocating promiscuous intercourse of the sexes" now operate under the Court's "constitutional" protection. For example, consider these excerpts from books and materials that *Planned Parenthood* recommends for adolescents 6 :

Boys and Sex

...more and more people are coming to understand that having sex is a joyful and enriching experience at any age. (p. 2)

Playing with girls sexually before adolescence...increases the chances for a satisfactory sex life when a boy grows up. (p. 38)

Premarital intercourse does have its definite values as a training ground for marriage...boys and girls who start having intercourse when they're adolescents...will find that it's a big help... it's like taking a car out on a test run before you buy it. (p. 117)

...premarital intercourse among adolescents is often helpful in later life because it's easier to learn things in our earlier years. (p. 118)

When people want to get close to each other, intercourse is the closest they can get. (p. 129)

Girls and Sex:

Girls understand now that they are far more likely to make good social and sexual adjustments to life if they learn to be warm, open, responsive, and sexually unafraid. They're learning to be sexual partners of men...(p. 10-11)

...everyone's agreed...that teenage sex should be a learning experience...(p. 15)

Sex play with boys...can be exciting, pleasurable, and even worthwhile...it will help later sexual adjustment. (p. 48)

For those who plan on marriage eventually, early intercourse can also be a training ground. (p. 95)

Another reason for intercourse is the fact that...it's a means of learning how to live with people. (p. 96)

You've Changed the Combination:

There are only two basic kinds of sex: sex with victims and sex without. Sex with victims is always wrong. Sex without is always right (p. 10).

One way to avoid having victims is, of course, to have sexual relationships only with your friends (p. 12).

It has been estimated that up to 80 percent of American public schools use materials available from *Planned Parenthood.* Publications like these are provided to adolescents, complete with photographs, illustrations, and graphics showing them how to accomplish sexual activity easily, encouraging types of sexual activity that are still illegal in many states even today. The effect that groups like *Planned Parenthood* have had on the nation in recent years (under Court protection) is seen through statistics published in *Parade* on December 18, 1988:

> Two-thirds of America's 11 million teenage boys say they have had sex with a girl...The first time for most of them was when they were around 15. By the time they are 18, on the average, boys have had sex with five girls.

The contemporary Court is a party to the decline of America's morality. It has upheld the "rights" of groups to propagate teachings on immorality and has prohibited schools from presenting Biblical teachings on morality. With the Court protecting groups who "advocate promiscuous intercourse," immorality has become so much a part of our society that, according to the same article:

> There are 20,000 scenes with suggested sexual acts on television each year, all of them without regard to outcome...

A study conducted by Lou Harris, entitled "Sexual Material on American Network Television During the 1987-1988 Season," found the number of sexual instances on television tallied over 27 per hour.

The Court had protected morality based on Biblical standards for more than a century-and-a-half; it reflected the beliefs of the Founders that morality provides our government its greatest protection. As Abraham Lincoln expressed it:

> The only assurance of our nation's safety is to lay our foundation in morality and religion. [7]

Lincoln continued:

> At what point then, is the approach of danger to be expected? If it ever reaches us, it must spring up from among us, it cannot come from abroad. If destruction is our lot, we must ourselves be its author and finisher; as a nation of free men, we must live through all time or die by suicide. [8]

Murphy v. Ramsey & Others, 1885
United States Supreme Court

This case again dealt with polygamy, but this time in the territory of Utah. It represented the same dilemma: whether to use the standards of traditional Biblical morality or to discard them. The Court again upheld and used God's standards. Notice its strong declaration on the importance of upholding legislation protecting the family according to Biblical teachings:

...certainly no legislation can be supposed more wholesome and necessary in the founding of a free, self-governing commonwealth...than that which seeks to establish it on the basis of the idea of the family, as consisting in and springing from the union for life of one man and one woman in the holy estate of matrimony; [the family is] the sure foundation of all that is stable and noble in our civilization; the best guarantee of that reverent morality which is the source of all beneficent progress in social and political improvement...

Ironically, legal action now goes directly against establishing family on "the union for life of one man and one woman in the holy estate of matrimony."

Current Courts have now rejected the previously held Biblical standards of morality. As a result, much opposition is now raised against former positions on morality. For example, in 1988, California was considering adopting legislation requiring that whenever sex education was taught in public schools that:

Course material and instruction shall stress that monogamous heterosexual [one man and one woman] intercourse within marriage is a traditional American value.

The Senator promoting this bill received a letter from an active legal organization protesting this provision. The excerpt below is from a copy of their letter; the letterhead bears the logo of the ACLU and is dated April 18, 1988. Why did the ACLU oppose the bill?

It is our position that teaching that monogamous, heterosexual intercourse within marriage as a traditional American value is an unconstitutional establishment of a religious doctrine in public schools. There are various religions which hold contrary beliefs with respect to marriage and monogamy. We believe SB 2394 violates the First Amendment.

Again, as in previous cases, the argument was raised that *any* moral standard is protected under the free exercise of religion. The difference is that the contemporary Courts sustain this argument! Groups who claim Jefferson and Madison as their heroes for allegedly advancing the complete separation of religious principles from the state would probably be horrified to read what the Court stated in many of the polygamy cases (this particular excerpt is from *Reynolds v. United States, 1878. United States Supreme Court):*

...it is a significant fact that on the 8th of December, 1788, after the passage of the act establishing religious freedom, and after the convention of Virginia had recommended as an amendment to the Constitution of the United States the declaration in a bill of rights that "all men have an equal, natural, and unalienable right to the free exercise of religion, according to the dictates of conscience," the legislature of that State substantially enacted the...death penalty...[for polygamy]...

Jefferson and Madison, the men many idolize as heroes who allegedly argued free conscience for any and all religious beliefs, were party to enacting the death penalty for bigamy and polygamy! Traditional Biblical morality had always been embodied in our Founder's legislation and upheld by the Courts. What would our Founders think if they could see us now?

City of Charleston v. S.A. Benjamin, 1846
Supreme Court of South Carolina

This controversy focused on the violation of a law best described by a quotation from the case:

"An Ordinance for the better observance of the Lord's day, commonly called Sunday." Specifically: "No person or persons whatsoever shall publicly expose to sale, or sell... any goods, wares or merchandise whatsoever upon the Lord's day..."

The defendant was accused of selling a pair of gloves in his shop on a Sunday. The defense used in the case is one that is frequently raised today: laws that prefer or support Christianity are a violation of the religious rights of others. The defense attorney argued that the Sunday law was a violation of the constitution and an infringement on his client's religious rights because the defendant was a Jew, and observed the seventh day of the week. On the other side, the city's attorneys responded that:

...Christianity is a part of the common law of the land, with liberty of conscience to all. It has always been so recognized...If Christianity is a part of the common law, its disturbance is punishable at common law. The U.S. Constitution allows it as a part of the common law. The President is allowed ten days [to sign a bill], with the exception of Sunday. The Legislature does not sit, public offices are closed, and the Government recognizes the day in all things ...The observance of Sunday is one of the usages of the common law, recognized by our U.S. and State Governments...The Sabbath is still to be supported; Christianity is part and parcel of the common law...Christianity has reference to the principles of right and wrong...it is the foundation of those morals and manners upon which our society is formed; it is their basis. Remove this and they would fall... [morality] has grown upon the basis of Christianity.

The Court commended the defendant for his religious devotion, but pointed out that in the United States, Sunday is a particularly important day because it is:

...the Lord's day, the day of the Resurrection to us who are called Christians, the day of rest after finishing a new creation. It is the day of the first visible triumph over death, hell and the grave! It was the birth day of the believer in Christ, to whom and through whom it opened up the way which, by repentance and faith, leads unto everlasting life and eternal happiness! On that day we rest, and to us it is the Sabbath of the Lord--its decent observance, in a Christian community, is that which ought to be expected.

Then, addressing the defendant's assertion that all religions are to be treated equally under the Constitution, the Judge directed attention to the source of the tolerance described in the Constitution:

What gave to us this noble safeguard of religious toleration...? It was Christianity...But this toleration, thus granted,
is a religious toleration; it is the free exercise and enjoyment
of religious profession and worship, with two provisos, one of
which, that which guards against acts of licentiousness, testifies to the Christian construction, which this section should
receive!   What are acts "of licentiousness" within the
meaning of this section? Must they not be such public acts,
as are calculated to shock the moral sense of the community, where they take place? The orgies of Bacchus, among
the ancients, were not offensive! At a later day, the Carni-
vals of Venice went off without note or observation. Such
could not be allowed now! Why? Public opinion, based on
Christian morality, would not suffer it!

What constitutes the standard of good morals? Is it not
Christianity? There certainly is none other. Say that it cannot
be appealed to, and I don't know what would be good morals.
The day of moral virtue in which we live would, in an instant, if
that standard were abolished, lapse into the dark and murky
night of Pagan immorality.

In the Courts over which we preside, we daily acknowledge Christianity as the most solemn part of our administration. A Christian witness, having no religious scruples about
placing his hand upon the book, is sworn upon the holy
Evangelists, the books of the New Testament, which testify
of our Savior's birth, life, death, and resurrection; this is so
common a matter, that it is little thought of as an evidence of
the part which Christianity has in the common law.

...I agree fully to what is beautifully and appropriately said
in Updegraph v. The Commonwealth,--Christianity, general
Christianity, is, and always has been, a part of the common
law: "not Christianity founded on any particular religious
tenets; not Christianity with an established church...but
Christianity with liberty of conscience to all men."

Since Christianity was the source of the religious tolerance found
both in the United States and in its Constitution, the Court could not
allow it to become an equal among other religions; Christianity must
remain foremost in the laws and statutes. The Court then addressed
the charge that laws preferring Christianity violated the free exercise
of religion:

...it is said [that Sunday laws] violated the free exercise and enjoyment of the religious profession and worship of the Israelite. Why? It does not require him to desecrate his own Sabbath. It does not say, "you must worship God on the Christian Sabbath." On the contrary, it leaves him free on all these matters. His evening sacrifice and his morning worship, constituting the 7th day, he publicly and freely offers up, that there is none to make him afraid. His Sundays are spent as he pleases, so far as religion is concerned.

It is however fancied that in some way this law is in derogation of the Hebrew's religion, inasmuch as by his faith and this statute, he is compelled to keep two Sabbaths. There is the mistake. He has his own, free and undiminished! Sunday is to us our day of rest. We say to him, simply, respect us, by ceasing on this day from the pursuit of that trade and business in which you, by the security and protection given to you by our [Christian] laws, make great gain...

There is therefore no violation of the Hebrew's religion, in requiring him to cease from labor on another day than his Sabbath, if he be left free to observe the latter according to his religion.

The Commonwealth v. Wolf, 1817
Supreme Court of Pennsylvania

Though this case occurred nearly three decades before *Charleston v. Benjamin,* the circumstances in the two cases were almost identical, as were the defense arguments. The Court, in addressing the seventh day sabbath of the Jewish religion vs. the first day sabbath of the Christian religion, returned to the Scriptures to show that it could not be argued that Saturday, or any other day, was *the* day commanded by the Scripture. No, the Sabbath could be any day, as long as it occurred every seventh. However, in this, a Christian nation, Sunday was that day. The Court emphasized the importance of a uniform national sabbath:

Laws cannot be administered in any civilized government unless the people are taught to revere the sanctity of an oath, and look to a future state of rewards and punishments for the deeds of this life. It is of the utmost moment, therefore, that they should be reminded of their religious duties at stated periods...A wise policy would naturally lead to the formation of laws calculated to subserve those salutary purposes. The invaluable privilege of the rights of conscience secured to us by the constitution of the commonwealth, was never intended to shelter those persons, who, out of mere caprice, would directly oppose those laws for the pleasure of showing their contempt and abhorrence of the religious opinions of the great mass of the citizens.

Again, the same conclusion was reached as in the previous cases: the rights of conscience and exercise of religion do not shelter those opposed to Christianity. All rights and beliefs were protected insofar as they did not oppose the advancement of Christianity.

United States v. Macintosh, 1931
United States Supreme Court

This case, concerning a Canadian who was applying for naturalization in the United States, occurred more than 140 years after the ratification of the Constitution, yet the Court was still articulating the same message:

We are a Christian people, according to one another the equal right of religious freedom, and acknowledging with reverence the duty of obedience to the will of God.

Zorach v. Clauson, 1952
United States Supreme Court

Although this case occurred after the 1947 case *Everson v. Board of Education* (the case in which the Court announced, for the first time in its history, that it would pursue "a wall of separation between church and state"), the Court did not deviate completely from the longstanding practice of commingling Christianity with education. The Court upheld the constitutionality of students receiving religious instruction during the school day. However, the Court did take a step toward separation and away from historical precedent by declaring that the instruction must occur off campus. Nonetheless, its ruling was still light-years away from the position now held by the Court. Notice these comments during what was still the adolescent stage of the Court's now well-developed position on separation:

...The First Amendment, however, does not say that in every and all respects there shall be a separation of Church and State...Otherwise the state and religion would be aliens to each other--hostile, suspicious, and even unfriendly...
We are a religious people whose institutions presuppose a Supreme Being...When the state encourages religious instruction or cooperates with religious authorities by adjusting the schedule of public events to sectarian needs, it follows the best of our traditions. For it then respects the religious nature of our people and accommodates the public service to their spiritual needs. To hold that it may not would be to find in the Constitution a requirement that the government show a callous indifference to religious groups. That would be preferring those who believe in no religion over those who do believe...we find no constitutional requirement which makes it necessary for government to be hostile to religion and to throw its weight against efforts to widen the effective scope of religious influence.

The Court concluded that the argument for separation of church and state did not apply to religious instruction for school students during school hours...

...unless separation of Church and State means that public institutions can make no adjustments of their schedules to accommodate the religious needs of the people. We cannot read into the Bill of Rights such a philosophy of hostility to religion.

The fifteen case excerpts above are only a few of hundreds of similar cases. Contemporary Courts lack no legal precedents to help establish the constitutional intent of the First Amendment. The simple fact is that the historical precedents disprove what the Court wishes to enact, and therefore are disregarded or avoided!

Early Supreme Court Justices

In addition to the extensive number of early cases available, there are also records providing the opinions of many of the earliest Judges who served on the Supreme Court. Their individual statements are as clear and concise as are those from the early Courts.

For example, consider the statements of John Jay, the first Chief Justice of the first Supreme Court. Jay was appointed by President

George Washington, which is in itself probably a sufficient endorsement. George Washington has been characterized as the man best portraying the true spirit of the Constitutional Convention, and as President of the Convention, he was probably more familiar with the intent of our Constitution than anyone else. Those he selected were not only those best qualified to serve, but were also those who would help establish the ideas birthed in Constitution Hall in Philadelphia. Although his selection by Washington was a high commendation, Jay could stand on his own accomplishments.

Jay, along with James Madison and Alexander Hamilton, authored *The Federalist Papers.* These three men, through their writings, probably did more to secure the ratification of the Constitution than any other group of men. They explained to America what would be achieved through the new form of government and how it would function to benefit the entire nation. If there were "heroes" in the effort to establish a new national government, John Jay would have to be placed near the top. Notice what this first Chief Justice of the Supreme Court declared:

> Providence has given to our people the choice of their rulers, and it is the duty, as well as the privilege and interest, of a Christian nation to select and prefer Christians for their rulers. 9

Another Justice appointed by George Washington, James Wilson, was one of only six men who signed both the Declaration of Independence and the Constitution. He was extremely active at the Constitutional Convention, speaking 168 times, second only to Gouverneur Morris' 173 times. This particular quote concerning Judge Wilson appeared in the Pennsylvania Supreme Court records of *Updegraph v. Commonwealth, 1826:*

> The late Judge Wilson, of the Supreme Court of the United States, Professor of Law in the College in Philadelphia, was appointed in 1791, unanimously, by the House of Representatives of this state....He had just risen from his seat in the convention which formed the constitution of the United States, and of this state; and it is well known, that for our present form of government we are greatly indebted to his exertions and influence. With his fresh recollections of both constitutions, in his Course of Lectures (3d vol. of his works, 122), he states that...Christianity is part of the common-law.

Quite impressive credentials! Not only did he participate in the birth of the nation and in its constitutional establishment, he was unanimously confirmed as George Washington's choice to serve on the Supreme Court. Having helped frame the Constitution, he was intimately aware of its intent, and he explicitly stated that Christianity is part of the "common law." The "common law" is the basis on which all other laws are built; it is the foundation. According to Justice James Wilson, our foundation is Christianity. It is ludicrous for anyone to assert that since the building is now complete, it would cause no damage to remove its foundation!

Another early Justice was Joseph Story. Justice Story was appointed by President James Madison and served on the Supreme Court for 34 years. Logic assures us that James Madison, as the "Chief Architect of the Constitution," would not have selected someone opposed to the principles of the new Constitution. Notice what Justice Story, who was also a professor at Harvard Law School, wrote concerning the First Amendment in his 1833 *Commentaries on the Constitution of the United States:*

> We are not to attribute this prohibition of a national religious establishment [in the First Amendment] to an indifference to religion in general, and especially to Christianity, *which none could hold in more reverence than the framers of the Constitution...*Probably at the time of the adoption of the Constitution and of the Amendments to it, the general, if not universal, sentiment in America was that Christianity ought to receive encouragement from the State...Any attempt to level all religions, and to make it a matter of state policy to hold all in utter indifference, would have created universal disapprobation, if not universal indignation. [10]
>
> It remains yet a problem to be solved in human affairs, whether any free government can be permanent, where the public worship of God and the support of religion constitute no part of the policy or duty of the state in any assignable shape. [11]

His statement is worth repeating: "Christianity ought to receive encouragement from the state" because it is doubted "whether any free government can be permanent" where "the support of religion constitute no part of the policy or duty of the state."

Perhaps the most famous of all Chief Justices of the Supreme Court was John Marshall. Marshall was active in the Revolutionary

War as a captain, fought in many campaigns in several states, and went through the infamous winter of 1777-1778 at Valley Forge with General George Washington. He was very active with James Madison in urging ratification of the Constitution at Virginia's ratifying convention. Marshall served in the House of Representatives and declined an appointment from George Washington to be Attorney General. Before being appointed by President John Adams as Chief Justice of the Supreme Court, he was Adams' Secretary of State.

Marshall served on the Court for 34 years. It was through his efforts that the Court moved from its fledgling beginnings to its position as a viable third branch of government. Elegant carvings of Marshall, which now adorn the outside of the Supreme Court building, commemorate his years of distinguished service to the Court. Peter Marshall and David Manuel, in their book *Sea to Shining Sea,* recount a story of Justice John Marshall that appeared in the *Winchester Republican* which described:

> ...an incident in McGuire's Hotel in that city, when Marshall arrived in that hotel's tavern, having suffered a mishap on the road:
>
> The shafts of his ancient gig were broken and held together by withes formed from the bark of a hickory sapling. He was negligently dressed, his knee buckles loosened. In the tavern, a discussion arose among some young men, concerning the merits of the Christian religion...No one knew Marshall, who sat quietly listening. Finally, one of the youthful combatants turned to him and said, "Well, my old gentleman, what think you of these things?"
>
> Marshall responded with a most eloquent and unanswerable appeal. He talked for an hour, answering every argument urged against the teachings of Jesus. In the whole lecture, there was so much simplicity and energy, pathos and sublimity, that not another word was uttered.
>
> The listeners wondered who the old man could be. Some thought him a preacher, and great was their surprise when they learned afterwards that he was the Chief Justice of the United States.
>
> In his stalwart defense of the Christian faith, Marshall was following in the footsteps of the first Chief Justice of the United States, John Jay. 12

Observers from the Outside

In addition to the records of the Supreme Court Justices, there are interesting observations recorded by visitors to this nation in its early years. The observations of one of these visitors, Alexis de Tocqueville, are preserved in his famous work *Democracy in America.* He was more than a mere "tourist" visiting America:

> I did not study America just to satisfy curiosity; I sought there lessons from which we might profit. 13

De Tocqueville, a French historian, traveled the length and breadth of the nation, observing and recording what made America so distinctive and great among the nations of the world. Pertinent to this chapter is an observation he made on the judicial system in the United States:

> While I was in America, a witness called at assizes of the county of Chester (state of New York) declared that he did not believe in the existence of God and the immortality of the soul. The judge refused to allow him to be sworn in, on the ground that the witness had destroyed beforehand all possible confidence in his testimony. Newspapers reported the fact without comment. This is how the New York *Spectator* of August 23, 1831, reported the matter:
> > The court of common pleas of Chester county (New York) a few days since, rejected a witness who declared his disbelief in the existence of God. The presiding judge remarked that he was not before aware that there was a man living who did not believe in the existence of God; that this belief constituted the sanction of all testimonies in a court of justice; and that he knew of no cause in a Christian country, where a witness had been permitted to testify without such belief. 14

His observations again confirm the Christian standards that were applied in America's Courts from its founding.

The cases presented in this chapter, representing only the "tip of the iceberg," accurately portray what was typical in America's Courts and legal system during its first 150 years under our Constitution. These cases (and the hundreds like them), the records of the early Supreme Court Justices, and the writings of the pioneers of

American legal practice, leave no doubt about where our Founders stood on Christian principles in government, education, and public affairs. Our Fathers intended that this nation should be a Christian nation; not because all who lived in it were Christians, but because it was founded on and would be governed and guided by Christian principles.

~ 5 ~
Other "Organic Utterances"

In the previous chapter, legal records establishing this country as a Christian nation were examined. In *Church of the Holy Trinity v. United States,* 1892, the Court stated:

> ...this is a religious people. This is historically true. From the discovery of this continent to the present hour, there is a single voice making this affirmation...these are not individual sayings, declarations of private persons: they are organic utterances; they speak the voice of the entire people...these and many other matters which might be noticed, add a volume of unofficial declarations to the mass of organic utterances that this is a Christian nation...

The Court said "organic utterances" proved that this is a Christian nation; what is an "organic utterance"? "Organic," in a legal sense, simply means, "belonging to the fundamental or constitutional law." It is the base on which the laws are built and therefore is part of the law; it is "organic" to the law itself. It is what judges call the "common law."

The organic utterances were comprised of "these and many other matters" that would "add a volume of unofficial declarations" proving their official declaration that "this is a Christian nation." This chapter presents some of the "volume" and "mass" of declarations.

The historical material (organic utterances) available for proving that this is a Christian nation is of such a quantity that one would be tempted to say, as did the Apostle John when writing about Jesus, that if everything "were written down, I suppose that even the whole world would not have room for the books that would be written." Several selections typical of the mass have been chosen for presentation in this chapter, but they only "skim the surface" of what is available. The reader can become his own investigator and student of history and quickly discover how much more could be added to that presented here.

The selections are presented in the order mentioned by the Court: "...from the discovery of the continent to the present hour." The records of each era, when combined together in this chapter, form a choir of voices declaring Christianity to be the base of our nation, government, and education. The reader will also be convinced of what the Supreme Court was convinced: "...this is a Christian nation."

America's Discovery

The decision by Columbus to embark on such an unprecedented and potentially dangerous journey could not have been an easy one to make. Popular opinion claimed the world to be flat--surely he must have considered the possibility that they were right. Why, then, did he set out at such risk and peril? Excerpts from his own diary provide the answer:

It was the Lord who put it into my mind--I could feel His hand upon me--the fact that it would be possible...All who heard of my project rejected it with laughter, ridiculing me...There is no question that the inspiration was from the Holy Spirit, because He comforted me with rays of illumination from the Holy Scriptures...It was simply the fulfillment of what Isaiah had prophesied...the fact that the Gospel must still be preached to so many lands in such a short time--this is what convinces me. No one should fear to undertake a task in the name of our Savior, if it is just and if the intention is purely for His service. [1]

America's First Colonies

Following Columbus' discovery of America, other explorers ventured into the new continent, making property claims for their own nation. When colonization began, groups of prospective Colonists would approach their sovereign to receive land charters in the new nation. In 1606, a charter was obtained from King James I for a permanent settlement in Virginia. That charter reflects the Colonists' reasons for traveling to the new world:

...to make habitation...and to deduce a colony of sundry of our people into that Part of America commonly called Virginia...in propagating of Christian religion to such people as yet live in darkness...[to] bring...a settled and quiet Government. [2]

In 1609, another charter was granted for Virginia:

...because the principal effect which we can expect or desire of this action is the conversion...of the people in those parts unto the true worship of God and the Christian religion. [3]

The charter for the Pilgrims in 1620, also signed by King James I, reflected the same intent:

...to advance the enlargement of the Christian religion, to the glory of God Almighty...[4]

The Pilgrims arrived in America on the Mayflower in November of 1620. Before disembarking, they wrote and signed the Mayflower Compact. It was brief and to the point. In it, they proclaimed their purpose for coming to America and their commitment to that purpose:

...having undertaken for the glory of God, and advancement of the Christian faith...a voyage to plant the first colony in the northern parts of Virginia...combine ourselves together into a civil body politic for...furtherance of the ends aforesaid. [5]

The First Charter of Massachusetts, dated March 1629, reflects similar goals. It was granted so that:

...our said people...may be so religiously, peaceably, and civilly governed, as their good life and orderly conversation may win and incite the natives of country to the knowledge and obedience of the only true God and Savior of mankind, and the Christian Faith, which is our royal intention, and...the principal end of this plantation...[6]

The group called Puritans arrived nearly a decade after the Pilgrims. During their journey to America, their leader, John Winthrop, authored a work, the title of which described their role in America--*A Model of Christian Charity.*

This love among Christians is a real thing, not imaginary... We are a company, professing ourselves knit together by this bond of love...we are entered into covenant with Him for this work...[7]

Winthrop warned that, since they were declaring to the world that they were witnesses of the Christian lifestyle, there was an awesome responsibility resting upon them:

For we must consider that we shall be as a city upon a hill, the eyes of all people are upon us, so that if we shall deal

falsely with God in this work we have undertaken, and so
cause Him to withdraw His present help from us, we shall be
made a story and a by-word through the world. 8

Those words are relevant and significant for this nation even
today. The charters of other early Colonies reflected similar commit-
ments. In 1632, the Charter of Maryland issued by King Charles
described Lord Baltimore and his goals for the Colony:

> Our well beloved and right trusty subject Caecilius Calver,
> Baron of Baltimore...being animated with a laudable and
> pious zeal for extending the Christian religion...hath humbly
> besought leave of us that he may transport...a numerous
> colony of the English nation to a certain region...partly
> occupied by savages having no knowledge of the Divine
> Being. 9

In 1633, on arriving in the land designated by the charter:

> The governor, leading the expedition sent by Lord Baltimore,
> took possession of the country "for our Lord Jesus Christ"
> and made "Christianity the established faith of the land."
> One of the leaders wrote: "bearing on our shoulders a huge
> cross, which we had hewn from a tree, we moved in proces-
> sion to a spot selected...and erected it as a trophy to Christ
> our Savior...10

In 1647, William Bradford, the leader of the Pilgrims, collected his
notes from earlier years and compiled them into *Of Plymouth
Plantation,* an historical account of why the Pilgrims came to the new
world:

> ...a great hope and inward zeal they had of laying some
> good foundation...for the propagating and advancing the
> gospel of the kingdom of Christ...their desires were set on
> the ways of God, and to enjoy his ordinances...they rested
> on his providence and knew whom they had believed. 11

Quakers and other Christian "minority" denominations began to
settle in North Carolina in 1653. Several years later they obtained a
charter confirming what was already obvious, that the settlement was
established for:

...the propagation of the gospel...in the parts of America not yet cultivated and planted...[12]

The Charter of Rhode Island, granted by King Charles II in July 1663, reflected the same goals as the other charters:

The colonies are to pursue with peace and loyal minds their sober, serious, and religious intentions...in holy Christian faith...A most flourishing civil state may stand and best be maintained...rightly grounded upon Gospel principles. [13]

In 1731, some 100 settlers moved into the Georgia area and were soon followed by Moravians and other Christian minority groups. What did they do on their arrival in the new territory?

...when they touched shore, kneeled in thanks to God. They said, "Our end in leaving our native country is not to gain riches and honor, but singly this: to live wholly to the glory of God." The object...was "to make Georgia a religious colony" ...they invited John and Charles Wesley and Rev. George Whitefield over to serve as chaplains, oversee Indian affairs and build orphanages, etc. When Whitefield died, the legislature attempted to have him buried there at public cost in honor of his influence. [14]

The charters of Connecticut, New Hampshire, and New Jersey were virtually a restatement of the Christian goals reflected in the other charters. [15]

America's First Governments

As the number of Colonists and settlements increased, so did the need for government. Though relying heavily on the personal self-control and integrity of the individual members of each respective Colony, the people recognized the benefit of civil regulations. Thus resulted the first legitimate constitution ever written in the United States: The Fundamental Orders of Connecticut. Our own federal Constitution is "in lineal descent more nearly related to that of Connecticut than to any of the other thirteen Colonies." [16] This constitution, written primarily by Puritan minister Thomas Hooker, was the beginning of American government. The instructions delivered to the committee that convened to frame the laws was to make them:

...as near the law of God as they can be. [17]

On January 14, 1639, the men from Hartford, Weathersfield, and Windsor gathered in Hartford and adopted this constitution. Its preamble proclaimed their reason for establishing this government:

...well knowing where a people are gathered together the word of God requires that to maintain the peace and union of such a people there should be an orderly and decent government established according to God...18

It went on to explain how this was to be attained:

...entering into combination and confederation together, to maintain and preserve the liberty and purity of the gospel of our Lord Jesus which we now profess...[that] gospel is now practiced amongst us; as also in our civil affairs to be guided and governed according to such laws, rules, orders, and decrees...19

When the Colonists of Exeter, New Hampshire, established their government seven months later, they expressed the same rationale:

...considering with ourselves the holy will of God and our own necessity, that we should not live without wholesome laws and civil government among us, of which we are altogether destitute, do, in the name of Christ and in the sight of God, combine ourselves together to erect and set up among us such government as shall be, to our best discerning, agreeable to the will of God...20

A similar proclamation was made when Massachusetts, Connecticut, New Plymouth, and New Haven formed the New England Confederation in 1643:

We all came into these parts of America with one and the same end and aim, namely, to advance the kingdom of our Lord Jesus Christ...21

In 1644, the New Haven Colony adopted rules for their Courts:

...the judicial laws of God as they were delivered by Moses... [are to] be a rule to all the courts in this jurisdiction...22

In 1662, the Fundamental Constitution of South Carolina was drawn up by John Locke. It required people to: (1) believe that there is a God, (2) in Court, recognize Divine justice and human responsibility, and (3) be a church member in order to be a freeman of the Colony. [23]

In 1665 the New York legislature passed an act to uphold "...the public worship of God" and instruction of "...the people in the true religion." [24]

In 1681, the Quaker minister William Penn received a land grant giving him the land between New York and Maryland, the area later called Pennsylvania. On receiving this new land, Penn professed:

> ...God that has given it to me...will, I believe, bless and make it the seed of a nation. [25]

The following year, Penn wrote the Frame of Government for this new territory. It was to:

> ...make and establish such laws as shall best preserve true Christian and civil liberty, in all opposition to all unchristian...practices...[26]

The laws were very simple--whatever was Christian was legal, whatever was not Christian was illegal. Penn also told the Russian Czar, Peter the Great, that:

> "...if thou wouldst rule well, thou must rule for God, and to do that, thou must be ruled by him." Penn also said that "those who will not be governed by God will be ruled by tyrants." [27]

An article on Penn that appeared in the *Biographical Review* in London in 1819 stated that he:

> ...established an absolute toleration; it was his wish that every man who believed in God should partake of the rights of a citizen; and that every man who adored Him as a Christian, of whatever sect he might be, should be a partaker in authority...[28]

The distinction is clear: whoever believed in God could be a citizen, but only Christians could be part of the civil authority. The "absolute toleration" to which they referred was illustrated by the inclusion of Christians in government "of whatever sect they might be." As with so many of the Founders, Penn felt the issue was not whether an individual was from the correct denomination, but whether he was Christian.

In New Jersey in 1697, the governor made a proclamation "...in obedience to the laws of God" which enacted statutes "...encouraging of religion and virtue, particularly the observance of the Lord's day..."[29] The influence of Christianity and the Bible on New Jersey is seen even in the inscription that appeared on their provincial seal: Proverbs 14:34--"Righteousness exalteth a nation." [30]

Christians played vital roles in the early growth and orderly development of the new world: colonization, government, education, etc. Nearly every significant achievement in our early years was accomplished under the influence of Christianity.

The Founding of Education in America

In Europe, the Reformation had occurred because men like Martin Luther wanted the common man to read the scriptures for himself. It had been the illiteracy of the people and their inability to read the Bible for themselves that allowed so many abuses to occur in the name of Christianity. The civil atrocities that had occurred because the people did not know the Scriptures were not ancient history to the settlers in America--they were still fresh in their minds.

The settlers wanted to preclude the possibility of a repetition in America. Therefore, in 1647 in Massachusetts, one of the first laws providing education for children of Colonists was enacted. It was a calculated attempt to prevent illiteracy and to avoid the abuse of power that can be imposed on an illiterate people. This law, called the "Old Deluder Satan Law," had a specific intent:

> It being one chief project of the old deluder, Satan, to keep men from the knowledge of the Scriptures, as in former times...It is therefore ordered...[that] after the Lord hath increased [the settlement] to the number of 50 householders, [they] shall then appoint one within their town to teach all such children as shall resort to him to write and read...and it is further ordered [that] where any town shall increase to the number of 100 families or householders, they shall set up a grammar school...to instruct youth so far as they may be fitted for the university. [31]

This law for the establishment of schools was enacted to make sure that students knew how to read the Bible. The inseparability of education and Christianity was seen in America not only in grammar schools, but in every level of American education. Consider America's first college as an example: Harvard College in Massachusetts. It was established by the Puritans only a decade after their arrival in America. A pamphlet made available to prospective students indicated the rules to be observed by every student enrolled in Harvard. Notice some of their requirements:

Let every student be plainly instructed and earnestly pressed to consider well the main end of his life and studies is to know God and Jesus Christ which is eternal life, Joh. 17:3, and therefore to lay Christ in the bottom, as the only foundation of all sound knowledge and learning.

And seeing the Lord only giveth wisdom, Let every one seriously set himself by prayer in secret to seek it of him. Prov. 2,3.

Every one shall exercise himself in reading the Scriptures twice a day, that he shall be ready to give such an account of his proficiency therein...[32]

The official motto of Harvard was "For Christ and the Church" and prior to the Revolution, ten of its twelve presidents were ministers. [33]
In 1692, the College of William & Mary was founded in Williamsburg, Virginia, through the efforts of Rev. James Blair. It was chartered that:

...the youth may be piously enacted in good letters and manners, and that the Christian faith may be propagated...to the glory of God. [34]

In 1701, Yale was founded in Connecticut by ten Congregational ministers. Until 1898, every president of Yale was a minister. Its purpose was:

...to plant and under the Divine blessing to propagate in this wilderness the blessed reformed Protestant religion...[35]

Like Harvard, Yale also had guidelines and requirements for its students:

Seeing God is the giver of all wisdom, every scholar, besides private or secret prayer, where all we are bound to ask wisdom, shall be present morning and evening at public prayer in the hall at the accustomed hour...
...the Scriptures...morning and evening [are] to be read by the students at the times of prayer in the school...studiously endeavoring in the education of said students to promote the power and the purity of religion...36

In 1746, Princeton was founded by Presbyterians with the official motto "Under God's Power She Flourishes." The Rev. Jonathan Dickinson became its first president, declaring "Cursed be all that learning that is contrary to the cross of Christ!" Until 1902, every president after him was a minister.

In 1766, through the efforts of Rev. Theodore Frelinghuysen, Rutgers University was founded; it's official motto: "Son of Righteousness, Shine upon the West also." 37

An incident that occurred in 1779 with George Washington shows our Founders' commitment to include Christianity in education. Some chiefs of the Delaware Indian tribe visited him at his military encampment and brought him three Indian youth for training in American schools. Washington, speaking to the chiefs:

...assured them that Congress would "look upon them as their own children" and then made the following suggestion: "You do well to wish to learn our arts and way of life, and above all, the religion of Jesus Christ. These will make you a greater and happier people than you are. Congress will do everything they can to assist you in this wise intention..." 38

These are not isolated examples--these represent the norm:

One hundred and six of the first one hundred and eight colleges in America were founded on the Christian faith. By the time of the Civil War, non-religious universities could be counted on one hand. College presidents were almost always clergymen until around 1900. A study entitled "An Appraisal of Church and Four-year Colleges" (1955) stated that "nearly all of those institutions which have exerted a decided influence, even in our literary and political history, were established by evangelical Christians." 39

To substantiate that Christian education "exerted a decided influence...in our...political history" we need proceed no further than John Witherspoon, President of Princeton.   Not only did Witherspoon sign the Declaration of Independence and serve on over 100 committees in Congress, he also trained many of the nation's leaders while he was at Princeton:

1 President, 1 Vice President, 3 Supreme Court Justices, 10 Cabinet members, 12 Governors, 60 Congressmen (21 Senators and 39 Representatives), plus many members of the Constitutional Convention and many state congressmen. [40]

Each of these men had been trained in the college that declared "Cursed be all learning that is contrary to the cross of Christ!" And this is only one example from one college!   Christian education trained our statesmen and patriots, and to it we owe the form of government that established this nation as a world leader.

The Struggle for Independence

During the era of independence, there was probably no individual more influential than Samuel Adams.   Adams worked actively in behalf of liberty for over 20 years.   He helped America understand not only the oppression it was under, but also the solution to that tyranny.   His unparalleled efforts and leadership in America's fight for independence earned him the title, "The Father of the American Revolution."

In the years immediately preceding the Revolution, when English oppression was mounting and injustices were increasing, there was no reliable source for the Colonists to receive accurate information or patriotic inspiration.   It was to meet this need that Samuel Adams formed Committees of Correspondence.   The original Committee in Boston had a three-fold goal: (1) to delineate the rights the Colonists had as men, as Christians, and as subjects of the crown, (2) to detail how these rights had been violated, and (3) to publicize throughout the Colonies the first two items.

This Committee was replicated in numerous other localities. Through this network of Committees, their three primary goals and other "news flashes" were uniformly communicated throughout the towns and parishes in each state.   These Committees provided the unity and cohesion necessary for the Colonies to stand as one in a time when communication was difficult and unreliable.

Samuel Adams assumed oversight for the first goal of the
Committees: the exposition of their rights. His resulting letters, "The
Rights of the Colonists," were circulated in 1772. In explaining their
rights as Christians, Adams declared:

> These may be best understood by reading and carefully
> studying the institutes of the great Law Giver and Head of
> the Christian Church, which are to be found clearly written
> and promulgated in the New Testament. 41

He believed that to understand how to change a situation from evil
to good, one should:

> ...study and practice the exalted virtues of the Christian
> system. 42

Adams declared that their rights could be understood from the
New Testament, and that to bring about proper change they needed
to study and practice Christianity.   Not only did he feel that
Christianity was vital to the birth of the nation, he believed it to be
vital to its longevity:

> While the people are virtuous they cannot be subdued; but
> when once they lose their virtue they will be ready to
> surrender their liberties to the first external or internal
> invader...If virtue and knowledge are diffused among the
> people, they will never be enslaved. This will be their great
> security. 43

He never separated the struggle for freedom from Biblical principles. During conflicts between the Colonists' provincial congresses
and the governors of the crown, Adams would set aside days of
prayer and fasting to seek the Lord and His intervention on America's
behalf. 44   There was no separation between "political" activities and
"spiritual" activities.

The provincial congresses held sentiments no different from those
of Adams. They proclaimed to the nation:

> Our cause is just and it was...a Christian duty to defend it...45

As men responded to their Christian duty to defend the cause,
they organized into small militia groups. The groups were frequently
comprised of the men in a church and became known as the

"minutemen." A deacon in the local church was generally responsible for drilling the men. Their military exercise was not separated from their spiritual beliefs:

> On the days of drill the citizen soldiers sometimes went from the parade ground to the church where they listened to exhortation and prayer. 46

The charge given to the Minutemen by the Provincial Congress indicates how closely the national policy was tied to Christian principles:

> You are placed by Providence in the post of honor, because it is the post of danger...The eyes not only of North America and the whole British Empire, but of all Europe, are upon you. Let us be, therefore, altogether solicitous that no disorderly behavior, nothing unbecoming our characters as Americans, as citizens and Christians, be justly chargeable to us. 47

This was a charge from the government to the military to remember to maintain their Christian witness during the struggle! Congress did not want anyone to lay an accusation of misbehavior to the cause of Christianity in the United States.

That patriots were strongly influenced by Christianity is evidenced by a letter written from Abigail Adams to Mercy Warren in late 1775:

> ...A patriot without religion in my estimation is as great a paradox as an honest man without the fear of God...The Scriptures tell us righteousness exalteth a Nation. 48

Commander-in-Chief George Washington expressed similar sentiments when, in his general orders to his troops calling for services each Sunday, he declared:

> To the distinguished character of a Patriot, it should be our highest glory to add the more distinguished character of a Christian. 49

So inseparable were the ideas of civil institutions and religious principles that the description of the inhabitants of a town in Massachusetts seemed to describe the entire nation:

...civil and religious principles [were] the sweetest and essential part of their lives, without which the remainder was scarcely worth preserving. 50

In December 1773, in opposition to taxes, the Colonists held the infamous Boston Tea Party. Tensions escalated rapidly and led to open reprisals between the Colonies and Great Britain. In early 1774, Parliament passed the Boston Port Bill to blockade Boston harbor and eliminate all trade to or from the port. The Committee of Correspondence quickly instructed its members to inform the rest of the Colonies of the plight facing Bostonians. How did the other Colonies respond to this crisis?

The first action of the colonies was to call for a Day of Fasting and Prayer for June 1, 1774, the day on which the Boston Port blockade would take affect. Thus the colonies turned immediately "to seek divine direction and aid."

Secondly, the cities and towns of the sister colonies responded to Boston with letters affirming their support and sending them whatever supplies they could. Every colony contributed something for a period of over six months-- voluntarily--to strangers.

Third, there was an immediate move to join together in a general Congress in Philadelphia on September 5, 1774. 51

By August, the men of Pepperell, Massachusetts, had already sent many loads of rye. Their leader, William Prescott, must have summed up the feelings of a great many Americans, when he wrote to the men of Boston:

We heartily sympathize with you, and are always ready to do all in our power for your support, comfort and relief, knowing that Providence has placed you where you must stand the first shock. We consider that we are all embarked in [the same boat] and must swim or sink together. We think if we submit to these regulations, all is gone. Our forefathers passed the vast Atlantic, spent their blood and treasure, that they might enjoy their liber-ties, both civil and religious, and transmit them to their posterity...Now if we should give them up, can our children rise up and call us blessed?...Let us all be of one heart, and stand fast in the liberty wherewith Christ has made us free. And may He, of His infinite mercy, grant us deliverance out of all our troubles. 52

Boston gratefully responded to this outpouring of spiritual encouragement and material support:

> The Christian sympathy and generosity of our friends through the Continent cannot fail to inspire the inhabitants of this town with patience, resignation, and firmness, while we trust in the Supreme Ruler of the universe, that he will graciously hear our cries, and in his time free us from our present bondage and make us rejoice in his great salvation. [53]

It may well have been these open declarations of their reliance on Christ that caused one Crown-appointed governor to write to the Board of Trade in England stating:

> If you ask an American, who is his master? He will tell you he has none, nor any governor but Jesus Christ. [54]

That letter may well have given rise to the cry soon passed throughout the Colonies by the Committees of Correspondence:

> "No King but King Jesus!" [55]

As time progressed, the inevitable became obvious: there could be no reconciliation with Britain. Armed hostility had already begun at Lexington and Concord. A clean break was the only solution. Thus, on July 4, 1776, the distinguished representatives from throughout the Colonies officially declared their independence from Great Britain. They were not foolish; they realized that they were facing a monumental, and perhaps impossible, task by facing up to Britain's superior, well-honed fighting machine. They already knew they could *not* win this struggle solely through their own efforts. They would need help, and they knew just where to go to receive it. The final sentence of the Declaration of Independence announced the source of their aid:

> For the support of this Declaration, with a firm reliance on the protection of Divine Providence, we mutually pledge to each other our Lives, our Fortunes, and our sacred Honor.

They were entering into this commitment with more than just a token acknowledgement of God; they had a "*firm* reliance on the protection of Divine Providence." In fact, several places in that document reflected their commitment to God:

While reviewing Thomas Jefferson's original draft of the Declaration, the committee assigned to the task added the words, "they are endowed by their Creator with certain unalienable rights." Then, when the Declaration was debated before Congress, they added the phrase, "appealing to the Supreme Judge of the World, for the rectitude of our intentions," as well as the words "with a firm reliance on the protection of divine Providence." 56

Congress had not been content with Jefferson's version; more about God needed to be included in it. After all, this was a declaration to the world! Though much of the remainder of Jefferson's draft remained intact, the revisions Congress made reflected their firm conviction that God and civil government were inseparable. The Declaration was actually a dual declaration--it was a Declaration of *Independence* from Britain and a Declaration of *Dependence* on God.

The Declaration had been approved on July 4, 1776. At that time it was signed only by the President of the Congress, John Hancock. Four days later, July 8th, the Declaration was read publicly outside Independence Hall. On July 19th, Congress ordered the Declaration to be engrossed in beautiful script on parchment so that it could be signed by the entire Congress. On August 2, 1776, with the final wording having been approved and the final draft written, the members of the Continental Congress jointly placed their hands to the document in its support. As it was being signed, Samuel Adams summarized their sentiments when he declared:

We have this day restored the Sovereign to whom all men ought to be obedient. He reigns in heaven, and from the rising to the setting of the sun, let His kingdom come. 57

At the time of the Declaration, armed conflict had already been occurring for over a year. The "shot heard 'round the world" had been fired between the Colonists and the British on April 19, 1775. Knowing they were facing a war, Congress contemplated their choice for a qualified leader for their "military." On June 14th, 1775, John Adams heartily recommended and then nominated George Washington as Commander-in-Chief of the Continental Army. The following day, the 15th, Congress unanimously approved Washington, and on the 16th he gave his acceptance speech. Congress could have made no finer choice to command the disorganized and fledgling army. His first general order to his troops contained an admonition similar to the one Congress had delivered to the Minutemen. He called on:

...every officer and man...to live and act as becomes a Christian soldier, defending the dearest rights and liberties of his country. 58

As time progressed, incredible things happened to the American army. Somehow they avoided situations where they should have been crushed by the British. On one occasion, an unexplained thick fog appeared, allowing the Americans to escape what appeared to be certain defeat in the powerful, closing jaws of the Redcoat army. On other occasions, unexplained storms and torrential downpours appeared from nowhere to halt the British and prevent their escape, allowing the Continentals to surround them. Such instances are documented quite well in *The Light and the Glory* by Peter Marshall and David Manuel. So obvious was the help they received from their "firm reliance on Divine Providence" that George Washington proclaimed in March of 1778:

The hand of Providence has been so conspicuous in all this, that he must be worse than an infidel, and more than wicked, that has not gratitude enough to acknowledge his obligation. 59

At the conclusion of the War, in a circular letter addressed to the Governors of all the states, Washington stated:

I now make it my earnest prayer that God would have you, and the State over which you preside, in his holy protection...that he would most graciously be pleased to dispose us all to do justice, to love mercy, and to demean ourselves with that charity, humility, and pacific temper of mind, which were the characteristics of the Divine Author of our blessed religion, and without an humble imitation of whose example in these things, we can never hope to be a happy nation. 60

What an unusual way to close a war! It certainly would have been appropriate for Washington to express exultant joy, and to extend congratulations. Yet Washington chose to conclude the War by praying for the Governors and their states, and by reminding them that without the humble imitation of Christ, we could never be a happy nation.

Washington, while definitely worthy to be the "Father of the Country," would not have been able to lead the nation had it not approved of him and the things for which he stood. His spirit and beliefs reflected the entire nation, as confirmed in a pamphlet written by Benjamin Franklin while serving as emissary in France. The pamphlet, *Information to Those Who Would Move to America,* was written for those who were considering a move to America, or who might send their children there for studies and further opportunity. Franklin was in France--land of the enlightenment, land of the rejection of religion, land of atheism and marital immorality. Notice his description of America for the French:

...bad examples to youth are more rare in America, which must be a comfortable consideration to parents. To this may be truly added, that serious religion, under its various denominations, is not only tolerated, but respected and practised. Atheism is unknown there; infidelity rare and secret; so that persons may live to a great age in that country without having their piety shocked by meeting with either an Atheist or an Infidel. And the Divine Being seems to have manifested his approbation of the mutual forbearance and kindness with which the different sects treat each other, by the remarkable prosperity with which he has been pleased to favor the whole country. 61

One of the most famous symbols of the Revolution which still exists today is probably the Liberty Bell. It is undoubtedly the most famous bell in America; most people can recognize it in a photo without the aid of an identifying caption. It rang, proclaiming liberty, when the Declaration of Independence was first read publicly on July 8, 1776. But why did they choose to ring it in conjuction with the reading of the Declaration of Independence? Why does this bell symbolize freedom? Because the inscription emblazoned on its side was a perfect reflection of the document declaring our freedom. Most do not even realize that the Liberty Bell bears an inscription, much less that the inscription is a Bible verse:

Proclaim liberty throughout the land unto all the inhabitants thereof. Leviticus 25:10.

The symbol most closely associated with the Revolution proclaims that the Bible and civil government were bound together.

Official Acts of Continental Congress

Just as the records of individuals in the Revolutionary era are both interesting and revealing, so are the official records of government for that period. For example, when the representatives to the *very first* Continental Congress met together for the *very first* time, what was the *very first* thing that these patriots did?

The first act of the first session of the Continental Congress was to pass the following resolution:

Tuesday, September 6, 1774--Resolved, that the Rev. Mr. Duché be desired to open Congress tomorrow morning with prayer, at Carpenter's Hall, at nine o'clock.

Wednesday, September 7, 1774, A.M.--Agreeable to the resolve of yesterday, the meeting was opened with prayer by the Rev. Mr. Duché. 62

John Adams, in a letter to his wife, described what happened on that Wednesday morning:

...Accordingly next morning he appeared with his clerk, and his pontificals, and read the Psalter for the seventh day of September, which was the 85th Psalm. You must remember this was the next morning after we had heard the rumor of the horrible cannonade of Boston. I never saw a greater effect produced upon an audience. It seemed as if Heaven had ordained that Psalm to be read on that morning. After this, Mr. Duché, unexpectedly to everybody, struck out into extemporary prayer which filled the bosom of every man present: "Be Thou present O God of Wisdom and direct the counsel of this Honorable Assembly. Enable them to settle all things on the best and surest foundations; that the scene of blood may be speedily closed; that order, harmony and peace may be effectually restored, and truth and justice, religion and piety, prevail and flourish among the people. Preserve the health of their bodies, and the vigor of them in this world, and crown them with everlasting glory in the world to come. All this we ask in the name and through the merits of Jesus Christ Thy Son and our Savior, Amen."

Washington was kneeling there, and Henry, Randolph, Rutledge, Lee, and Jay, and by their side there stood, bowed in reverence, the Puritan Patriots of New England, who at that moment had reason to believe that an armed soldiery was wasting their humble households...They prayed fervently "for America, for Congress, for the Province of Massachusetts Bay, and especially for the town of Boston," and who can realize the emotions with which they turned imploringly to Heaven for Divine interposition. It was enough to melt a heart of stone. I saw the tears gush into the eyes of the old grave pacific Quakers of Philadelphia. 63

This incident is typical of the spirit and mind of the men who guided the nation through the Revolution. Both the national and state congresses called regularly for days of prayer and fasting or prayer and thanksgiving, depending upon the circumstances. Their written records calling for such days were far from pluralistic--they were Christian. Notice this Massachusetts proclamation, given in April 1775, when the ominous stormclouds of war were evident to the entire nation:

Concord, April 15, 1775
In circumstances dark as these, it becomes us, as Men and Christians, to reflect that, whilst every prudent measure should be taken to ward off the impending judgments...all confidence must be...reposed only on that God who rules in the Armies of Heaven, and without whose blessing the best human counsels are but foolishness--and all created power vanity;

It is the happiness of his Church that, when the Powers of Earth and Hell combine against it...the Throne of Grace is of the easiest access--and its appeal thither is graciously invited by the Father of Mercies, who has assured it, that when his Children ask bread he will not give them a stone:

Resolved, that it be, and hereby is recommended to the good people of this colony of all denominations, that thursday the eleventh day of May next be set apart as a day of public humiliation, fasting and prayer...to confess the sins...to implore the forgiveness of all our transgressions...and a blessing on the husbandry, manufactures, and other lawful employments of this people, and especially that the union of the American Colonies in defence of their rights (for which hitherto we desire to thank Almighty God) may be preserved and confirmed...and that America may soon behold a gracious interposition of Heaven...

By Order of the Provincial Congress,
John Hancock, President. 64

In May 1776, Congress appointed a day of fasting and prayer so that the nation might:

...by a sincere repentance...and through the merits and mediation of Jesus Christ obtain His pardon and forgiveness. 65

After the birth of the new and independent nation was announced through the Declaration, a committee composed of John Adams, Thomas Jefferson, and Ben Franklin, was appointed to draft a seal for the newly united states. The seal was to reflect the philosophy and belief of the new nation. Although Congress eventually delayed the adoption of any seal, the suggestions offered by the members of that committee again reflect the belief that the Bible was inseparable from civil government. Franklin proposed:

Moses standing on the shore, and extending his hand over the sea, thereby causing the same to overwhelm Pharaoh who is sitting in an open chariot, a crown on his head and a sword in his hand. Rays from a pillar of fire in the clouds reaching to Moses, to express that he acts by command of the Deity. Motto: Rebellion to tyrants is obedience to God. 66

Jefferson proposed:

...the children of Israel in the wilderness, led by a cloud by day, and a pillar of fire by night. 67

The following year, two significant events occurred in Congress on the same day. Congress already, as its first official act, had authorized chaplains to open Congressional meetings. However, after that act, the Continental Army had become the responsibility of Congress. Since Congress opened with prayer and issued proclamations calling the people to prayer, how could they conceive of any less for the military? They, too, needed prayer and chaplains--prayer was part of the national posture! Thus, Congress authorized chaplains for the Continental Army. Washington responded quickly and appointed chaplains for each regiment. 68

The second action of that same day was also of spiritual significance. From the arrival of the first Colonists, the Bible had been an integral part of America, in public and personal realms. The Revolution had now continued for over two years, and the impact from having lost Britain as their major trading partner was being felt in the Colonies. Their Bibles had been imported from England and now were in short supply. A request was placed before Congress to print or import more. The request was referred to a special committee which examined the possibilities and then reported:

...that the use of the Bible is so universal and its importance so great...the Committee recommend that Congress will order the Committee of Congress to import 20,000 Bibles from Holland, Scotland, or elsewhere, into the different parts of the States of the Union. Whereupon it was resolved accordingly to direct said Committee to import 20,000 copies of the Bible. 69

Congress acted in the same day to promote prayer and to provide more Bibles throughout the nation. Less than six weeks later, on November 1, 1777, Congress called for a national day of thanksgiving and prayer for the victory at Saratoga. As with previous proclamations, their words were neither religiously neutral nor pluralistic:

Forasmuch as it is the indispensable duty of all men to adore the superintending Providence of Almighty God; to acknowledge with gratitude their obligation to him for benefits received and to implore such further blessings as they stand in need of...70 ...[to ask] Jesus Christ mercifully to forgive and blot out [our sins] and to prosper the means of religion for the promotion and enlargement of that Kingdom which consisteth in righteousness, peace, and joy in the Holy Ghost... 71

As the war continued, further evidences of God's aid to the nation were recognized and gratefully acknowledged. The following series of documents shows how America's leaders reacted to the discovery of the plot by Benedict Arnold to betray them to the British. The first is a message from George Washington delivered to his troops through General Greene:

General Orders--Head Quarters, Orangetown, Tuesday, September 26, 1780.
     Treason of the blackest dye was yesterday discovered! General Arnold who commanded at Westpoint, lost to every sentiment of honor, of public and private obligation, was about to deliver up that important Post into the hands of the

enemy. Such an event must have given the American cause a deadly wound if not a fatal stab. Happily the treason has been timely discovered to prevent the fatal misfortune. The Providential train of circumstances which led to it affords the most convincing proof that the liberties of America are the object of Divine Protection. [72]

This Congressional response, taken from the *Journals of Congress*, followed on Wednesday, October 18, 1780.

Whereas it hath pleased Almighty God, the Father of all mercies, amidst the vicissitudes and calamities of war, to bestow blessings on the people of these states, which call for their devout and thankful acknowledgments, more especially in the late remarkable interposition of his watchful providence, in rescuing the person of our Commander in Chief and the army from imminent dangers, at the moment when treason was ripened for execution...It is therefore recommended to the several states...a day of public thanksgiving and prayer; that all the people may assemble on that day to celebrate the praises of our Divine Benefactor; to confess our unworthiness of the least of his favours, and to offer our fervent supplications to the God of all grace...to cause the knowledge of Christianity to spread over all the earth. [73]

As the Revolution continued, for a second time there arose a need for Bibles. Robert Aiken, publisher of *The Pennsylvania Magazine*, petitioned Congress in 1781 for permission to print the Bibles. Congress approved, and the next year the Bibles rolled off the press. That edition is now called the "Bible of the Revolution" and is one of the world's rarest books, being a purely American printing. [74] On September 10, 1782, Congress issued this endorsement of the new Bible:

The Congress of the United States approves and recommends to the people *The Holy Bible* printed by Robert Aiken of Philadelphia, a neat edition of the Holy Scriptures for the use of schools.
  Whereupon, Resolved that the United States in Congress... recommend this edition of the Bible to the inhabitants of the United States, and hereby authorize him to publish this recommendation in the manner he shall think proper. [75]

America's premier group of statesmen and patriots assembled in Congress was not ashamed of nor reticent about placing their whole-hearted endorsement on the use of the Bible for schools and citizens. Again, the government was encouraging Christianity.

Not only did Congress encourage the principles of Christianity, the states also encouraged them. This proclamation, issued by John Hancock, Governor of Massachusetts, was in response to the end of the war with Britain:

Boston, November 10, 1783
A Proclamation for a Day of Thanksgiving:
Whereas...these United States are not only happily rescued from the danger and calamities to which they have been for long exposed, but their freedom, sovereignty and independence ultimately acknowledged.
And whereas...the interposition of Divine Providence in our favor hath been most abundantly and most graciously manifested, and the citizens of these United States have every reason for praise and gratitude to the God of their salvation;
Impressed therefore with an exalted sense of the bless-ings by which we are surrounded, and of our entire depen-dence on that Almighty being from whose goodness and bounty they are derived; I do, by and with the advice of the council, appoint Thursday the eleventh day of December next, (the day recommended by the Congress to all the States,) to be *religiously* observed as a Day of Thanksgiving and prayer...he hath been pleased to continue to us the light of the blessed Gospel...that we also offer up fervent supplications, to cause pure religion and virtue to flourish...and to fill the world with his glory.
John Hancock, Esquire
Governor of the Commonwealth of Massachusetts 76

Establishing a Stronger Government

With the cessation of hostilities and the victorious conclusion of the campaign against Britain, it was time to turn the full attention of the legislators toward securing the new freedom and liberty they had gained. The Declaration of Independence had declared their rights, but now it was time to secure them. To respond to this need, delegates from each state arrived in Philadelphia to revise the

Articles of Confederation under which the government currently functioned. As time progressed in their deliberations, it became evident that the Articles would not be sufficient for the new nation. Consequently, attention was turned toward the creation of a new pact of government. Although this Convention had not been convened to write a new constitution, it ultimately did, and therefore became known historically as the Constitutional Convention.

This Convention had begun in a manner quite different from the First Continental Congress. The first act of the earlier Congress had been to seek God, and that same attitude of reliance on God had been carried throughout the Revolution. But now, perhaps as a consequence of the nation's recent successes, they did not commence this endeavor as they had their previous ones. They neither requested God's aid nor acknowledged their dependence on Him.

From all historical accounts, there had been very little progress in their effort to establish a new government until one specific incident provided a new spirit for their endeavors. James Madison, a delegate to the Convention, kept fastidious personal records of its events and debates. It is his narrative that provides the description of the turning point in the Convention--a stinging rebuke by the 81 year-old Ben Franklin on June 28, 1787. At the time of Franklin's address, the delegates were embroiled in a heated debate over how the representation of each state in the new government would be decided. The dispute had caused great animosity and pitted the larger states against the smaller ones, creating bitter and hostile feelings between the states' delegations. Addressing George Washington, Franklin declared:

Mr. President:

The small progress we have made after four or five weeks close attendance and continual reasonings with each other--our different sentiments on almost every question, several of the last producing as many nayes as ayes, is methinks a melancholy proof of the imperfection of the human understanding. We indeed seem to feel our own want of political wisdom, since we have been running about in search of it. We have gone back to ancient history for models of government, and examined the different forms of those Republics which having been formed with the seeds of their own dissolution now no longer exist. And we have viewed modern states all round Europe, but find none of their constitutions suitable to our circumstances.

In this situation of this Assembly, groping, as it were, in the dark to find political truth, and scarce able to distinguish it when presented to us, how has it happened, Sir, that we have not hitherto once thought of humbly applying to the Father of lights to illuminate our understanding! In the beginning of the contest with Great Britain, when we were sensible of danger, we had daily prayer in this room for the Divine protection. --Our prayers, Sir, were heard, and they were graciously answered. All of us who were engaged in the struggle must have observed frequent instances of a superintending Providence in our favor. To that kind providence, we owe this happy opportunity of consulting in peace on the means of establishing our future national felicity. And have we now forgotten this powerful Friend? Or do we imagine we no longer need His assistance?

I have lived, Sir, a long time, and the longer I live, the more convincing proofs I see of this truth--*that God governs in the affairs of men.* And if a sparrow cannot fall to the ground without His notice, is it probable that an empire can rise without his aid? We have been assured, Sir, in the Sacred Writings, that "except the Lord build the house, they labor in vain that build it." I firmly believe this; and I also believe that without His concurring aid, we shall succeed in this political building no better than the builders of Babel: We shall be divided by our little partial local interests; our projects will be confounded; and we ourselves shall become a reproach and by word down to future ages. And what is worse, mankind may hereafter from this unfortunate instance, despair of establishing governments by human wisdom and leave it to chance, war, and conquest.

I therefore beg leave to move--that henceforth prayers imploring the assistance of Heaven, and its blessings on our deliberations, be held in this Assembly every morning before we proceed to business, and that one or more of the clergy of this city be requested to officiate in that service. 77

How did the delegates respond to this rebuff? One of them, Jonathan Dayton of New Jersey, reported:

The doctor sat down; and never did I behold a countenance at once so dignified and delighted as was that of Washington at the close of the address; nor were the members of the convention generally less affected. The words of the venerable Franklin fell upon our ears with a weight and authority even greater than we may suppose an oracle to have had in the Roman Senate. 78

Roger Sherman, of Connecticut, seconded Franklin's motion for prayer. 79 Edmund Jennings Randolph, of Virginia, further proposed:

...that a sermon be preached, at the request of the Convention, on the fourth of July, the anniversary of Independence, and thence forward prayers be read in the Convention every morning. 80

Someone then pointed out that the Convention had no funds and therefore could not pay the clergy. Notwithstanding, some clergy of the city, in response to the delegates' desire to convene with prayer, and having no desire for monetary remuneration, agreed to their request. Did these measures have an effect? Notice Dayton's records for July 2, after they had turned their attention toward God and initiated daily prayer at the Convention:

...we assembled again; and...every unfriendly feeling had been expelled, and a spirit of reconciliation had been cultivated...81

On July 4, in accordance with the proposal by Edmund Jennings Randolph, the entire Convention assembled in the Reformed Calvinistic Church and heard a sermon by Rev. Williams Rogers. His prayer reflected the sentiment which had now gripped the delegates following Franklin's admonition:

...we fervently recommend to Thy Fatherly notice...our federal convention...favor them from day to day, with Thy inspiring presence; be their wisdom and strength; enable them to devise such measures as may prove happy instruments in healing all divisions and prove the good of the great whole...that the United States of America may form one example of a free and virtuous government...May we... continue, under the influence of republican virtue, to partake of all the blessings of cultivated and Christian society. 82

Franklin's rebuff and the delegates response to it had been the turning point for the future of the nation. While neglecting God, their efforts had been surrounded with frustration and selfishness. With their repentance came a desire to begin each morning of official government business with prayer and even to attend church *en mass,* as government officials, to hear a minister inspire and challenge them. After returning God to their deliberations, were they able to effectively frame a new government?

"We, the people of the United States..." Thus begins what has become the oldest written constitution still in effect today...the greatest legal minds of two centuries have continued to marvel at it as being almost beyond the scope and dimension of human wisdom. When one stops to consider the enormous problems the Constitution somehow anticipated and the challenges and testings it foresaw, that statement appears more understated than exaggerated. For not even the collective genius of the fledgling United States of America could claim credit for the fantastic strength, resilience, balance, and timelessness of the Constitution. And most of them knew it. 83

As was seen in judicial rulings in the·last chapter, those who participated in the Convention unequivocally declared that Christianity was part of and the basis for the Constitution. Did this really have any effect on our form of government? Would it have made any difference if our Founders had embraced the enlightenment philosophy so prevalent in France that taught the complete separation of religious principle from government and education?

If our Founding Fathers had been smitten with the idealism of the Enlightenment...we would have established the same unstable form of government experienced by France, which has endured seven different governmental systems during the two hundred years that America has enjoyed only one. 84

Additional evidence that Christianity is the basis of the Constitution is seen in Article 1, Section 7, Paragraph 2, which states that the President shall have ten days to consider a bill, "Sundays excepted." To most people today, the provision of "Sundays excepted" does not declare a strong Christian construction of the Constitution. However, that was not the sentiment in earlier years, as evidenced by this excerpt from a January 19, 1853, Senate Judiciary Committee report commenting on the "Sundays Excepted" provision:

In the law, Sunday is a *"dies non"* ...The executive department, the public establishments, are all closed on Sundays;
on that day neither House of Congress sits...Here is a recognition by law, and by universal usage, not only of a Sabbath,
but of the Christian Sabbath, in exclusion of the Jewish or
Mahammedan Sabbath...The recognition of the Christian
Sabbath [by the Constitution] is complete and perfect.

Not only did the Senate view Sunday recognition as an important
aspect indicating the Christian basis of the government, even the
Courts declared the same.   Recall the *Charleston* case from the
previous chapter:

...the Lord's day, the day of the Resurrection to us who are
called Christians, the day of rest after finishing a new
creation. It is the day of the first visible triumph over death,
hell and the grave! It is the birth day of the believer in Christ,
to whom and through whom it opened up the way which, by
repentance and faith, leads unto everlasting life and eternal
happiness! On that day we rest, and to us it is the Sabbath
of the Lord...

For the most part, citizens of the United States no longer see
Sunday as a major reflection of Christianity. In *McGowan v. Maryland,
1960,* the Court said Sunday closing laws had no real religious significance, but only represented a national day of rest, relaxation, and
recreation (such an opinion contradicted even the case just quoted).
Understanding Sunday's importance in former years establishes why
earlier Courts and Congresses viewed the "Sundays excepted" provision as a clear declaration of Christianity in the government.

The activities surrounding the inauguration of George Washington
continued to reflect the infusion of Christianity into governmental
affairs. The April 23, 1789 edition of the *Daily Advertiser* reported:

...On the morning of the day on which our illustrious
President will be invested with his office, the bells will ring at
nine o'clock, when the people may go up and in a solemn
manner commit the new Government, with its important train
of consequences, to the holy protection and blessings of the
Most High. An early hour is prudently fixed for this peculiar
act of devotion, and it is designed wholly for prayer...[85]

The day before the inauguration, April 29, 1789, Congress passed the following:

Resolved, that, after the oath shall be administered to the President...the Speaker and the members of the House of Representatives, will accompany him to St. Paul's Chapel, to hear divine service performed by the chaplains. [86]

George Washington's inaugural speech, delivered to a joint session of Congress on April 30, 1789, reflected the same spirit and conviction which had characterized every previous act of government:

...it would be peculiarly improper to omit, in this first official act, my fervent supplications to that Almighty Being who rules over the universe, who presides in the councils of nations and whose providential aids can supply every human defect...No people can be bound to acknowledge and adore the Invisible Hand which conducts the affairs of men more than the people of the United States. Every step by which they have advanced to the character of an independent nation seems to have been distinguished by some token of providential agency...We ought to be no less persuaded that the propitious smiles of Heaven can never be expected on a nation that disregards the eternal rules of order and right which heaven itself has ordained...[87]

Following his election as President, the Baptists sent him a letter of congratulations. Washington's reply to them confirms the convictions prevalent among the delegates of the Constitutional Convention:

If I could have entertained the slightest apprehension that the Constitution framed by the Convention, where I had the honor to preside, might possibly endanger the religious rights of any ecclesiastical society, certainly I would never have placed my signature on it...[88]

Washington, as had been his custom in earlier years, remained outspoken and adamant in his promotion of the importance of Christianity to government. For example, when addressing the general committee representing the United Baptist Churches in Virginia in May 1789, he declared:

While just government protects all in the religious rights, true religion affords to government its surest support. [89]

He also declared:

It is impossible to rightly govern...without God and the Bible. [90]

Washington was convinced of God's importance to this nation:

I am sure that never was a people who had more reason to acknowledge a Divine interposition in their affairs than those of the United States; and I should be pained to believe that they have forgotten the agency which was so often manifested in the Revolution. [91]

In Washington's first year in office, Congress contemplated requesting him to declare a day for national thanksgiving. The *Journals of Congress* record the sentiments of one of its members on this issue:

Mr. Sherman justified the practice of thanksgiving on any signal even, not only as a laudable one in itself, but as warranted by precedents in Holy Writ: for instance, the solemn thanksgiving and rejoicing which took place in the time of Solomon after the building of the temple was a case in point. This example he thought worthy of imitation on the present occasion. [92]

For the Congress, since such an act was precedented in the Scriptures, it was worthy of emulation for the United States. They unanimously adopted the following resolution and delivered it to President Washington:

Sept. 25, 1789. Day of Thanksgiving.
Resolved. That a joint committee of both Houses... request that he recommend to the people of the United States a day of public thanksgiving and prayer, to be observed by acknowledging, with grateful hearts, the many signal favors of Almighty God, especially by affording them an opportunity peaceably to establish a constitution of government for their safety and happiness. [93]

Washington, heartily concurring with the resolution of Congress, gladly issued the following proclamation:

> Whereas it is the duty of all nations to acknowledge the providence of Almighty God, to obey his will, to be grateful for his benefits, and humbly to implore his protection and favor...Now, therefore, I do recommend and assign Thursday, the twenty-sixth day of November next, to be devoted by the people of these States...that we then may all unite unto him our sincere and humble thanks for his kind care and protection of the people of this country previous to their becoming a nation; for the signal and manifold mercies and the favorable interpositions of his providence in the course and conclusion of the late war; for the great degree of tranquility, union, and plenty which we have since enjoyed; for the peaceable and rational manner in which we have been enabled to establish constitutions of government for our safety and happiness, and particularly the national one now lately instituted; for the civil and religious liberty with which we are blessed...
>
> And, also, that we may then unite in most humbly offering our prayers and supplications to the great Lord and Ruler of Nations, and beseech him to pardon our national and other transgressions...to promote the knowledge and practice of true religion and virtue...
>
> Given under my hand, at the city of New York, the third day of October, in the year of our Lord one thousand seven hundred and eighty-nine.
>
> George Washington. [94]

Washington's proclamations for national days of prayer and thanksgiving were not unusual. For example, on January 1, 1795, he proclaimed a day of prayer and thanksgiving when America avoided being pulled into a war involving France, Great Britain, Spain, and the Netherlands. He issued another proclamation when the Jay Treaty with England was ratified and proclaimed another when Alexander Hamilton, leading the militia, squelched the Whiskey Insurrection in western Pennsylvania. [95]

During his years as President, he skillfully guided the nation through many tenuous situations and precarious circumstances. Probably in a manner no one else could have, he secured the nation in overall peace and stability. In addition to having personally traversed many stressful situations, he had observed many others. The French Revolution, with its proponents of amorality and atheism, had turned into a bloodbath and spectacle of horrors. Not only did Washington never want to see anything similar in the United States, he also did not want to see the philosophy that had caused it to infiltrate the thinking of Americans. Therefore, in his farewell address, he delivered an articulate warning to the nation summarizing the difference between the successful American government and the embarrassing French spectacle:

> Of all the dispositions and habits which lead to political prosperity, religion and morality are indispensable supports. In vain would that man claim the tribute of patriotism, who should labor to subvert these great pillars of human happiness...The mere politician...ought to respect and cherish them. Who that is a sincere friend to it can look with indifference upon attempts to shake the foundation of the fabric?...Whatever may be conceded to the influence of refined education on minds...reason and experience both forbid us to expect that national morality can prevail, in exclusion of religious principle.
> George Washington
> Farewell Address, September 19, 1796 96

Famous Founding Fathers

Thus far, the records from each era of America's history have declared that this is a Christian nation. However, there are still many more eras in our history, with still more "organic utterances" proving the Court's statement. While men like Samuel Adams and George Washington have already been quoted, there is still much more that they could say, as well as many of the other famous Founders.

SAMUEL ADAMS

Not only did Samuel Adams organize the Committees of Correspondence (discussed earlier in this Chapter), he also instigated the Boston Tea Party, signed the Declaration of Independence, called for the first Continental Congress in 1774, and served as a member of those Congresses until 1781. His participation in politics continued well after the War. He was active in Massachusetts, helping draft the state constitution, serving as a delegate to the state ratifying convention for the federal Constitution, serving as Lieutenant Governor under John Hancock, and then becoming Governor. Having given over two decades of his life and energy to the cause of America and liberty, he wanted to ensure that America never lost the things for which it had fought. He described the nation's true enemy:

A general dissolution of principles and manners will more surely overthrow the liberties of America than the whole force of the common enemy. While the people are virtuous they cannot be subdued; but when once they lose their virtue they will be ready to surrender their liberties to the first external or internal invader...If virtue and knowledge are diffused among the people, they will never be enslaved. This will be their great security. 97

With virtue and knowledge being the chief protection against the loss of their liberties, how could they be diffused among the people? What means should they use, and what standard would they use for virtue?

Let divines and philosophers, statesmen and patriots, unite their endeavors to renovate the age by impressing the minds of men with the importance of educating their little boys and girls, of inculcating in the minds of youth the fear and love of the Deity...and, in subordination to these great principles, the love of their country...in short, of leading them in the study and practice of the exalted virtues of the Christian system... 98

The plan could not be clearer: education based on Christianity.

JOHN WITHERSPOON

In addition to signing the Declaration of Independence, Witherspoon was a member of the Continental Congress for six years, where he served on over 100 Congressional Committees. Earlier in this chapter, his influence on the nation while President of Princeton was documented in that he trained 87 men for national positions, including those of President, Vice-President, Supreme Court Justices, cabinet members, U.S. Senators and Congressmen, not to mention a multitude of state officials. How did he feel about mixing politics and Christianity?

...it is in the man of piety and inward principle that we may expect to find the uncorrupted patriot, the useful citizen, and the invincible soldier--God grant that in America true religion and civil liberty may be inseparable...[99]

While this statement is strong, he had something much more forceful to declare:

> What follows from this? That he is the best friend to American liberty who is most sincere and active in promoting true and undefiled religion, and who sets himself with the greatest firmness to bear down on profanity and immorality of every kind. Whoever is an avowed enemy of God, I scruple not [would not hesitate] to call him an enemy to his country. [100]

PATRICK HENRY

Patrick Henry, known for the fiery speech in which he declared, "Give me liberty, or give me death!", was active in American politics until his death. He was a member of the Continental Congress, Commander-in-Chief of Virginia's military, helped write the first constitution of Virginia, and served many years in Virginia's House of Burgesses and General Assembly. He also holds a distinction held by none other: he was elected Governor of Virginia for five terms. He was so popular that, in spite of his refusal to run for re-election, the people elected him to the Governorship for a sixth term (which he refused to serve). In addition, although he declined the positions, George Washington selected him as the nation's Secretary of State and as the first Chief Justice of the Supreme Court. He also declined an appointment to the U.S. Senate, as Minister to France, and Minister to Spain. He was largely responsible for the adoption of the first ten amendments to the Constitution--the Bill of Rights. Since he was a great force behind the First Amendment, did he see it as separating church and state? And how did he feel about mixing public affairs with Christianity?

> It cannot be emphasized too strongly or too often that this great nation was founded, not by religionists [pluralism], but by Christians; not on religions, but on the gospel of Jesus Christ! For this very reason peoples of other faiths have been afforded asylum, prosperity, and freedom of worship here.   [101]

In assessment of Henry's life and work for America, his grandson, William Wirt Henry, said that Patrick Henry:

...looked to the restraining and elevating principles of Christianity as the hope of his country's institutions. [102]

Another of Henry's grandsons, Patrick Henry Fontaine, said that his grandfather had given himself to:

...earnest efforts to establish true Christianity in our country. [103]

Patrick Henry himself had declared:

The Bible is worth all other books which have ever been printed. [104]

JOHN JAY

John Jay, briefly presented in the last chapter, is worthy of further examination. Not only was he one of the three authors of *The Federalist Papers* and George Washington's selection as the first Chief Justice of the United States Supreme Court, he was also a member of the First and Second Continental Congresses and even served as its President. Along with Ben Franklin and John Adams, he negotiated the final peace treaty with England. He was Governor of New York, authored the New York Constitution of 1777, served as Secretary of Foreign Affairs under the Articles of Confederation, was Minister to Spain, and negotiated the 1794 treaty, now called the Jay Treaty, which kept the young nation from being pulled back into a war between England and France. Did he believe Christianity should be part of public affairs?

Providence has given to our people the choice of their rulers, and it is the duty, as well as the privilege and interest, of a Christian nation to select and prefer Christians for their rulers. [105]

He served as President of the American Bible Society for several years before his death. On his deathbed, when asked if he had any final words for his children, he replied, "They have the Book." [106]

JAMES MADISON

James Madison, because of his efforts at the Convention, is called "The Chief Architect of the Constitution" or "The Father of the Constitution." In addition to being one of the three authors of *The Federalist Papers,* he served eight years in Congress, eight years as Secretary of State, and eight years as President of the United States. While attending Princeton, he was trained by Rev. John Witherspoon. The fact that Madison chose to attend a college which had declared, "Cursed be all learning contrary to the cross of Christ!" is probably a sufficient statement of the importance of Christianity to him. What did he say about the relationship between God and civil institutions?

> ...religion...[is] the basis and foundation of government... before any man can be considered as a member of civil society, he must be considered as a subject of the Governor of the Universe. [107]

With his intimate knowledge of the Constitution, he would surely know if there was an intent to separate Christianity and the Constitution. Yet, he declared:

> We have staked the whole future of American civilization, not upon the power of government, far from it. We have staked the future of all of our political institutions upon the capacity of mankind for self-government; upon the capacity of each and all of us to govern ourselves, to control ourselves, to sustain ourselves according to the Ten Commandments of God. [108]

Madison believed the future of America did not rest on the Constitution, but on the ability of every individual to conduct himself according to the Ten Commandments! Yet, in *Stone v. Gramm* in 1980, the Court ruled that it was unconstitutional for school students to read the Ten Commandments on school property. Amazing! The Father of the Constitution says our institutions are built on keeping the Ten Commandments, and the Court says that is unconstitutional for students to see them. A reasonable question would be: "Who knows more about the Constitution, James Madison or the current Supreme Court?" Further information on the statements and actions of James Madison and Thomas Jefferson will be presented in Chapter 9.

GOUVERNEUR MORRIS

Gouverneur Morris was a Pennsylvania delegate to the Constitutional Convention. He was the most prolific member of the Convention in that he spoke 173 times on the Convention floor. As head of the Committee on Style, he was responsible for drafting and providing the final wording of the Constitution. In a physical sense, he actually "wrote" the Constitution. He also served in the Continental Congress, helped write the New York State Constitution, and served as a U.S. Senator from New York.

Having been intimately involved with the formation of the new successful government in the United States, in his *Observations on Government, Applicable to the Political State of France* and *Notes on the Form of a Constitution for France,* he offered some suggestions to the French in their efforts to establish their new government. What was his recommendation to them for providing success in a self-governing nation?

> Religion is the only solid basis of good morals; therefore education should teach the precepts of religion, and the duties of man toward God. 109

The man who "wrote" the Constitution declares that for self-government to work, **education** should teach the precepts of religion and the duties of man toward God. Now the Courts have taken exactly the opposite view!

ROGER SHERMAN

Roger Sherman holds a unique and distinguished position among the Founding Fathers. He is the only one who signed the nation's four major documents: the Articles of Association in 1774, the Declaration of Independence in 1776, the Articles of Confederation in 1777, and the Constitution in 1787. At the Convention, he was the one who seconded Franklin's motion to commence each day with prayer. He also proposed the compromise between the larger and the smaller states whereby one house of Congress would have representation based on population and the other house would have equal votes between states--our current system. He served in the U.S. House of Representatives, the U.S. Senate, and fourteen years as a judge in Connecticut. Did he believe that Christianity had any place in government? Did the Bible hold any relevancy for governmental policy?

While in Congress, he objected to a War Committee report which recommended 500 lashes as a punishment to be imposed by court-martials. Sherman successfully argued that Deuteronomy 25:3 limits the number of lashes to forty: "Forty stripes he may give him, and not exceed: lest, if he should exceed, and beat him above these with many stripes, then thy brother should seem vile unto thee." [110]

In 1776, when serving on a congressional committee which wrote instructions for an embassy going to Canada, Sherman included an order that the delegation was "further to declare that we hold sacred the rights of conscience, and may promise to the whole people, solemnly in our name, the free and undisturbed exercise of their religion," but added that all civil rights and the right to hold office were to be extended to persons of any *Christian* denomination. [111]

This is yet another example of a Founding Father with strong opinions about basing governmental and public policy on Christianity!

JOHN ADAMS

It was John Adams who personally urged Thomas Jefferson to write the Declaration of Independence. Adams not only signed the Declaration, he also served in the Continental Congress, was the U.S. Minister to France, and, along with John Jay and Ben Franklin, negotiated the final treaty ending the war with Britain. Afterwards, while serving as the U.S. Minister to Britain, he wrote a three-volume work entitled *A Defense of the Constitutions of the Government of the United States,* urging the nation to ratify the Constitution. It is widely believed that this work was read by most of the delegates to the state ratifying conventions.

After 10 years of representing the United States abroad, he returned home to serve two terms as Vice-President under George Washington. He was elected the second President of the United States, succeeding George Washington, and was the first President to live in the White House. During his Presidency, the Department of the Navy was organized and the Library of Congress was established.

Not only did he participate in the establishment of American government on Christian principles, as Minister to France, he worked closely with the French government. This provided him the opportunity to observe government conducted without Christian principles and to compare it with the government in the United States. Adams did not believe a republican form of government would work in France. He expressed concern over what might happen to "a republic of thirty million atheists." [112] He also believed that widespread French immorality would keep the French Revolution from producing a successful lasting government. It was religion and morality that made America distinctively different from France.

It was his personal experiences with both styles of government that, in a Presidential address to the military in October 1798, enabled him to state with firm conviction:

> We have no government armed with power capable of contending with human passions unbridled by morality and religion. Avarice, ambition, revenge or gallantry would break the strongest cords of our Constitution as a whale goes through a net. Our Constitution was made only for a moral and religious people. It is wholly inadequate to the government of any other. [113]

Notice other statements he made about the inclusion of Christianity in politics and public affairs:

> Statesmen may plan and speculate for liberty, but it is religion and morality alone which can establish the principles upon which freedom can securely stand. The only foundation of a free constitution is pure virtue. [114]

> The Christian religion is, above all the religions that ever prevailed or existed in ancient or modern times, the religion of wisdom, virtue, equity, and humanity...[115]

> Suppose a nation in some distant region should take the Bible for their only law Book, and every member should regulate his conduct by the precepts there exhibited...What a Eutopa, What a Paradise would this region be! [116]

> ...religion and virtue are the only foundations, not only of republicanism and of all free government, but of social felicity under all governments and in all the combinations of human society. [117]

In a letter to his son, John Quincy Adams, who was at that time Ambassador to Russia, the elder Adams admonished him:

> It is essential, my son...that you should form and adopt certain rules or principles...It is in the Bible, you must learn them, and from the Bible how to practice them. [118]

There is no doubt where John Adams stood on the importance of Christianity to politics and public affairs.

ALEXANDER HAMILTON

During the Revolution, Hamilton was a captain of a New York artillery unit, and later became secretary and personal assistant to General George Washington.   While a member of Congress, Hamilton called for the Constitutional Convention. He served as a delegate to the Convention and, as one of the three authors of *The Federalist Papers,* was responsible for almost two-thirds of its content. It was largely through his efforts in these papers that the nation understood the purpose of the new Constitution.   After Washington became President, he appointed Hamilton as the first Secretary of the Treasury. Since Hamilton helped Washington write his farewell address, that address reveals the beliefs which were Hamilton's as well as Washington's:

> Of all the dispositions and habits which lead to political prosperity, religion and morality are indispensable supports. In vain would that man claim the tribute of patriotism, who should labor to subvert these great pillars of human happiness...The mere politician...ought to respect and cherish them. Who that is a sincere friend to it can look with indifference upon attempts to shake the foundation of the fabric? ...reason and experience both forbid us to expect that national morality can prevail, in exclusion of religious principle. [119]

In a letter to James Bayard in April 1802, Hamilton outlined plans for a "Christian Constitutional Society" to promote the two factors that had been most influential in America: Christianity and the rule of law under the Constitution. [120]

JOHN QUINCY ADAMS

John Quincy Adams received an early start in politics. In 1788, when he was eleven, his mother, Abigail Adams, sent him to France to be with his father, John Adams, who was then serving as Minister to France. Within three years, at age fourteen, he had become so skilled that he received a Congressional appointment to a post in the Court of Catherine the Great of Russia. In addition to his diplomatic service in Russia, he was Ambassador to Britain and France.

He also served eighteen years in the House of Representatives, was Secretary of State under James Monroe, and was elected the sixth President of the United States. Having been in politics from his earliest years, having grown up during the Revolution as the son of a Patriot, and having served in national office for over three decades, what relationship did he see between Christianity and public affairs? Was there to be a separation between the two?

> The highest glory of the American Revolution was this: it connected, in one indissoluble bond, the principles of civil government with the principles of Christianity. 121

NOAH WEBSTER

Although he is most frequently associated with the dictionary bearing his name, few realize that he was also an active politician. He served nine terms as a member of the Connecticut General Assembly, three terms in Massachusetts' Legislature, four years as a judge, and was a strong influence in the ratification of the Constitution. What did he say about the relationship between Christianity and government?

> The religion which has introduced civil liberty, is the religion of Christ and his apostles, which enjoins humility, piety, and benevolence; which acknowledges in every person a brother, or a sister, and a citizen with equal rights. This is genuine Christianity, and to this we owe our free constitutions of government. 122

> The moral principles and precepts contained in the Scriptures ought to form the basis of all our civil constitutions and laws. All the miseries and evils which men suffer from vice, crime, ambition, injustice, oppression, slavery, and war, proceed from their despising or neglecting the precepts contained in the Bible. 123

The Strengthening of Education

After the Revolution, education gained more of a national perspective, as did nearly everything else in the Colonies. While states remained the highest authority, the new national consciousness caused common ideas and programs to be adopted among the individual states. Some of the pioneers of early education under the new government included Noah Webster, Jedediah Morse, and William Holmes McGuffey. What were their contributions to American education? What convictions did they hold about a sound educational system?

NOAH WEBSTER

Due to his extensive efforts in establishing sound education in America, Noah Webster has been titled "America's Schoolmaster." He authored textbooks and resource books for schools--dictionaries, spellers, catechisms, history books, and much more.

While teaching school in New York in the 1780's, he wrote his first speller. These spellers would change the entire nation. Millions of them were sold and they were used by virtually every educational group in America. Prior to these spellers, there was no objective standard in spelling--no right way or wrong way to spell a word. The same word might be spelled several different ways within a single document. It was through his efforts that spelling and pronunciation were standardized throughout the nation.

Having helped in establishing the nation's successful constitutional government, Webster recognized that education must continue to transmit the principles that gave birth to the nation. He believed that education was the guardian of true republican principles and that the success of our government depended upon the quality of our education. What did he believe to be crucial in any sound educational system?

In my view, the Christian religion is the most important and one of the first things in which all children, under a free government, ought to be instructed...No truth is more evident to my mind than that the Christian religion must be the basis of any government intended to secure the rights and privileges of a free people. 124

While in the Massachusetts Legislature, he worked to secure permanent funding for education. He wanted to see an educational system adopted that would:

...discipline our youth in early life in sound maxims of moral, political, and religious duties. 125

Webster's educational materials never divorced learning from Biblical perspectives. Notice his comments in the Preface of his *History of the United States:*

The brief exposition of the constitution of the United States will unfold to young persons the principles of republican government; and it is the sincere desire of the writer that our citizens should early understand that the genuine source of correct republican principles is the Bible, particularly the New Testament or the Christian religion. 126

It is extremely important to our nation, in a political as well as religious view, that all possible authority and influence should be given to the scriptures, for these furnish the best principles of civil liberty, and the most effectual support of republican government. The principles of all genuine liberty, and of wise laws and administrations are to be drawn from the Bible and sustained by its authority. The man therefore who weakens or destroys the divine authority of that book may be accessory to all the public disorders which society is doomed to suffer. 127

An examination of the original version of his *American Dictionary of the English Language* again illustrates his inclusion of Christianity in education. He regularly used Bible verses to clarify the context in which a word was used. Notice the examples he utilized to establish the individual connotations of the word "faith":

Being justified by *faith.* Rom. v.
Without *faith* it is impossible to please God. Heb. xi.
For we walk by *faith,* not by sight. 2 Cor. v.
With the *heart* man believeth to righteousness. Rom. x.
They heard only, that he who persecuted us in times past, now preacheth the *faith* which once he destroyed. Gal. i.

Shall their unbelief make the *faith* of God without effect?
Rom. iii.
Your *faith* is spoken of throughout the whole world. Rom. i.
Hast thou *faith?* Have it to thyself before God. Rom. xiv.
Children in whom is no *faith.* Deut. xxxii.

Since its original publication in 1828, this dictionary has undergone much censoring to remove the Christian perspective that it originally contained. Although the most popular dictionary in America continues to bear his name, it no longer reflects the spirit of the original.

JEDEDIAH MORSE

Dr. Jedidiah Morse, while teaching school in the early 1780's in New Haven, became dissatisfied with the treatment of American geography in the textbooks then available to schools. He took his own lectures and, in 1784, published them in the book *Geography Made Easy.* The book was a great success, as evidenced by the 25 successive reprints that followed. He continued his writing, mainly on American geography and history, authoring *The American Geography, Elements of Geography, The American Gazetteer, A New Gazetteer of the Eastern Continent, A Compendious History of New England,* and *Annals of the American Revolution.* His efforts deservingly earned him the title of "The Father of American Geography." What did this influential educator say about the importance of Christianity in education?

> To the kindly influence of Christianity we owe that degree of civil freedom, and political and social happiness which mankind now enjoys. In proportion as the genuine effects of Christianity are diminished in any nation...through...the neglect of its institutions; in the same proportion will the people of that nation recede from the blessings of genuine freedom...Whenever the pillars of Christianity shall be overthrown, our present republican forms of government, and all the blessings which flow from them, must fall with them. [128]

Notice that he said that if Christianity is neglected in the nation's institutions, the blessings over those institutions would recede. To confirm the truth of that statement, one need only observe the decline in American education that has resulted since the Court, in 1962, began disallowing Christianity in schools.

WILLIAM HOLMES McGUFFEY

Educator William Holmes McGuffey, best known for the *McGuffey Readers,* was professor and chairman of a department at Miami University of Ohio, formed the first teachers' association in that part of the nation, was President of Ohio University, and was a professor at the University of Virginia. His *Readers,* first printed in 1836, sold 122 million copies in 75 years. It was through his *Readers* that stories like those of George Washington and the cherry tree became famous. His efforts in education have prompted many to title him "The Schoolmaster of the Nation." In the Preface to his fourth *Reader,* he revealed what he felt was an essential ingredient in education:

> From no source has the author drawn more copiously, in his selections, than from the sacred Scriptures. For this, he certainly apprehends no censure. In a Christian country, that man is to be pitied, who at this day, can honestly object to imbuing the minds of youth with the language and spirit of the Word of God...129

In the foreword of one of the *Readers,* McGuffey wrote:

> The Christian religion is the religion of our country...On its doctrines are founded the peculiarities of our free institutions. 130

The nation's outstanding educational leaders (Webster, Morse, McGuffey, etc.) not only verbalized the importance of Christianity to education, they included it in their academic instructional materials.

What Did the Fathers Say to Teach?

In addition to what educational professionals had said, the Founding Fathers also delivered their own significant declarations on what should be part of education in America. Notice this statement from Samuel Adams:

> Let divines and philosophers, statesmen and patriots, unite their endeavors to renovate the age by impressing the minds of men with the importance of educating their little boys and girls, of inculcating in the minds of youth the fear and love of

the Deity and...the love of their country...in short, of leading
them in the study and practice of the exalted virtues of the
Christian system...[131]

Gouverneur Morris, the Pennsylvania statesman who was so
active in the formation of the Constitution, declared:

Religion is the only solid basis of good morals; therefore
education should teach the precepts of religion, and the
duties of man toward God. [132]

Thomas Jefferson, while President, also chaired the school board
for the District of Columbia. He authored its plan of education that
used the Bible and Watt's Hymnal as reading texts. [133] Notice his
comment on why the Bible should be included in any plan of
education:

The Bible is the cornerstone of liberty...students perusal of
the sacred volume will make us better citizens. [134]

Congress also believed that Christianity should be part of education, as evidenced by its endorsement of the "Bible of the Revolution":

The Congress of the United States approves and recommends to the people *The Holy Bible* printed by Robert Aiken
of Philadelphia, *a neat edition of the Holy Scriptures for
the use of schools.* [135]

Congress again emphasized the importance of Christianity in
education when it passed the Northwest Ordinance (the same day it
approved the First Amendment), declaring that religion, morality, and
knowledge were to be encouraged throughout the nation by the
schools and other means of education.

When Alexis de Tocqueville, the French observer of America,
examined the role that ministers held in the nation in the 1830's, he
commented that "the greater part of education is entrusted to the
clergy." [136] An 1854 report delivered by the House Judiciary
Committee of Congress reconfirmed the relationship between education and Christian ministers. After examining the historical role of
chaplains in Congress and the military, the Committee referred to the
Act of 1838 which stipulated that "the chaplain is also to discharge
the duties of schoolmaster." Not only was education not separated
from Christianity, it was not separated from Christian ministers!

An 1853 report by the Senate Judiciary Committee of Congress, delivered the year before the House version, described the influence of Christianity in American education:

> ...we are a Christian people...not because the law demands it, not to gain exclusive benefits or to avoid legal disabilities, but from choice and *education;* and in a land thus universally Christian, what is to be expected, what desired, but that we shall pay a due regard to Christianity...?

America's education system clearly included Christianity in its academics. Is there any indication that this system was successful?

In the 1840 census, about 90 percent of white adults were listed as literate. [137]

That percentage, despite the difficult and demanding lifestyles that faced Americans in the 1840's, is better than the percentage recorded today. The current educational system no longer receives high marks for national literacy. Project Literacy United States (PLUS) reports that the *illiteracy* rate in America is currently higher than any other industrial nation in the world. According to the National Institute of Education, the pool of *additional* illiterates in America is growing at the rate of 2.3 million per year!

So successful had been the system of education in America that John Adams remarked as early as 1765:

> [A] native of America who cannot read or write is as rare as a comet or an earthquake. [138]

The success resulting from including Christianity in all aspects of American life evinced this observation from Alexis de Tocqueville:

> America is still the place where the Christian religion has kept the greatest real power over men's souls; and nothing better demonstrated how useful and natural it is to man since the country where it now has widest sway is both the most enlightened and the freest. [139]

That the nation where Christianity had the greatest influence was also the world's most enlightened and freest was no coincidence!

Congressional Investigations

There were those in America who did seek, as the enlightenment had taught, a total separation of church and state. Their attempts to use the Courts to gain any semblance of a separation of Christianity from the government and public affairs had been completely unsuccessful (as evidenced in the previous chapter). Our Founders made it clear that Christianity was not to be separated from any portion of public affairs.

Having failed in the Courts, those seeking a separation of church and state turned their efforts to different channels. They petitioned Congress to separate church and state--to remove chaplains from the Congressional halls and from the military. These petitions were referred to the appropriate committees of Congress for consideration: the Committees on the Judiciary. Those Committees conducted extensive investigations into historical records and laws to determine if it would be appropriate to separate church and state. Excerpts from their final reports are given below. The reports are given in their entirety in the 1864 history book by B.F. Morris. [140] What did each of these committees conclude after their investigations?

In the Senate of the United States, January 19, 1853, Mr. Badger made the following report:
The ground on which the petitioners found their prayer is, that the provisions of law...are in violation of the first amendment of the constitution of the United States, which declares that "Congress shall make no law respecting an establishment of religion, or prohibiting the free exercise thereof."
It thus becomes necessary to inquire whether the position of the petitioners be correct.
The clause speaks of "an establishment of religion." What is meant by that expression? It referred, without doubt, to that establishment which existed in the mother-country, and its meaning is to be ascertained by ascertaining what that establishment was. It was the connection, with the state, of a particular religious society [denomination]...
*...we are a Christian people...*not because the law demands it, not to gain exclusive benefits or to avoid legal disabilities, but from choice and education; *and in a land thus universally Christian, what is to be expected, what desired, but that we shall pay a due regard to Christianity...?*

...The whole view of the petitioners seems founded upon mistaken conceptions of the meaning of the Constitution... They intended, by this amendment, to prohibit "an establishment of religion: such as the English Church presented, or any thing like it. *But they had no fear or jealousy of religion itself, nor did they wish to see us an irreligious people...they did not intend to spread over all the public authorities and the whole public action of the nation the dead and revolting spectacle of atheistic apathy.* Not so had the battles of the Revolution been fought and the deliberations of the Revolutionary Congress been conducted. (emphasis added)

March 27, 1854. Mr Meacham, from the [House] Committee on the Judiciary:

The Committee on the Judiciary...had the subject under consideration, and, after careful examination, are not prepared to come to the conclusion desired by the memorialists. Having made that decision, it is due that the reason should be given.

At the adoption of the Constitution, we believe every State--certainly 10 of the 13--provided as regularly for the support of the Church as for the support of the Government...*Had the people, during the Revolution, had a suspicion of any attempt to war against Christianity, that Revolution would have been strangled in its cradle. At the time of the adoption of the Constitution and the amendments, the universal sentiment was that Christianity should be encouraged, not any one sect.*

It [Christianity] must be considered as the foundation on which the whole structure rests. Laws will not have permanence or power without the sanction of religious sentiment-- without a firm belief that there is a Power above us that will reward our virtues and punish our vices. *In this age there can be no substitute for Christianity:* that, in its general principles, is the great conservative element on which we must rely for the purity and permanence of free institutions. *That was the religion of the founders of the republic, and they expected it to remain the religion of their descendants.* There is a great and very prevalent error on this subject in the opinion that those who organized the Government did not legislate on religion.

...the great vital and conservative element in our system is the belief of our people in the pure doctrines and divine truths of the gospel of Jesus Christ... (emphasis added)

Those wanting to divorce God from government found no allies in either the Courts or the Congress!

Outside Observers

In addition to those intimately involved in the birth and establishment of the nation, there were many others who made interesting observations on the relationship between Christianity and the government. Consider for example, Daniel Webster. Although he had no part in framing the Constitution, he was very active in government in the early years under the new Constitution. He served in the House of Representatives, the Senate, and as Secretary of State for three different Presidents. His political career spanned more than three decades.

In December of 1820, while delivering a speech at Plymouth commemorating the arrival of the Pilgrims, he described the legacy they had left the nation:

Cultivated mind was to act on uncultivated nature; and more than all, a government and a country were to commence, with the very first foundations laid under the divine light of the Christian religion. Happy auspices of a happy futurity! Who would wish that his country's existence had otherwise begun? [141]

What a rhetorical question! The overwhelming and resounding response from those then present would have been that no one could possibly have wished that the Country had begun differently! They were proud that this country had been founded on the Christian religion! Such a rhetorical question would be awkward today, for the answer would no longer be clear and obvious.

He concluded his address by summarizing the reasons the Pilgrims came to America:

Our fathers were brought hither by their high veneration for the Christian religion. They journeyed by its light, and labored in its hope. They sought to incorporate its principles with the elements of their society, and to diffuse its influence through all their institutions, civil, political, or literary. [142]

Another observer with an interesting perspective on America was Alexis de Tocqueville. As noted earlier, he traveled throughout the nation in the early 1830's and published his observations in *Democracy in America.* His writings, unveiling what America was *really* like 50 years after its inception as an independent nation, make fascinating reading. Notice these excerpts:

> The religious atmosphere of the country was the first thing that struck me on arrival in the United States. The longer I stayed in the country, the more conscious I became of the important political consequences resulting from this novel situation. In France I had seen the spirits of religion and freedom almost always marching in opposite directions. In America I found them intimately linked together in joint reign over the same land. [143]
> For Americans the ideas of Christianity and liberty are so completely mingled that it is almost impossible to get them to conceive of the one without the other...[144]
> Religion...should therefore be considered as the first of their political institutions...[145]
> ...they therefore brought...a Christianity which I can only describe as democratic and republican...From the start politics and religion agreed, and they have not since ceased to do so. [146]
> I do not know if all Americans have faith in their religion--for who can read the secrets of the heart?--but I am sure that they think it necessary to the maintenance of republican institutions. That is not the view of one class or party among the citizens, but of the whole nation; it is found in all ranks. [147]
> ...Christianity reigns without obstacles, by universal consent...[148]

It was obvious, even to a foreign observer fifty years after the Constitution, that Christianity was the _first_ of their **political** institutions! American historians from the same period reached identical conclusions and offered similar commentaries:

> This is a Christian nation, first in name, and secondly because of the many and mighty elements of a pure Christianity which have given it character and shaped its destiny from the beginning. It is preeminently the land of the Bible, of the Christian Church, and of the Christian Sabbath.

...The chief security and glory of the United States of America has been, is now, and will be forever, the prevalence and domination of the Christian Faith. 149   *B.F. Morris, 1864*

The government of the United States is acknowledged by the wise and good of other nations, to be the most free, impartial, and righteous government of the world; but all agree, that for such a government to be sustained for many years, the principles of truth and righteousness, taught in the Holy Scriptures, must be practiced. 150   *Emma Willard, 1843*

The North American Review, a magazine popular in 1867, stated:

The American government and Constitution is the most precious possession which the world holds, or which the future can inherit. This is true--true because the American system is the political expression of Christian ideas. 151

The selections in this chapter represent only a minute portion of what could be cited to establish why the 1892 Supreme Court declared:

...this is a religious people. This is historically true. From the discovery of this continent to the present hour, there is a single voice making this affirmation...these are not individual sayings, declarations of private persons: they are organic utterances; they speak the voice of the entire people...these and many other matters which might be noticed, add a volume of unofficial declarations to the mass of organic utterances that this is a Christian nation...

No other conclusion is possible after an honest study of America's history! Nonetheless, the contemporary Courts, in their strong war against Christianity, have been forceful and effective in promoting propaganda on separation of church and state. Not only does the nation *not* realize that separation of church and state is unconstitutional, as a whole we are not even aware that the privilege to exercise religious freedom *is* constitutional! A 1987 study showed that "only a third [of the nation's citizens] knew freedom of religion was guaranteed by the Constitution's First Amendment." 152 How did this nation's attitude toward Christianity and government get turned upside-down? How did we ever abandon our roots?

~6~
Protection from the Absurd

The move away from our clearly Christian roots began when the contemporary Courts refused to heed the warnings given through earlier Courts to rule by the intent of laws and not merely their wording. When the intent for which a law has been framed is discarded or ignored, that law can be applied in a manner that its sponsors would neither have imagined nor approved. The early Courts had ruled in such a way as to ensure that the people were protected from the results that come when rulings are based on absurd interpretations and applications of a law.

The *Holy Trinity* case was an excellent example of the Court ruling by the intent of a law and not merely its wording. The U.S. Attorney had attempted to prosecute the church under a law which originally had been enacted for an entirely different purpose. Recall that in 1887, when the Church of the Holy Trinity in New York employed a clergyman from England as their pastor, they had technically violated the law that stated:

> ...it shall be unlawful for any...corporation, in any manner whatsoever...to in any way assist or encourage the importa-tion...of any alien or...foreigners, into the United States...to perform labor or service of any kind...

While the church argued that the law was never intended to affect ministers, the prosecution persisted that the church had violated the written, black-and-white wording of the statute. The Court searched for the law's intent and discovered, from the Congressional records, that its enactment was to correct a specific abuse in the domestic railway labor market by prohibiting the importation of slave-type labor.

Although the church's actions did fall within the literal and technical wording of the law, they did not fall within the intent of that law. Therefore, the Court ruled that a prosecution of the church would be an absurd application of that law--a misuse of that law. The Court commented on the principle that guided its decision:

> It is a familiar rule that a thing may be within the letter of the statute and yet not within the statute, because not within its spirit, nor within the intention of its makers...for frequently

words of general meaning are used in a statute, words broad enough to include an act in question, and yet a consideration of the whole legislation, or of the circumstances surrounding its enactment, or of the absurd results which follow from giving such broad meaning to the words, which makes it unreasonable to believe that the legislator intended to include the particular act.

The *Holy Trinity* Court excerpted two other cases which had reached similar conclusions, though based on very different laws:

In the case of the *State v. Clark,* "The language of the act, if construed literally, evidently leads to an absurd result. If a literal construction of the words of a statute be absurd, the act must be so construed as to avoid the absurdity..." In *United States v. Kirby,* "All laws should receive a sensible construction. General terms should be so limited in their application as not to lead to injustice, oppression or an absurd consequence. It will always, therefore, be presumed that the legislature intended exceptions to its language which would avoid results of this character. The reason of the law in such cases should prevail over its letter..."

The Court established that whenever attempting to settle a dispute arising from a law, it must first determine the spirit of that law by examining:

...the evil which was intended to be remedied, the circumstances surrounding the appeal to Congress, the reports of the committee of each house...the intent of Congress...

Legislators are not able to consider every circumstance that might arise under the enforcement of a law they enact. There is a natural tendency for those developing solutions to problems to believe that the law springing from their extensive discussion and debate communicates more clearly than it actually does. They vividly recall the context in which the legislation was framed, and they could never envision its being interpreted or applied in a manner other than the one that led to its construction. However, those later called upon to enforce that law do not always see the intent that the legislators felt was so obvious.

Early Courts understood this. Five times in the brief excerpts given above from the *Holy Trinity* case, the Court specifically referred to the absurd results that could occur when a law is applied apart from its original intent. Those early Courts, unlike the contemporary ones, recognized the responsibility to interpret a law by its spirit, even if their decision appeared to disregard the literal wording of the law.

The two cases to which the *Holy Trinity* Court referred in its discussion of "absurd" applications of laws are presented below.

The State vs. Smith Clark, 1860

The offense is described from the case:

> The first count charges that the defendant did maliciously and willfully...break down...twenty panels of rail fence belonging to and in the possession of George Arnwine.
> The section of the act upon which this indictment was found provides that if any person or persons [who] shall willfully... break down...or destroy any fences...belonging to...any other person...shall be deemed guilty of a misdemeanor...

This is a very concise description of the law and of its violation by Smith Clark. Even common sense says it is wrong to go around destroying other people's fences. At this point, the defendant would be found guilty, for he has violated the law. However, there is more to this case:

> ...The defendant [Smith Clark] offered to show, by way of defence, that at the several times when he broke down the fence he had title to the land upon which it was built, and...that the fence which was destroyed was erected...upon the land of the defendant.

That puts a different light on it! The fence that Clark broke down was built by someone else on his property, property to which Clark held clear legal title. Clark had engaged in many "discussions" with his neighbor, George Arnwine, who persisted in building his fences off his property and on Smith Clark's property. Even though Smith Clark had literally and technically violated the law, the law had not been constructed to keep him from tearing down someone else's fences erected on his own property. It was Arnwine who was the real abuser of its intent. The Court recognized this as a violation of the "letter" of the law, but not of its "spirit":

> ...The language of the act, if construed literally, evidently leads to an absurd result. If a literal construction of the words of a statute be absurd, the act must be so construed as to avoid the absurdity...No one but a trespasser can be amenable to the provisions of the act.

The legislature had not included the word "trespasser" in the law, for it evidently felt the intent of the law was obvious. It could never have foreseen this attempt to misapply its law. Had the Court applied the law solely by its wording, and not according to its spirit, it would have created an injustice while supposedly administering "justice."

United States v. Kirby, 1868

This was the second case excerpted in *Holy Trinity*. The offense is described from the case:

> The defendants were indicted for...willfully obstructing...the passage of the mail and of a mail carrier...
> The act of Congress...provides "that, if any person shall knowingly and willfully obstruct or retard the passage of the mail, or of any driver or carrier...he shall, upon conviction, for every such offence, pay a fine not exceeding one hundred dollars..."
> The indictment contained four counts, and charged the defendants with knowingly and willfully obstructing the passage of the mail of the United States...and with knowingly and willfully obstructing...the passage of one Farris, a carrier of the mail, while engaged in the performance of his duty; and with knowingly and willfully retarding...the steamboat General Buell, which was then carrying the mail of the United States from the city of Louisville, in Kentucky, to the city of Cincinnati, in Ohio.

The law stated that no one could interfere with a mail-carrier delivering mail, and that no one could intentionally delay the delivery of the mail on a steamboat. Congress clearly intended that "the mail must go through!" Testimony in the case revealed that the defendant, Kirby, and the three with him, had definitely and deliberately interfered with Farris, the mail-carrier, and with the steamboat, the General Buell. Under the law, those violations should be punished! However, there is more to this case. The defendants argued that:

> ...two indictments were found by the grand jury of the county against the said Farris [the mail-carrier] for murder...and placed in the hands of Kirby...who was then sheriff of the county, commanding him to arrest the said Farris and bring him before the court to answer the indictments; that in obedience to these warrants he arrested Farris, and was accompanied by other defendants as a posse, who were lawfully summoned to assist him in effecting the arrest; that they entered the steamboat Buell to make the arrest, and only used such force as was necessary to accomplish this end...

That puts a different light on it! Kirby, the Sheriff, and the three men in his posse, did indeed interfere with the delivery of the mail by Farris, thus causing a delay for the steamship. Their actions indisputably constituted a literal violation of the wording of the law. But are we to believe that the law was intended to keep the Sheriff from arresting Farris, who had two murder indictments against him? It could be argued that if Congress had wanted an exception to its law, it would have provided for it. Isn't that a logical assertion? Obviously not! As in the previous case, the Court agreed that this was a violation of the "letter" of the law, but not of its "spirit":

> ...All laws should receive a sensible construction. General terms should be so limited in their application as not to lead to injustice, oppression, or an absurd consequence. It will always, therefore, be presumed that the legislature intended exceptions to its language which would avoid results of this character. The reason of the law in such cases should prevail over its letter.
>
> The common sense of man approves the judgment mentioned by Puffendorf [a Christian philosopher quoted by several of the Founding Fathers], that the...law which enacted, "that whoever drew blood in the streets should be punished with the utmost severity," did not extend to the surgeon who opened the vein of a person that fell down in the street in a fit. The same common sense accepts the

ruling...which enacts that a prisoner who breaks prison shall be guilty of felony does not extend to a prisoner who breaks out when the prison is on fire--"for he is not to be hanged because he would not stay to be burnt." And we think that a like common sense will sanction the ruling we make, that the act of Congress which punishes the obstruction or retarding of the passage of the mail, or of its carrier, does not apply to a case of temporary detention of the mail caused by the arrest of the carrier upon an indictment for murder.

The *Holy Trinity* Court cited an additional thirteen cases involving conflicts over the "letter of the law" vs. the "spirit of the law." These will not be excerpted here, but it is interesting to note that the Court went to great lengths to emphasize that the intent of the law must prevail over its literal construction. The Supreme Court stressed the responsibility resting on every Court:

...the legislature used general terms...and thereafter, unexpectedly, it is developed that the general language thus employed is broad enough to reach cases and acts which the whole history and life of the country affirm could not have been intentionally legislated against. It is the duty of the courts, under those circumstances, to say that, however broad the language of the statute may be, the act, although within the letter, is not within the intention of the legislature, and therefore cannot be within the statute.

When our Fathers enacted the First Amendment, the abuse they intended to avoid was that of having one, and only one, denomination of Christianity selected, protected, and promoted by the government. This was the evil they had experienced in England and planned to avoid in America.

Through their political writings and legal decisions they made clear their intent--to keep Christianity as the basis of government and public institutions, yet protect freedom of conscience to all individuals within the broad confines of basic Christian principles. For example, the argument for freedom of conscience was not allowed to protect immorality, polygamy, blasphemy, the promotion of lewdness, etc. Freedom of conscience stopped where violation of Biblical principles of morality began. However, their laws prescribed nothing on baptism, the role of the Holy Spirit in a believer's life, the structure or organization of a church; these were denominational questions, not part of the basic principles of Christianity. Nor did they dictate where, how often, or even if a person chose to worship God. As stated in *Updegraph v. The Commonwealth, 1826:*

> Chief Justice Raymond said, "I would have it taken notice of, that we do not meddle with the difference of opinion, and that *we interfere only where the root of Christianity is struck at."* The great and wise and learned judge observes, "The true principles of natural religion are part of the common law; the essential principles of revealed religion are part of the common law; so that a person vilifying, subverting or ridiculing them may be prosecuted at common law; but temporal punishments ought not to be inflicted for mere opinions." Thus this wise legislature framed this great body of laws, for a Christian country and Christian people. (emphasis added)

It was the basic principles of Christianity that were adopted by the governments and expressed in the various state constitutions:

> PENNSYLVANIA. Each legislator before he takes his seat, shall make and subscribe the following declaration: "I do believe in one God, the creator and governor of the universe, the rewarder to the good and the punisher of the wicked. And I do acknowledge the Scriptures of the Old and New Testament to be given by Divine inspiration."
> DELAWARE. Every person who shall be chosen a member of either house...shall make and subscribe the following declaration: "I, _____, do profess faith in God the Father, and in Jesus Christ His only Son, and in the Holy Ghost, one God, blessed for evermore; and I do acknowledge the holy scriptures of the Old and New Testament to be given by divine inspiration."
> NORTH CAROLINA. That no person who shall deny the being of God or the truth of the [Christian] religion, or the divine authority either of the Old or New Testaments...shall be capable of holding any office or place of trust or profit in the civil department within this State.

These were not declarations of denominational doctrine--these were declarations of Christian consensus. When someone was prosecuted under the laws of the nation, it was because of a violation of civil laws--Bible-based civil laws; it was not for spiritual reasons or to give spiritual correction.

The well-documented intent of the Founders has not been enough to deter the contemporary Court's absurd application of the First Amendment. Because the Framers did not actually include words stipulating that the First Amendment pertained only to denominations within Christianity, and not to Christianity as compared to other beliefs (atheism, humanism, Islam, etc.), the Court has been able to promote the letter of the law and circumvent and destroy its spirit. Our Fathers never envisioned that the First Amendment could be interpreted the way it is now--a weapon against the expansion of Christianity. As George Washington had stated to the Baptists of Virginia:

> If I could have entertained the slightest apprehension that the Constitution framed by the Convention, where I had the honor to preside, might possibly endanger the religious rights of any ecclesiastical society, certainly I would never have placed my signature on it...[1]

And as Congress observed in 1853:

> Had the people, during the Revolution, had a suspicion of any attempt to war against Christianity, that Revolution would have been strangled in its cradle. At the time of the adoption of the Constitution and the amendments, the universal sentiment was that Christianity should be encouraged, not any one sect. [2]

The Courts have now rejected and abandoned the spirit of the First Amendment, ignoring the massive documentation of our Founders that reveals its intent. We now find ourselves under the "absurd results" that inevitably follow such a repudiation of original intent.

~7~
The Absurd Becomes Reality--
Dismantling the First Amendment

Since 1947, the Court's rulings on the First Amendment have completely opposed its spirit and intent, now placing society under the absurd results forewarned by previous Courts. Eight cases will be excerpted in this chapter, illustrating that the decisions now regularly reached by the Courts not only qualify as "absurd," they even defy common sense. Unless otherwise footnoted, the quotes in each section in this chapter come from within the case being discussed.

Engel v. Vitale, 1962

This was the first case in which the Court applied its innovation of separation to overturn a longstanding tradition: school prayer. The issue in this case was New York students' use of a simple 22-word prayer that somehow didn't seem very dangerous:

Almighty God, we acknowledge our dependence upon Thee, and we beg Thy blessings upon us, our parents, our teachers and our Country.

Understand that when the Court declares something unconstitutional, it is saying that it is against the will and design of the Founders embodied through the Constitution. If the Court rules the use of this prayer unconstitutional, it will be saying that our Founders would have opposed it. It seems improbable that the Founders would find fault with the students' use of this prayer, particularly considering the details surrounding its use:

...the schools did not compel any pupil to join in the prayer over his or his parents' objection...

The Court not only established that this prayer was voluntary, it further stated that it was non-denominational--it merely acknowledged God. An accurate description of this relatively "bland" prayer appeared eight years later in 1970, in *Board of Education v. Netcong Board of Education:*

...In Engel v. Vitale...this 22-word prayer, requiring less than ten seconds of reading time, is as innocuous, nonsectarian and universal as could possibly be formulated. One commentator has described the prayer as a "to-whom-it-may-concern" prayer.

This prayer, by being voluntary and non-denominational, has met the requirements of the First Amendment. And what was the Court's ruling on this "to-whom-it-may-concern" prayer?

Neither the fact that the prayer may be denominationally neutral nor the fact that its observance on the part of the students is voluntary can serve to free it from the limitations of the Establishment Clause...[it] ignores the essential nature of the program's constitutional defects...prayer in its public school system breaches the constitutional wall of separation between Church and State.

The Court has declared that our Founders would have opposed this prayer! The Court was not satisfied with merely declaring the use of this prayer unconstitutional--it felt a need to disperse more propaganda about *its* doctrine of separation:

...a union of government and religion tends to destroy government and to degrade religion...

Did our Founders agree that a union between government and religion would degrade government and destroy religion?

...true religion affords to government its surest support... *George Washington* [1]

...religion and virtue are the only foundations...of republicanism and of all free government...*John Adams* [2]

...religion...[is] the basis and foundation of government... *James Madison* [3]

God grant that in America true religion and civil liberty may be inseparable, and the unjust attempts to destroy the one, may in the issue tend to the support and establishment of both. *Dr. John Witherspoon* [4]

Our Constitution was made only for a moral and religious people. It is wholly inadequate to the government of any other. *John Adams* 5

There is a definite disagreement between our Founders and this Court! The Court's contempt for the Founders is seen in this remark:

It is true that New York's...prayer...does not amount to a total establishment of one particular religious sect to the exclusion of all others...that prayer seems relatively insignificant when compared to the governmental encroachments upon religion which were commonplace 200 years ago.

The Court claims that this prayer was only a minor violation of the Constitution when compared to the encroachment by the Founders 200 years ago! This Court, by accusing the Founders of violating the principles of the Constitution, purports to understand the Constitution better than those who wrote it!

Courts nearly always cite previous cases as precedents--it is the means by which the past is used to give credibility to the present and also serves as a foundation upon which to build current decisions. A significant legal note to this case is that not one single precedent was used by the Court. That the Court was able to overturn 340 years of school history in America without the aid of a single reference was an unprecedented accomplishment of which it was proud, as evidenced by a comment made the following year in the *Abington v. Schempp* case:

Finally, in *Engel v. Vitale,* only last year [1962], these principles were so universally recognized that the Court, *without the citation of a single case*...reaffirmed them.

Why did the Court not include a precedent? There were no previous cases to support its decision in this case! The Court had refused to acknowledge the existence of opinions by the Founders, Congress, previous Courts, and others, because those opinions conflicted with the position the Court now assumed. This ruling was simply a declaration of the Court's new policy, revealing the way it would now interpret the First Amendment.

The Court employed an effective strategy to help create acceptance of its policy: the *appearance* of its widespread public support.

Advertising agencies frequently use this tactic, publicizing phrases such as "Everybody's doing it!"; "Everybody has one!"; "Don't be the last one in your neighborhood to get one!"; etc. to apply subtle pressure to accept their product. The Court had utilized the same soft-sell approach. Recall its comment? "...these principles [of separation of church and state] are so *universally recognized*..." In other words, "*Everybody* knows this is right--the whole world!" Without legal precedents to aid them, the Court relied on purveying an image of universal acceptance and support of its new policy. This was a patent misrepresentation. None of the states, reflecting the views of their citizens, had ever adopted this position. To the contrary, state laws represented a view opposite to the Court's. The Court had employed an effective strategy, but not an honest one!

How could such an absurd decision occur--a decision declaring voluntary prayer unconstitutional? Because these Justices were political judges, not constitutional judges. As Edwin S. Corwin pointed out in *The Constitution of the United States,* this Court, which during its tenure was able to completely remove God from education by a series of unprecedented decisions, *did not have a single judge with any prior judicial experience!* 6 Despite the oath the Justices took when entering office, the Court did not intend to follow the original intent and uphold the Constitution. It intended to make the nation's policies reflect its own personal philosophical views. In a superficial attempt to justify the decision in this case, the Court quoted James Madison:

> "[A]ttempts to enforce...acts obnoxious to so great a propor-
> tion of Citizens tend to enervate the laws in general and to
> slacken the bands of Society..."

The Court was proposing that students saying the 22-word prayer was an act so obnoxious to the nation's citizens that it would weaken society. The Court disproved its own statement the following year with statistics it presented in *Abington v. Schempp, 1963.* Since this prayer was merely a generic acknowledgment of God, how many in the nation might have objected to such an acknowledgment?

> ...Indeed, only last year an official survey of the country
> indicated that 64% of our people have church membership,
> while *less than 3% profess no religion whatever.*
> (emphasis added)

Contrary to the Court's assertion, that 22-word voluntary prayer was *not* an act "obnoxious to so great a proportion of citizens"--it did not weaken society. This case consisted of a series of ill-advised statements made by the Court.

School District of Abington Township v. Schempp, 1963

This case involved another voluntary activity by students: Bible reading. Occurring less than a year after the *Engel* case, it provided the Court further opportunity to solidify its new doctrine. At issue was a school policy which stated:

> At least ten verses from the Holy Bible shall be read, without comment, at the opening of each public school on each school day...Participation in the opening exercises...is voluntary. The student reading the verses from the Bible may select the passages and read from any version he chooses...There are no prefatory statements, no questions asked or solicited, no comments or explanations made and no interpretations given at or during the exercises. The students and parents are advised that the student may absent himself from the classroom or, should he elect to remain, not participate in the exercises.

As with the prayer used in the previous case, this too seemed to be a relatively innocent action. It was voluntary; the Bible was read without comment by one of the students from a version of his choice; and there was no instruction other than what was contained within the ten verses. Nonetheless, the Court produced testimony that this action was dangerous to the children:

> Dr. Solomon Grayzel testified that...if portions of the New Testament were read without explanation, they could be, and...had been, psychologically harmful to the child...

This was a very unorthodox action by the High Court: it quoted from individual testimony. The Court rarely quotes common individuals unless they are historically important or Justices commenting from previous cases. However, in this case it quoted a Dr. Solomon Grayzel. The Court was not using that quote to establish legal precedent--it was using it to present its own feelings. Contrast its feelings about the Bible with those of the Founders:

The Bible is the cornerstone of liberty...students perusal of the sacred volume will make us better citizens. *Thomas Jefferson* 7

It is impossible to rightly govern...without God and the Bible. *George Washington* 8

The Bible is worth all other books which have ever been printed. *Patrick Henry* 9

Suppose a nation in some distant Region should take the Bible for their only law Book, and every member should regulate his conduct by the precepts there exhibited...What a Eutopa, what a Paradise would this region be! *John Adams* 10

The Congress of the United States approves and recommends to the people *The Holy Bible*...for the use of schools. *Congress, 1782* 11

The moral principles and precepts contained in the Scriptures ought to form the basis of all our civil constitutions and laws. All the miseries and evils which men suffer from vice, crime, ambition, injustice, oppression, slavery, and war, proceed from their despising or neglecting the precepts contained in the Bible. *Noah Webster* 12

Here is another radical disagreement between this Court and our Founders. But the Court was not finished with its opinions. After its declaration of the Bible's psychological harm to children, it proclaimed:

"The [First] Amendment's purpose was not to strike merely at the official establishment of a single sect...It was to create a complete and permanent separation of the spheres of religious activity and civil authority...

Again, contrast this statement by the Court with what the Founders actually said:

The highest glory of the American Revolution was this: it connected, in one indissoluble bond, the principles of civil government with the principles of Christianity. *John Quincy Adams* 13

Whoever shall introduce into public affairs the principles of primitive Christianity will change the face of the world. *Benjamin Franklin* 14

Had the people during the revolution had a suspicion of any attempt to war against Christianity, that Revolution would have been strangled in its cradle. At the time of the adoption of the Constitution and the amendments, the universal sentiment was that Christianity should be encouraged, not any one sect. *House Judiciary Committee, 1854* 15

In this age there can be no substitute for Christianity: that, in its general principles, is the great conservative element on which we must rely for the purity and permanence of free institutions. *House Judiciary Committee, 1854* 16

The recent Court's statement is so historically inaccurate that it defies logic, as do many of its comments. The Court was attempting to create the appearance that it was doing something rational and logical--something that would have been widely accepted by our Founders. Untrue on all counts! The Court's pronouncements are sensible only to those attempting to subvert the intent of the Constitution and would have been universally rejected by the Founders. This Court further stated, as though it were a matter of common knowledge:

Almost 20 years ago in *Everson [1947]*, the Court said "...neither a state nor the Federal Government...can pass laws which aid one religion, aid all religions, or prefer one religion over another."

Another conflict between this Court and those who authored and originally applied the Constitution. The early Courts did prefer one religion above the others:

By our form of government, the Christian religion is the established religion; and all sects and denominations of Christians are placed upon the same equal footing. *Runkel v. Winemiller, 1799*

Christianity, general Christianity, is and always has been part of the common law...The laws and institutions are built on the foundation of reverence for Christianity. *Updegraph v. Commonwealth, 1826*

Providence has given to our people the choice of their rulers, and it is the duty, as well as the privilege and interest, of a Christian nation to select and prefer Christians for their rulers. *John Jay, First Chief Justice of the Supreme Court* [17]

The Court also stated in the *Abington* case:

It is true that religion has been closely identified with our history and government. As we said in *Engel v. Vitale,* "The history of man is inseparable from the history of religion."

In this instance, the Court is correct; American history *cannot* be separated from religion. However, the results of research conducted through a Department of Education grant regarding religion in students' textbooks does not substantiate that fact. The research on textbooks revealed:

...that not one of the...ten thousand pages had one *text* reference to a primary religious activity occurring in representative contemporary American life. [18]

To illustrate this finding, this excerpt, one of the many supplied by the researchers, indicates what is typical in high school textbooks:

Laidlaw, *A History of Our American People* (1981)...Of 642 listed events, only six refer to religion...The following supposedly important dates in American history are listed in this book: 1893, Yale introduces ice hockey; 1897, first subway completed in Boston; 1920, United States wins first place in Olympic Games; 1930, Irish Sweepstakes becomes popular; 1960, Pittsburgh Pirates win World Series; 1962, Twist--a popular dance craze. The above categories make it clear that such trivia is given more emphasis than any aspect of religion...[19]

The Court has effectively censored textbooks by the pressure it has placed on publishers through its rulings. This rewriting of America's history could never have occurred without the anti-Christian sentiment promoted by the contemporary Courts. The absurdity of the Court's decisions in prohibiting the students' actions in the *Engel* and *Abington* cases can be proven by proposing an absurd scenario. The Court frequently allows someone not directly involved in a case to speak in behalf of one of the sides through briefs of *amicus curiae*. Suppose that George Washington, Benjamin Franklin, and Thomas Jefferson filed briefs to appear before these Justices to express their feelings.

Begins George: "Although I firmly believe the basis of our government is religion and morality, and despite saying I would never have signed the Constitution if I believed it would ever have encroached on the rights to exercise religious principles, and despite passing the Northwest Ordinance saying that religion was to be promoted in schools on the same day that we approved the First Amendment, I firmly support your efforts to rid our schools of voluntary prayer and Bible reading. Clearly, this violates the First Amendment; and who should know better than I? Yes, you must prohibit prayer and Bible reading in schools and act to protect these young, impressionable students from religion. I urge you to disregard our history, our laws, and our traditions!"

"Let me add my support to what George has stated," says Ben. "Despite the fact that I said the principles of Christianity must be included in public affairs, despite calling for prayer for each of our sessions at the Constitutional Convention, and although I declared that I don't believe we can possibly succeed without God's aid and assistance, we definitely need to keep these students away from prayer and the Scriptures! Even though what I am now encouraging you to do is contradictory to everything I did during my long and extended years of public service, you must ignore what we did in the Constitutional Convention and in Congress; protect these students from the influence of religion!"

Thomas echoes, "Yes! And it doesn't even matter that this prayer came with the consent of the governed, that it was upheld by the state's own legislature and state's own Courts--you must act! You must go against the consent of the governed, against the 97 percent in this nation. Do not let these students pray, even if they want to!"

Obviously, we cannot picture our Founders making such appeals! Yet when the Court declares these items unconstitutional, this is what it would have us believe!

Stone v. Gramm, 1980

This case occurred 17 years after the banning of voluntary Bible reading in schools. Nationwide, schools had succumbed to judicial pressure and had now stopped the active use of the Bible. However, this case did not deal with its active use, but its passive use. Specifically, was it a violation of the Constitution to display the Ten Commandments on the walls of a school? After all, the Ten Commandments are not solely religious--it is an historical fact that they are the basis of the civil laws of the entire western world. When confronted with the argument of the secular importance of the Ten Commandments, the Court showed an emotional outburst of religious prejudice:

> The pre-eminent purpose for posting the Ten Commandments on schoolroom walls is plainly religious in nature. The Ten Commandments are undeniably a sacred text in the Jewish and Christian faiths, and no legislative recitation of a supposed secular purpose can blind us to that fact.

The Court pointed out the problem with displaying the Ten Commandments:

> If the posted copies of the Ten Commandments are to have any effect at all, it will be to induce the schoolchildren to read, meditate upon, perhaps to venerate and obey, the Commandments...this...is not a permissible state objective under the Establishment Clause.

Wouldn't it be terrible if the students were to somehow read, think about, respect, or even obey the Ten Commandments? What might happen if they were to respect their parents? Or not steal? Or perhaps not even murder someone, or not become involved in adultery? God forbid! If these children were to read and obey the Ten Commandments, it would apparently be in violation of the First Amendment (so says the Court):

> ...the mere posting of the copies...the Establishment Clause prohibits.

A single quote by James Madison will demonstrate the absurdity of the Court's statement. Madison, the "Father of the Constitution," also authored the essential elements of the First Amendment. Certainly he would know what it forbids. Did it prohibit children from viewing the Ten Commandments?

We have staked the whole future of American civilization, not upon the power of government, far from it. We have staked the future...upon the capacity of each and all of us to govern ourselves, to sustain ourselves, according to the Ten Commandments of God. [20]

Madison did not believe viewing the Ten Commandments was a violation of the Constitution; he believed obeying them was its basis! The Court declared unconstitutional the very thing Madison said supported our form of government. How ludicrous to think that this Court has a better understanding of the First Amendment than the one who wrote it!

State Board of Education v. Board of Education of Netcong, New Jersey, 1970

Following *Engel, Abington,* and several other similar cases, many still believed that there had to be a constitutional manner in which voluntary prayer and Bible reading could be allowed. After all, the First Amendment states that no law may be made which would "prohibit the free exercise [of religion]." With such clear Constitutional protection, it should not be too difficult to construct a statute acceptable even within the interpretations used by contemporary Courts. Notice this effort made by the Netcong school board:

On each school day before class instruction begins, a period of not more than five minutes shall be available to those teachers and students who may wish to participate voluntarily in the free exercise of religion as guaranteed by the United States Constitution. This freedom of religion shall not be expressed in any way which will interfere with another's rights. Participation may be total or partial, regular or occasional, or not at all. Non-participation shall not be considered evidence of non-religion, nor shall participation be considered evidence of or recognizing an establishment of religion. The purpose of this motion is not to favor one religion over another nor to favor religion over non-religion but rather to promote love of neighbor, brotherhood, respect for the dignity of the individual, moral consciousness and civic responsibility, to contribute to the general welfare of the community and to preserve the values that constitute our American heritage.

The plan was implemented by the school in the following manner:

At 7:55 A.M. in the Netcong High School gymnasium, immediately prior to the formal opening of school, students who wish to join in the exercise either sit or stand in the bleachers. A student volunteer reader, assigned by the principal on a first come, first serve basis, then comes forward and reads the "remarks"...of the chaplain from the *Congressional Record*...The selection of material to be read is made by the volunteer reader...The volunteer reader is free to add remarks concerning such subjects as love of neighbor, brotherhood and civic responsibility. At the conclusion of the reading the students are asked to meditate for a short period of time either on the material that has been read or upon anything else they desire.

Although this appears to be a sensible plan, the New Jersey Court found an ingenious way to declare it unconstitutional. The Court claimed *it* owned the children, and did not want *its* children exposed to religion:

It is hereby declared to be a principle governing the law of this state that children under the jurisdiction of said court are wards of the state...which may intervene to safeguard them from neglect or injury...

The Court was intervening to protect "its" children from the "neglect or injury" that might be caused by allowing them to voluntarily pray. But the U.S. Government has chaplains, and it is legal for them to lead Congress in prayer. Surely it can do no harm for students to hear the same prayers that our Congressmen hear. The Court did not agree:

...Public schools, unlike the halls of Congress, present a special case. This audience is without the maturity to express independence...What may be wholly permissible for adults therefore may not be so for children...

But the prayers the students read were part of the *Congressional Record*--part of the public record published by the United States Government and available to any citizens! It contains a record of the statements made on the floor of Congress. Despite being a public record--the Court prohibited students from reading it:

It is religious exercise to read from the *Congressional Record* "remarks" of the chaplain...reading from the *Congressional Record* may be an unconstitutional infringement upon the First Amendment.

But this was *completely* voluntary, and it occurred *before* school! That made no difference to the Court:

...[A] School program for religious exercises is not saved from being unconstitutional establishment of religion by providing for permissive attendance...[a] "period for the free exercise of religion"...was unconstitutional establishment of religion, and not essential to free exercise of religion.

The Court explained that only if it could be proven that the students would suffer harm by not being allowed to pray in the school gym would the Court entertain allowing "free exercise." This is further evidence that the Court is committed to thwarting *any* religious activity in schools! No matter how carefully worded, no matter how thoughtfully constructed, it appears that the Court will devise a way to forbid it!

Walz v. Tax Commission of the City of New York, 1970

This case considered the constitutionality of tax exemptions for churches. In reviewing the actions the Court had taken in previous cases, the Court complimented itself:

...we have been able to chart a course that preserved the autonomy and freedom of religious bodies while avoiding any semblance of established religion. This is a "tight rope" and one we have successfully traversed.

...the line we must draw between the permissible and the impermissible is one which accords with history and faithfully reflects the understanding of the Founding Fathers.

It seems incredible that the Court can seriously claim it has faithfully reflected the intent of the Founding Fathers, or that it has successfully walked the "tight rope" in the First Amendment! Its measurement of success is based on its own standards, not on the standards of the Founders. By removing any acknowledgment of God from the schools and public affairs of the nation, the Court considers itself successful. Its next statement again reflects not what the first Amendment says, but what the Court wants it to say:

...one of the mandates of the First Amendment is to promote a viable, pluralistic society and to keep government neutral, not only between sects, but also between believers and nonbelievers.

A pluralistic society is one which acknowledges no one religion above any other. Our Founders certainly were not pluralistic:

It cannot be emphasized too strongly or too often that this great nation was founded, not by religionists [pluralism], but by Christians; not on religions, but on the gospel of Jesus Christ! *Patrick Henry* 21

Let divines and philosophers, statesmen and patriots, unite their endeavors to renovate the age by...educating their little boys and girls...of leading them in the study and practice of the exalted virtues of the Christian system. *Samuel Adams* 22

You do well to wish to learn our arts and way of life, and above all, the religion of Jesus Christ...Congress will do everything they can to assist you in this wise intention. *George Washington* 23

The religion which has introduced civil liberty is the religion of Christ and his apostles...This is genuine Christianity, and to this we owe our free constitutions of government. *Noah Webster* 24

In this age there can be no substitute for Christianity...that was the religion of the Founders of the republic and they expected it to remain the religion of their descendants. *House Judiciary Committee, 1854* 25

Much, much more could be quoted, but the inaccuracy of the Court's comment is obvious. The promotion of a pluralistic society could not have been further from the intent of the First Amendment!

Wallace, Governor of Alabama v. Jaffree, 1984

This case dealt with an Alabama law authorizing a 1-minute period of silence in all public schools for meditation or voluntary prayer.

The Court declared the law unconstitutional, but the interesting part of this case is *why* the Court found it unconstitutional. Even though it conceded that a 1-minute period of silence for meditation was constitutional, the Court struck down the law. Why?

> ...It is not the activity itself that concerns us; it is the purpose of the activity that we shall scrutinize.

In reviewing the statements of the legislator who authored the bill, the Court established that:

> ...the statements of [the bill's] sponsor...indicate that the legislation was solely an "effort to return voluntary prayer" to the public schools...he intended to provide children the opportunity of sharing in their spiritual heritage of Alabama and of this country.

Having determined his intent when he authored the bill, the Court declared the statute:

> ...invalid because the sole purpose...was "an effort on the part of the State of Alabama to encourage a religious activity." [It] is a law respecting the establishment of religion and thus violates the First Amendment.

Even if the wording is constitutionally acceptable, a law may become unconstitutional if the sponsor's heart was "wrong"!

DeSpain v. DeKalb County Community School District, 1967

A kindergarten teacher had her students recite this poem:

> "We thank you for the flowers so sweet; We thank you for the food we eat; We thank you for the birds that sing; We thank you for everything."

Although the word "God" is not contained in this verse, the Court determined it was unconstitutional for the children to recite it. A Justice who dissented in this decision offered an interesting observation on the Court's ruling:

> Despite the elimination of the word "God" from the children's recital of thanks, [the] plaintiffs maintain...that that word is still there in the minds of the children. Thus we are asked as

a court to prohibit, not only what these children are saying, but also what plaintiffs *think* the children are *thinking*...One who seeks to convert a child's supposed thought into a violation of the constitution of the United States is placing a meaning on that historic doctrine which would have surprised the founding fathers.

The dissenting Justice was amazed that the Court could conclude it to be unconstitutional for school children to think about God!

McCollum *v.* Board of Education, 1948

In this case, religious classes had been offered as electives within schools:

In 1940 interested members of the Jewish, Roman Catholic, and a few of the Protestant faiths formed a voluntary association called the Champaign Council on Religious Education. They obtained permission from the Board of Education to offer classes in religious instruction to public school pupils in grades four to nine inclusive. Classes were made up of pupils whose parents signed printed cards requesting that their children be permitted to attend; classes were held weekly, thirty minutes for the lower grades, forty-five minutes for the higher. The council employed the religious teachers at no expense to the school authorities, but the instructors were subject to the approval and supervision of the superintendent of schools. The classes were taught in three separate religious groups by Protestant teachers, Catholic priests, and a Jewish rabbi...

Although the classes were voluntary, and students had to receive parents' written permission to attend the classes, the Court found these classes unacceptable:

...as we said in the *Everson* case, the First Amendment has erected a wall between Church and State which must be kept high and impregnable...Separation means separation, not something less...It is the Court's duty to enforce this principle in its full integrity...Illinois has here authorized the commingling of sectarian with secular instruction in the public schools. The Constitution of the United States forbids this...

After ruling in favor of McCullom and against the school program, the Court remanded the case to the lower Courts to implement its decision. A dissenting Justice argued that the Court had awarded McCullom too much. She had asked the Court to force the Illinois school board to:

> ...adopt and enforce rules and regulations prohibiting all instruction in and teaching of religious education in all public schools...in said district...

The Justice explained why he thought the Court had gone too far:

> The plaintiff, as she has every right to be, is an avowed atheist. What she has asked of the courts is that they not only end the "released time" plan but also ban every form of teaching which suggests or recognizes that there is a God. She would ban all teaching of the Scriptures. She especially mentions as an example of invasion of her rights "having pupils learn and recite such statements as, 'The Lord is my Shepherd, I shall not want.'" And she objects to teaching that the King James version of the Bible "is called the Christian's Guide Book, the Holy Writ and the Word of God," and many other similar matters. This Court is directing the Illinois courts generally to sustain plaintiff's complaint without exception of any of these grounds of complaint...

The Court ruled in favor of a single atheist who was not involved in any of the classes in question. She brought suit against the school district because she was personally offended by Christianity. She, a single individual, with the help of an eager Court, was able to "prohibit the free exercise [of religion]" in every school in the district! A concurring Justice in this decision commented that the Court was now assuming "the role of a super board of education for every school district in the nation."

These are eight representative cases selected from among many that show how the First Amendment is now being abused by the Court. The Court's current doctrine is foreign to our history and contrary to more than 300 years of practice. The Court has no historical or legal precedent for its decisions; it has created its own new standards for the First Amendment.

Recall the statue personifying Lady Justice? She is blindfolded, holding a balance in her hand. Why is she blindfolded? So that she cannot see the parties involved--so that she can administer justice impartially. The Court has now ruled that she may no longer remain blindfolded. She must remove her blindfold to see if a Christian group or a Christian principle is involved in the case. If so, she must rule against it. The absurd has become reality!

~8~
The Absurd Becomes The Standard

No longer is there any concern about isolated instances of absurd decisions--they are now the bench mark of the Court. The very things that our Founders would never have imagined have become matter-of-fact.

When the Court first struck down school prayer in the *Engel* case, it was unable to cite a single reference to justify the removal of that simple 22-word prayer. As will be seen through the following cases, a lack of precedents to cite is no longer a problem for the Court.

Wallace v. Jaffree, 1984

Recall that this was the case in which the Court ruled that an Alabama statute authorizing a 1-minute period of silence in schools for meditation or voluntary prayer was unconstitutional. When rendering this decision (22 years after the *Engel* case and 37 after announcing the doctrine of separation in *Everson)* the Court did not have any difficulty citing references. The Court used over 200 references to previous cases in this decision. By the sheer quantity of its citations, they appeared to have more than sufficient precedent to justify this decision.

An interesting question that might be posed would be: "What dates were on those 200 cases?" The dates reveal an amazing trend. The 200 cases fell into the following categories: cases before 1947 (the year the Court announced separation of church and state)--22; cases from 1947 to 1950--10; cases during the fifties--4; during the sixties--44; during the seventies--65; and during the eighties--55. Only 22 of the 200 citations occurred before 1947; the remaining 178 occurred after the Court's 1947 declaration! Of those cited before 1947, many came from the 1940 case, *Cantwell v. Connecticut,* in which the Court originally seized control of the First Amendment by means of the Fourteenth Amendment. The other pre-1947 cases deal with procedural questions and not issues specifically germane to school prayer.

Notice how the numbers increased as the years marched on: only 10 quoted from the fifties, but 65 from the seventies. The eighties appeared even more promising for this Court--by 1984 there were already 55 citations! The Court no longer has difficulty providing citations in a case--it has created its own pool on which it relies. This pattern occurs regularly in the Court's decisions.

Levitt v. Committee for Public Education, 1973

New York law mandated that all schools in the state, whether public or non-public, keep certain administrative records. The record requirements were purely secular, relating only to testing, attendance, etc. Obeying these laws cost the schools considerable financial expenditures and substantial amounts of staff time. Consequently, the legislature provided money for the public schools to cover these expenses and felt it should do as much for the non-public schools. After all, tax money had been collected from *all* families in the state, whether their children attended public or non-public schools. Therefore, the legislature:

> ...appropriated $28,000,000 to reimburse nonpublic schools in the State for...the preparation and submission to the state of various other reports as provided for or required by law or regulation.

Although the money was for non-religious activities, the Court ruled it unconstitutional because it went to religious groups. What precedents did the Court cite for this decision? **Pre-1947: 0; Post- 1947: 18.**

Committee for Public Education v. Nyquist, 1973

In order to ensure that students had safe facilities in which to attend school, the New York legislature had provided money solely for schools' maintenance of their physical facilities. The funding was available in large amounts for public schools and in nominal, token amounts for qualifying non-public schools. The money appropriated for the non-public schools was designated only for:

> ...maintenance and repair of facilities and equipment to ensure the students' health, welfare and safety...

The Court declared the legislature's actions unconstitutional. On which precedents? **Pre-1947: 1; Post-1947: 99.**

Stone V. Gramm, 1980

This was the case in which the Court ruled that it was unconstitutional for students to view the Ten Commandments at school. Only nine citations were used in this case. Six came from *Abington v. Schempp, 1963* (which removed prayer and Bible reading from schools); one referred to *Engel v. Vitale, 1962* (the first case on school prayer); and the other two were from *Lemon v. Kurtzman, 1971*, which established what the Court now calls "The Lemon Test," which declared that spiritual activities may be tolerated only if they have a predominately non-spiritual value (what the Court calls "secular legislative value"). **Pre-1947: 0; Post-1947: 9.**

Chambers v. Marsh, 1982

This case involved a challenge against the position of the chaplain in the Nebraska legislature. The Court ruled one aspect of the chaplaincy to be constitutional and another portion unconstitutional. Where did it find its precedents? **Pre-1947: 1; Post-1947: 32.**

Many, many other cases can be cited; the results differ little. The Court has established its own reservoir of cases to which it can scurry to declare a public religious expression unconstitutional.

Examining the history of the Court's decisions relating to matters of religion and government identifies three different eras. Two are very distinctive and easily identifiable; the other is somewhat blurred and serves as a transition between the other two. The first era can be described as pro-Christian, the middle era as Christian tolerant, and the last as anti-Christian. There are distinguishing traits in each era.

In the pro-Christian era, this nation was described by the Court as "a Christian nation" from its earliest rulings through the 1931 decision in *McIntosh*. The second era began following the *McIntosh* case. The Court changed its phraseology, indicating a change in philosophy. It moved from declaring us "a Christian nation" and "a Christian people" to describing us as only "a religious people" *(Zorach v. Clauson, 1952)*. In this transition period, the Court moved from the Christian definition that had been established, understood, and applied since our founding, to a pluralistic interpretation. In the anti-Christian years, even the watery acknowledgment that we are a religious people (much less a Christian people) is omitted. There no longer exists any religious base, as evidenced by "The Lemon Test" declaring that in order for anything spiritual to be tolerated, it must have substantial "secular legislative value" *(Lemon v. Kurtzman, 1971)*.

In the pro-Christian era, the Court's precedents were numerous and broad, often spanning two or more centuries. For example, in *Holy Trinity Church v. United States,* the Court quoted as many as 18 *different* founding sources and over 60 different *historical* precedents to rule that "this nation is a Christian nation...and no legislative action can be taken against Christianity." In the Christian-tolerant years, precedents covered a narrow band, being taken mainly from the decades immediately preceding the decisions. Few, if any, were cited from earlier times. In anti-Christian years, any decisions prior to 1947 are virtually ignored (since they would tend to disprove the Court's actions) and only its own decisions made since 1947 are cited. The anti-Christian Court has provided its own self-contained standards for proving what is "right."

In the early pro-Christianity years, the Court relied heavily on the intent of laws, placing the "spirit" above the "letter." It would search historical records to find the spirit of the law, quoting from numerous Founders and founding documents.

In the neutral and anti-Christian years, the only Founders quoted to show "intent" are James Madison and Thomas Jefferson, which is quite interesting, considering that Jefferson neither attended the Constitutional Convention nor participated in its framing or ratification. As pointed out earlier, had the enlightenment ideas in which Jefferson was tutored in France become part of our Constitution, we might have had the same results as France: seven different forms of government during the same period that we have had only one.

~9~
The Court's Defense of Its Position

The Court has employed a series of defenses to shield itself from attack and criticism when misapplying the First Amendment. This chapter will examine five defenses the Court utilizes in virtually every case dealing with the First Amendment: (1) its use of the Fourteenth Amendment, (2) its use of James Madison and his activities in Virginia, (3) its use of Thomas Jefferson, (4) its omission of major historical facts, and (5) its omission of important statements from both Madison and Jefferson. The Court has become skillful in its use of these five areas, having refined them well over the past four decades. Nevertheless, these defenses are not without fatal flaws which will be exposed in this chapter.

1. The Fourteenth Amendment

The Fourteenth Amendment was part of a quick succession of three Amendments at the conclusion of the Civil War. The Thirteenth, Fourteenth, and Fifteenth Amendments were written by Congress and ratified by the states within the five-year period, 1865-1870. All three dealt with the dominant issue that had precipitated the conflict: slavery. The Thirteenth abolished slavery, the Fourteenth guaranteed civil rights for former slaves, and the Fifteenth provided them voting rights. That the purpose of the Fourteenth Amendment was to secure civil rights for former slaves is established through the records of Congress and well-understood by historians, as illustrated by this explanation of the Fourteenth Amendment found in the *World Book Encyclopedia, 1986:*

> The principal purpose of this [Fourteenth] amendment was to make former slaves citizens of both the United States and the state in which they lived.

For some reason, in *Everson v. Board of Education, 1947,* the Court coupled the Fourteenth Amendment with the First Amendment. The Court stated that the Fourteenth Amendment enabled it to apply the First Amendment against the states:

> ...the First Amendment, made applicable to the states by the Fourteenth Amendment...Prior to the adoption of the Fourteenth Amendment, the First Amendment did not apply as a restraint against the states.

The Court further discussed the coupling of these two Amendments in *Abington v. Schempp, 1963:*

...this Court has decisively settled that the First Amendment's mandate that "Congress shall make no law respecting an establishment of religion, or prohibiting the free exercise thereof" has been made wholly applicable to the States by the Fourteenth Amendment.
The first Amendment declares that Congress shall make no law respecting an establishment of religion or prohibiting the free exercise thereof. The Fourteenth Amendment has rendered the legislatures of the states as incompetent as Congress to enact such laws...

Twenty-three years after the *Everson* case, in *Walz v. Tax Commission, 1970,* the Court reviewed the effects of this coupling:

...the Court largely overlooks the revolution initiated by the adoption of the Fourteenth Amendment...reversing the historic position that the foundations of those liberties rested largely in state law.
The process of the "selective incorporation" of various provisions of the Bill of Rights into the Fourteenth Amendment...has been a steady one...The Establishment Clause was not incorporated in the Fourteenth Amendment until *Everson v. Board of Education* was decided in 1947.
...And so the revolution occasioned by the Fourteenth Amendment has progressed as Article after Article in the Bill of Rights has been incorporated in it and made applicable to the States.

"The First Amendment made applicable to the states by the Fourteenth Amendment..."--such phraseology has now become commonplace. Any case concerning the First Amendment that appears before the Courts will contain this phrase.
Since the Fourteenth Amendment was ratified to guarantee civil rights for recently emancipated slaves, how could the Court combine it with the First Amendment? Because the Court used the wording of the Fourteenth, ignoring its intent. The Fourteenth specifically stated:

All persons born or naturalized in the United States, and subject to the jurisdiction thereof, are citizens of the United States and of the state wherein they reside. No state shall

make or enforce any law which shall abridge the privileges
or immunities of citizens of the United States...

Taking the wording of the Fourteenth Amendment, without regard
to its context or intent, the Court determined that the Constitutional
Amendments which previously pertained only to the federal government now pertained to the states also. Such an interpretation was
fundamentally opposed to the purpose of the first ten Amendments
(the Bill of Rights):

> The Bill of Rights was intended to be a restriction on the
> national government, not the states. Chief Justice John
> Marshall in the 1833 decision of *Barron v. Baltimore* empha-
> sized that the Bill of Rights restricted only the national govern-
> ment. But since the 1940s, the Supreme Court has interpreted
> Section I of the Fourteenth Amendment...as incorporating the
> Bill of Rights, i.e., making it applicable to the states. The
> Supreme Court has thus achieved precisely the opposite of
> what was intended by the framers of the Bill of Rights: instead
> of being solely a restriction on the national government, the
> Bill of Rights is now a restriction on the states. [1]

Did the Congress that framed the Fourteenth Amendment intend
to incorporate the First Amendment against the states? The answer
is an emphatic and resounding "No!" as evidenced by what was
called the Blaine Amendment. The Blaine Amendment, submitted to
Congress during the same time period as the Fourteenth
Amendment, was a specific attempt to apply the First Amendment to
the states. The Court quoted the Blaine Amendment in *McCollum v.
Board of Education, 1948:*

> No State shall make any law respecting an establishment of
> religion, or prohibiting the free exercise thereof...No public
> property, and no public revenue...shall be appropriated to...
> the support of any school...under the control of any religious
> or anti-religious sect, organization or denomination...And no
> such particular creed or tenets shall be read or taught in any
> school or institution supported...by such revenue...

What happened to that proposed Amendment, attempting to
separate church and state in each of the states? The Blaine

Amendment, as well as five similarly proposed ones, were voted down. The *McCollum* Court explained:

> The reason for the failure of these attempts seems to have been in part that the "provisions of the State constitutions are in almost all instances adequate on this subject, and no amendment is likely to be secured." *Id.* H.Res. 1, 44th Cong., 1st Sess. (1876).

The Congress rejected *six* attempts to make the First Amendment apply to the states. The reason given by Congress for their rejection was that "the State constitutions are in almost all instances adequate on this subject." The Court, using the Fourteenth Amendment to apply the First Amendment to the states, adopted what Congress opposed on six occasions. By not allowing the states and their constitutions to handle the issue, the Court is doing exactly the opposite of what Congress intended through the Fourteenth.

The legislators who framed the Fourteenth Amendment never imagined that their repeated opposition to attempts to apply the First Amendment to the states would be ignored by later Courts. The Court's current use of the Fourteenth Amendment is an affront to the intent of the Amendment, to the federal Congress which proposed it, and to the state congresses which ratified it. It is even an insult to the Court's own hero, Thomas Jefferson, who instructed:

> On every question of construction, carry ourselves back to the time when the Constitution was adopted, recollect the spirit manifested in the debates, and instead of trying what meaning may be squeezed out of the text, or invented against it, *conform to the probable one in which it was passed.* 2 (emphasis added)

For almost eight decades after the ratification of the Fourteenth Amendment, there had been no cases coupling the First to the Fourteenth. Since there were no previous decisions on which the Court might rely for guidance, it would have to make its own rules. For example, in *Murdock v. Pennsylvania, 1943,* the Court seemed unsure as to how far to advance its new doctrine:

> ...as a Court, we should determine what sort of liberty it is that the due process clause of the Fourteenth Amendment guarantees against state restrictions on speech and church.

The Court is saying, "Now, seventy-nine years *ex post facto,* we have figured out what they *really* meant to say in the Fourteenth. No Court before us has enforced it correctly, but we will!" This Court began doing what Congress had rejected on six occasions! This was an obvious case of usurpation--the Judges have taken over the role of the legislators in the making of laws. They strike down state laws they don't like and enact judicial laws they do.

The Court's own description given in *Walz v. Tax Commission, 1970,* is indeed accurate--there was a revolution initiated by the Court's use of the Fourteenth Amendment. Unfortunately, the revolution was not a revolution by the people, it was a revolution by the Courts, entirely outside the control of the governed.

2. James Madison and Virginia

A second ploy routinely utilized by the Court to give an image of credibility to its separation doctrine is to invoke James Madison and Thomas Jefferson. Notice this excerpt from *Walz v. Tax Commission, 1970:*

> ...Thomas Jefferson was President...and James Madison sat in sessions of the Virginia General Assembly...I have found no record of their personal views on the respective Acts. The absence of such a record is itself significant...Both Jefferson and Madison wrote prolifically about issues they felt important, and their opinions were well known to contemporary chroniclers.

When Madison is quoted, the Court focuses on his efforts in Virginia prior to the Constitutional Convention. These excerpts from *Everson, 1947,* and *Engel, 1962,* are illustrative:

> This Court has previously recognized that the provisions of the First Amendment, in the drafting and adoption of which Madison and Jefferson played such leading roles, had the same objective and were intended to provide the same protection against governmental intrusion on religious liberty as the Virginia statute. *(Everson)*

> In 1785-86, those opposed to the established Church, led by James Madison and Thomas Jefferson...[who] opposed all religious establishments by law on grounds of principle,

> obtained the enactment of the famous "Virginia Bill for
> Religious Liberty" by which all religious groups were placed
> on an equal footing so far as the State was concerned.
> Similar though less far-reaching legislation was being
> considered and passed in other States. *(Engel)*

The Court relies heavily on these two Founders and their activities
in Virginia prior to the Constitutional Convention. The Court presents
what was happening in Virginia as though it were standard throughout
the nation. What did occur in Virginia that brought such notoriety to
Madison?

In the years immediately preceding the Constitutional Convention,
Virginia was the *only* state that still had denominational laws:

> ...For the first 163 years of Virginia history, the Church of
> England was Virginia's only legal church. By law, every
> plantation or settlement had a house or a room set apart for
> the worship of God. That worship was legally bound to
> follow the English Book of Common Prayer, and everyone--
> man, woman and child--was ordered to attend. 3

At that time in Virginia, members of the Church of England, the
church in power, were numerically in the minority. Members of other
denominations (Baptists, Lutherans, Presbyterians, Quakers, etc.)
were more numerous than those of the Church of England.

Madison and Jefferson turned their efforts to assist the other
denominations. Jefferson authored the "Virginia Bill for Religious
Liberty," which would give all denominations in Virginia an equal
position, as was already the case in the rest of the states. Madison
worked hard for the bill's passage and wrote *Memorial and
Remonstrance* to delineate the reasons why the establishment of
one Christian denomination above others was wrong. When the vote
on the bill was taken:

> Thomas Jefferson was at his ambassadorial post in France,
> and James Madison was making one last eloquent plea on
> behalf of Jefferson's bill. Then the delegates began to vote.
> When the vote was counted, sixty-seven men had voted aye
> and twenty had voted no to disestablish the Church of
> England as the one legal state church, to end all taxation to
> support that church, and to grant religious freedom to
> the...settlers of Virginia. 4

From the Court's accounts, the situation in Virginia was typical of every state and, somehow, Madison and Jefferson singlehandedly corrected the entire nation. Untrue. What happened in Virginia was unusual--no other state had that practice. This was even backhandedly acknowledged in a one-line statement by the Court in *Engel:* "...less far-reaching legislation was being considered...in the other states." That was because the other states had already eliminated what Virginia was still embracing. The report by the 1854 Senate Judiciary Committee reaffirmed this, stating that Virginia was the *only* state which had a system of state-ordered tithes at the time of the Constitution.

The Court refers to the situation in Virginia and quotes the related statements by Madison and Jefferson without providing the proper context or setting. When statements are removed from the context in which they were spoken and without regard to the evil which they intended to correct, they cannot be equitably applied to different situations. Statements used out of context can be used to prove almost anything.

This is what has happened with the use of James Madison and his *Memorial and Remonstrance.* Madison was not fighting against Christianity, he was fighting *for* its free expression! He was representing the Baptists, Quakers, Presbyterians--he was representing Christians and fighting *for* Christians when he made the statements in Virginia which the Court now subverts.

3. Thomas Jefferson

As noted from the Court's excerpts, Jefferson's name usually appears in conjunction with Madison's. The statement of the *Everson* Court bears repeating:

> This Court has previously recognized that the provisions of *the First Amendment, in the drafting and adoption of which Madison and Jefferson played such leading roles,* had the same objective and were intended to provide the same protection against governmental intrusion on religious liberty as the Virginia statute.

As shown in Chapter 3, Jefferson did *not* play a leading role in either the First Amendment or the Constitution. Jefferson had been in Paris, serving as Secretary of State under George Washington. Jefferson *did* have much to say about the First Amendment, but evidently nothing the Court wants to quote in its decisions. Notice Jefferson's statements:

> *Kentucky Resolutions of 1798:* No power over the freedom of religion (is) delegated to the United States by the Constitution...
> *Second Inaugural Address, 1805:* "In matters of religion I have considered that its free exercise is placed by the Constitution independent of the powers of the General (i.e. national) Government."
> *Letter to Samuel Miller, 1808:* "I consider the government of the United States as interdicted [prohibited] by the Constitution from intermeddling with religious institutions, their doctrines, discipline, or exercises. This results not only from the provision that no law shall be made respecting an establishment or free exercise of religion, but from that also which reserves to the states the powers not delegated to the general government (10th Amendment). It must then rest with the states as far as it can be in any human authority..." 5

Jefferson's statements should not be considered "best evidence" when considering the Constitution and the First Amendment. However, if the Court is going to use Thomas Jefferson, it should "tell the truth, the whole truth, and nothing but the truth."

4. Omission of Facts

The fourth maneuver that the Court has effectively adopted is that of omission. It has been shown that the Court omits cases prior to 1947; equally absent from its discussions are *any* quotes from George Washington, Benjamin Franklin, John Adams, John Jay, Samuel Adams, Patrick Henry, or other Founders. In all of the research conducted by this author on the Court's recent decisions, the only additional historical figure quoted by the Court is Ulysses S. Grant (on two occasions), a source from nearly a century after the nation's founding. In one footnote, Alexander Hamilton was mentioned, but without any quote credited to him.

The Court's omission of the other Founders implies either that they were not qualified to speak to these issues or that there are no recorded statements from these Founders on the separation question. Since many records do exist, the alternative is that the Court is not willing to consider the testimony of other Founders. Dr.

Paul Vitz, who conducted the research presented earlier on the treatment of religion in textbooks, made an appropriate statement:

> Over and over, we have seen that liberal and secular bias is primarily accomplished by exclusion, by leaving out the opposing position. Such a bias is much harder to observe than a positive vilification or direct criticism, but it is the essence of censorship. It is effective not only because it is hard to observe--it isn't *there*--and therefore hard to counteract, but also because it makes only the liberal, secular positions familiar and plausible. [6]

5. Some Words from Jefferson and Madison about Religion

The Court portrays Madison and Jefferson as being opposed *en toto* to permitting any religious influence on government or public affairs. Such is not the case, as shown by Jefferson's actions while in office:

> While serving in the Virginia House of Burgesses, he was the one who personally introduced a resolution for a Day of Fasting and Prayer in 1774. Then while President, he also chaired the school board for the District of Columbia and authored its plan of education using the Bible and Watt's Hymnal as reading texts...When he established the University of Virginia, he encouraged the teaching of religion and set apart space in the Rotunda for chapel services. He also praised the use of the local courthouse in his home town for religious services. [7]

Jefferson included the Bible as part of the public school's curriculum. According to Jefferson:

> The Bible is the cornerstone of liberty...students perusal of the sacred volume will make us better citizens. [8]

Notice other actions Jefferson took while in government:

> In 1803 President Jefferson recommended that Congress pass a treaty with the Kaskaskia Indians which provided, among other things, a stipend of $100 annually for seven years from the Federal treasury for the support of a Catholic

priest to minister to the Kaskaskia Indians. This and two similar treaties were enacted during Jefferson's administration--one with the Wyandotte Indians and other tribes in 1806, and one with the Cherokees in 1807. In 1787, another act of Congress ordained special lands "for the sole use of Christian Indians" and reserved lands for the Moravian Brethren "for civilizing the Indians and promoting Christianity"...Congress extended this act three times during Jefferson's administration and each time he signed the extension into law. 9

During George Washington's administration, work had begun on the Treaty of Peace and Amity with Tripoli. The treaty was negotiated through Joel Barlow, U.S. Consul in Algiers. At issue had been the right of American ships to move freely through the waters off the Barbary Coast in northern Africa. The Muslims, with whom Barlow negotiated, demanded a provision in the treaty declaring that the United States "is, not in any sense, founded on the Christian religion." Negotiations were completed while Jefferson was President. When...

...the Treaty of Peace and Amity [was] signed in Tripoli, June 4, 1805, [the Senate had] struck out that clause in "virtual repudiation of the negative statement in the original treaty," an act all the more significant in that it came in Jefferson's administration...10

Jefferson understood the important relationship between religion and government. He stated that religion is "deemed in other countries incompatible with good government and yet proved by our experience to be its best support." 11 In the "Virginia Bill of Religious Liberties," Jefferson declared:

Can the liberties of a nation be thought secure when we have removed their only firm basis, a conviction in the minds of the people that these liberties are...the gift of God? That they are not to be violated but with his wrath? 12

Now the Court, supposedly on Jefferson's authority, absolutely prohibits students from being exposed to the idea that liberties are the gift of God. The Court also prohibits the things that Jefferson promoted and enacted while President (i.e., Bible reading in schools). Historical evidence shows that the man supposedly responsible for the separation doctrine didn't practice what the Court says he preached.

James Madison also said much about the necessity of including religious principles in public affairs:

Before any man can be considered as a member of Civil Society, he must be considered as a subject of the Governor of the Universe. [13]

...it is the mutual duty of all to practice Christian forbearance, love, and charity toward each other. [14]

Recall that it was Madison who declared that the success of our political institutions and government was based on keeping the Ten Commandments.

6. Some Words from Jefferson and Madison about the Court

Madison and Jefferson also had much to say about the proper role of the Court. However, since the Court omits their important quotes on religion, it is not surprising that their quotations about the Court are also deleted. If the Court sincerely accepts that Madison and Jefferson were Constitutional experts, then the Court should heed the following statements. In a letter written to Abigail Adams in 1804, Jefferson said:

Nothing in the Constitution has given them [the federal judges] a right to decide for the Executive, more than the Executive to decide for them. The opinion which gives the judges the right to decide what laws are unconstitutional and what are not, not only for themselves in their own sphere of action, but for the Legislature and the Executive also, in their spheres, would make the judiciary a despotic branch. [15]

Jefferson wrote to William Jarvis in 1820:

You seem to consider the judges as the ultimate arbiters of all constitutional questions; a very dangerous doctrine, indeed, and one which would place us under *the despotism of an oligarchy.* Our judges are as honest as other men, and not more so...and their power is the more dangerous, as they are in office for life and not responsible, as the other functionaries, to the elective control. The Constitution has erected no such single tribunal... [16]

And again:

> The germ of dissolution of our Federal government is in...the federal judiciary; an irresponsible body working like gravity by night and by day, gaining a little today and a little tomorrow, and advancing its noiseless step like a thief, over the field of jurisdiction, until all shall be usurped from the states, and the judges as the ultimate arbiters of all constitutional questions is a very dangerous doctrine indeed...[17]

Madison had much to say about judges not becoming lawmakers:

> The preservation of a free government requires not merely, that the metes and bounds which separate each department of power be invariably maintained; but more specially that neither of them be suffered to overleap the great Barrier which defends the rights of the people. The rulers who are guilty of such an encroachment, exceed the commission from which they derive their authority, and are tyrants. The people who submit to it are governed by laws made neither by themselves nor by an authority derived from them, and are slaves. [18]

We are now ruled by laws "neither made by themselves [the people] nor by an authority derived from them [the legislature]." In 1788, Madison warned:

> ...as the courts are generally the last in making the decision [on laws], it results to them by refusing or not refusing to execute a law, to stamp it with its final character. This makes the judiciary department paramount in fact to the legislature, which was never intended and can never be proper. [19]

History reveals that the defenses on which the Court relies so heavily in justifying separation are really no defense at all!

~10~
Dilemmas for the Court

Just as the current Court has opposed the beliefs, intents, and laws of the Founders, it has also opposed the ruling of its predecessors. Both the contemporary Courts and the earlier Courts based their decisions on the same Constitution and Bill of Rights, but the conclusions they reached on identical issues are radically different. The following selections are typical of the numerous conflicts that exist between current Courts and previous Courts.

ON PROFANITY

Notice the position of the current Court on profanity:

> Appellant was...wearing a jacket bearing the words "Fuck the Draft" in a corridor of the Los Angeles Courthouse. *Held:* ...the State may not...make the simple public display of this single four-letter expletive a[n]...offense...the [California statute prohibiting such use of words] infringed his rights to freedom of expression guaranteed by the First and Fourteenth Amendments of the Federal Constitution...This is not...an obscenity case...That the air may at times seem filled with verbal cacophony is, in this sense not a sign of weakness but of strength. *Cohen v. California, 1971*

The rulings of previous Courts differed significantly:

> ...Nothing could be more offensive to the virtuous part of the community, or more injurious to the tender morals of the young, than to declare such profanity lawful...and shall we form an exception in the particulars to the rest of the civilized world? *The People v. Ruggles, 1811*

Quite a difference of opinion! The current Court says protecting profanity like "f--- the draft" shows the strength of our society; the earlier Court said that such language injured the morals of youth and of the community.

ON LEWDNESS AND INDECENCY

In the case of *Erznoznik v. City of Jacksonville, 1975,* the city sought to restrict indecent movies shown in a public drive-in theater because:

...the screen...is visible from two adjacent public streets and a nearby church parking lot...

Jacksonville attempted to protect its children and citizens from this open lewdness and nudity by passing this ordinance:

It shall be unlawful...for any...drive-in theater in the City to exhibit...any motion picture...in which the human male or female bare buttocks, human female bare breasts, or human bare pubic areas are shown, if...visible from any public street or public place.

The Supreme Court ruled this ordinance:

...invalid...an infringement of First Amendment rights...Nor can the ordinance be justified as an exercise of the city...for the protection of children...

This ruling by the current Court was dramatically opposed to earlier rulings:

The destruction of morality renders the power of the government invalid...The corruption of the public mind, in general, and debauching the manners of youth, in particular, by lewd and obscene pictures exhibited to view, must necessarily be attended with the most injurious consequences...No man is permitted to corrupt the morals of the people...*The Commonwealth v. Sharpless, 1815*

ON BLASPHEMY

In the case of *Grove v. Mead School District, 1985,* Cassie Grove, a high school sophomore, had been required to read the book *A Learning Tree* in her English Literature class. She objected to portions of the book and filed suit to have it removed from the curriculum. She objected to several phrases, including those...

...declaring Jesus Christ to be a "poor white trash God," or "a long-legged white son-of-a-bitch"...

The Court refused to rule in her favor or to remove the book from the school's required curriculum. All students taking that class would continue to use the book. That ruling by the Court conflicted with previous Courts:

"Jesus Christ was a bastard, and his mother must be a whore"...Such words...were an offense at common law...it tends to corrupt the morals of the people, and to destroy good order. Such offenses...are treated as affecting the essential interests of civil society. *The People v. Ruggles, 1811*

ON DETERRING NO RELIGIOUS BELIEF

In *Walz v. Tax Commission, 1970,* the Court stated, as it frequently does, that all religious beliefs were to be tolerated:

The fullest realization of true religious liberty requires that government...effect no favoritism among sects or between religion and nonreligion, *and that it work deterrence of no religious belief.*

That statement contradicted earlier cases which declared that there were numerous religious beliefs which would *never* be tolerated in the United States:

There have been sects which denied as a part of their religious tenets that there should be any marriage tie, and advocated promiscuous intercourse of the sexes as prompted by the passions of its members...Should a sect of [this] kind ever find its way into this country, swift punishment would follow the carrying into effect of its doctrines, and no heed would be given to the pretence that...their supporters could be protected in their exercise by the Constitution of the United States. Probably never before in the history of this country has it been seriously contended that the whole punitive power of the government for acts, recognized by the general consent of the Christian world...must be suspended in order that the tenets of a religious sect...may be carried out without hindrance. *Davis v. Beason, 1889*

Every person who has a husband or wife living...and marries another...is guilty of polygamy, and shall be punished...no legislation can be...more wholesome and necessary...than that which seeks to establish it on the basis of the idea of the family as consisting in and springing from the union for life of one man and one woman in the holy estate of matrimony; the sure foundation of all that is stable and noble in our civilization...*Murphy v. Ramsey, 1885*

ON ATHEISM

The First Amendment's protection of free religious exercise was always understood to exclude atheism, since it was not a religion. However, in *Theriault v. Silber, 1977,* the Court determined that the First Amendment was too narrow in its wording. It decided, unilaterally and apart from Congressional action, that the meaning of the First Amendment should be expanded to cover others who have no religious beliefs. As a result:

Atheism may be a religion under the establishment clause...
Malnak v. Yogi, 1977

Secular humanism may be a religion for purposes of First Amendment. *Grove v. Mead School Dist., 1985*

Contrast these decisions with previous ones:

It [the First Amendment] embraces all who believe in the existence of God, as well...as Christians of every denomination. But clearly does not include atheists...this provision does not extend to atheists, because they do not believe in God or religion; and therefore that their sentiments and professions, whatever they may be, cannot be called *religious* sentiments and professions. *Commonwealth v. Abner Kneeland, 1838*

The Founders knew what the word "religion" meant, and atheism did not qualify. Their use of the word "religion" at the time of the First Amendment is revealed from Webster's original dictionary:

RELIGION. Includes a belief in the being and perfections of God, in the revelation of his will to man, and in man's obligation to obey his commands, in a state of reward and punishment, and in man's accountableness to God; and also true godliness or piety of life, with the practice of all moral duties...the practice of moral duties without a belief in a divine lawgiver, and without reference to his will or commands, is not religion. [7]

What was *not* a religion, and therefore *not* part of the First Amendment?

The practice of moral duties *without a belief in a divine lawgiver* and without reference to his will or his commands *is not religion.*

Neither atheism nor secular humanism qualified as "religions" in earlier decisions regarding the First Amendment.

ON SUNDAY LAWS

Notice the contemporary Courts' view of Sunday:

Laws setting aside Sunday as a day of rest are upheld, *not from any right of the government to legislate for the promotion of religious observances,* but from its right to protect all persons from the physical and moral debasement which comes from uninterrupted labor. *McGowan v. Maryland, 1960*

Sunday closing laws upheld as establishing uniform day-of-rest and recreation *with only remote or incidental religious benefit. Florey v. Sioux Falls School District, 1979*

Contrast these views with those of previous Courts:

...The Lord's day, the day of the Resurrection, is to us, who are called Christians, the day of rest after finishing a new creation. It is the day of the first visible triumph over death, hell and the grave! It was the birth day of the believer in Christ, to whom and through whom it opened up the way which, by repentance and faith, leads unto everlasting life and eternal happiness! On that day we rest, and to us it is the Sabbath of the Lord--its decent observance, in a Christian community, is that which ought to be expected. *City of Charleston v. S.A. Benjamin, 1846*

Another emphatic pronouncement concerning Sundays came from a report of the 1854 Senate Judiciary Committee:

Sunday, the Christian Sabbath, is recognized and respected by all the departments of the Government...Here is a recognition by law, and by universal usage, not only of *a* Sabbath, but of the *Christian* sabbath, in exclusion of the Jewish or Mahammedan Sabbath.

Conclusions

Not only has the current Court contradicted earlier stands of the Court, but by so doing, it has created some interesting dilemmas for itself. For example, consider the repercussions of declaring atheism and secular humanism as religions. First, the Court has been very emphatic in its position that no preference can be given between religion or non-religion. The following statements are typical of those found in cases on the First Amendment:

> This amendment mandates governmental neutrality between religion and religion, and between religion and nonreligion. *Epperson v. Arkansas, 1968*

> The fullest realization of true religious liberty requires that government...effect no favoritism among sects or between religion and nonreligion...*Walz v. Tax Commission, 1970*

Second, the Court had defined the religious practice of atheists as that of **no** religious practice and the religious practice of secular humanists as that of **excluding God** and including only a human perspective.

Take these two positions of the Court (neutrality toward all views, and atheism as a religion) and try to apply them jointly in schools. The Court has overturned the inclusion of *any* religious activities in schools. But if God and religious activities are excluded, then the religious practice of atheism has been established. Since the Court has installed practical atheism in schools, it has violated its own position of neutrality between non-religion and religion. It is impossible to apply both positions in practice! Whether the Court installed atheism and secular humanism in schools in an intentional or an ignorant manner is a matter of conjecture; but the fact remains, it has violated its own standards.

Another example of a dilemma the Court has created for itself regards a principal articulated by the 1892 Court:

> ...no purpose of action against religion can be imputed to any legislation, state or national...

This principle is widely accepted and understood. If Congress should pass a law dictating that youth below the age of 18 would not be allowed to pray, it would be declared unconstitutional. If a legislature should enact a law making it illegal for an adolescent between the ages of 10 and 17 to read the Bible, it would also be declared unconstitutional. These types of laws would never be tolerated.

It is ironic that the Court now does the very things impossible to do by law. Laws cannot ban voluntary Bible reading by youth--the Court can. Laws cannot prohibit adolescents from seeing and reading the Ten Commandments--the Court can. Laws cannot prohibit the free exercise of Christianity--the Court can. A Congress, duly elected by the people and responsible to them, the heart and soul of a democratic republic, cannot do these things. The Court, in an insult to our Constitutional form of government, *has* done it. The Court routinely enacts "legislation" that would be unconstitutional for the people's representatives even to consider!

~11~
Double Standards

Not only do the decisions by the current Court clash with both the Founders and earlier Courts, they even clash with themselves. Such unstable and fluctuating standards from the Court have created an uncertainty for society--a set of double standards. The following examples of double standards are illustrative of the many legal contradictions now existing within the judiciary.

ON CHAPLAINS

On the one hand, the prayers of the Congressional Chaplains are constitutional:

> The legislature by majority vote invites a clergyman to give a prayer; neither the inviting nor the giving nor the hearing of the prayer is making a law. On this basis alone...the saying of prayers, per se, in the legislative halls at the opening session is not prohibited by the First and Fourteenth Amendments. *Chambers v. Marsh, 1982*

But, on the other hand, hearing the prayers of the Chaplains is unconstitutional:

> ...students...would listen to "remarks" of the chaplain read from the *Congressional Record*...[this] was unconstitutional establishment of religion...*State Board of Educ. v. Board of Educ. of Netcong, 1970*

It is constitutional for Chaplains to pray prayers, but unconstitutional for students to hear those prayers.

ON THE TEN COMMANDMENTS

On the one hand, the display of the Ten Commandments on public property is constitutional:

> The exact origin of the Ten Commandments is uncertain, but ...a large portion of our population believes they are Bible based. Even so...it also has substantial secular attributes... the Ten Commandments is an affirmation of at least a precedent legal code.

...but this creed does not include any element of coercion concerning these beliefs, unless one considers it coercive to look upon the Ten Commandments. Although they are in plain view, no one is required to read or recite them.

It does not seem reasonable to require removal of a passive monument, involving no compulsion, because its accepted precepts, as a foundation for law, reflect the religious nature of an ancient era. *Anderson v. Salt Lake City Corporation, 1973*

However, on the other hand, the display of the Ten Commandments on public property is unconstitutional:

...the posting of a copy of the Ten Commandments...on the wall of each public school classroom...has no secular legislative purpose, and therefore is unconstitutional as violating the Establishment Clause of the First Amendment. While the state legislature required the notation in small print at the bottom of each display that "[t]he secular application of the Ten Commandments is clearly seen in its adoption as the fundamental legal code of Western Civilization and the Common Law of the United States," such an "avowed" secular purpose is not sufficient to avoid conflict with the First Amendment. Nor is it significant that the Ten Commandments are merely posted rather than read aloud...*Stone v. Gramm, 1980*

The descriptions of the passive use of the Ten Commandments are the same in both cases, but the conclusions are contradictory.

ON INVOCATIONS

On the one hand, invocations are constitutional:

...[the case] *Bogen v. Doty*...involved a county board's practice of opening each of its public meetings with a prayer offered by a local member of the clergy...This Court upheld that practice, finding that it advanced a clearly secular purpose of "establishing a solemn atmosphere and serious tone for the board meetings"...establishing solemnity is the primary effect of all invocations at gatherings of persons with differing views on religion. *Chambers v. Marsh, 1982*

On the other hand, invocations are unconstitutional:

> School district's inclusion of religious invocation and religious benediction as part of its graduation ceremonies violated establishment clause of First Amendment. *Graham v. Central Community School Dist., 1985*

> ...religious invocation...included in high school commencement exercise conveyed message that district had given its endorsement to prayer and religion, so that school district was properly [prohibited] from including invocation in commencement exercise...*Kay v. Douglas School Dist., 1986*

ON CHRISTMAS AND NATIVITY SCENES

On the one hand, it is constitutional to depict the origins of Christmas:

> The city of Pawtucket, R.I., annually erects a Christmas display in a park...The [nativity] display is sponsored by the city to celebrate the Holiday recognized by Congress and national tradition and to depict the origins of that Holiday; these are legitimate secular purposes...the creche...is no more an advancement or endorsement of religion than the congressional and executive recognition of the origins of Christmas...It would be ironic if...the creche in the display, as part of a celebration of an event acknowledged in the Western World for 20 centuries, and in this country by the people, the Executive Branch, Congress, and the courts for 2 centuries, would so "taint" the exhibition as to render it violative of the Establishment Clause. To forbid the use of this one passive symbol...would be an overreaction contrary to this Nation's history...*Lynch v. Donnelly, 1985*

On the other hand, it is unconstitutional for students to ask questions about the origins of Christmas, even if those questions are historically based:

> A variety of Christmas assemblies has been presented in the Sioux Falls public schools for a number of years. During the Christmas season of 1977, two Sioux Falls kindergarten classes rehearsed, memorized and then performed for

parents a Christmas assembly...including a responsive discourse between the teacher and the class entitled, "The Beginners Christmas Quiz." The "Quiz" consisted of the following:
TEACHER: Of whom did heav'nly angels sing,
And news about His birthday bring?
CLASS: Jesus.
TEACHER: Now, can you name the little town where they the Baby Jesus found?
CLASS: Bethlehem.
TEACHER: Where had they made a little bed for Christ, the blessed Savior's head?
CLASS: In a manger in a cattle stall.
TEACHER: What is the day we celebrate as birthday of this One so great?
CLASS: Christmas.
...the kindergarten program presented in 1977...exceeded the boundaries of what is constitutionally permissible under the Establishment Clause. *Florey v. Sioux Falls School District, 1979*

Furthermore, if there is to be a nativity scene at a school, it is to be at a time when students will not see it:

The Supreme Court...held that where Nativity Scene was not erected or displayed while school was in session...[it] was not unconstitutional as violating doctrine of separation of church and state. *Baer v. Kolmorgen, 1958*

While it is constitutional to depict publicly the origins of Christmas, a holiday created and endorsed by the government, it is unconstitutional for students to view those origins at school or to ask questions about those origins, despite the fact that the questions *are* historical and *do* relate to the reason Congress established the holiday.

ON PERSONAL APPEARANCE

On the one hand, the freedom to govern one's personal appearance is a fundamental constitutional right:

The Founding Fathers wrote an amendment for speech and assembly; even they did not deem it necessary to write an amendment for personal appearance...the Constitution guaranteed rights other than those specifically enumerated, and...the right to govern one's personal appearance is one of those guaranteed rights. *Bishop v. Colaw, 1971*

No right is held more sacred, or is more carefully guarded, by the common law, than the right of every individual to the possession and control of his own person, free from all restraint or interference of others...As well said by Judge Cooley [in *Union Pacific Railway Co. v. Botsford*]: "The right to one's person may be said to be a right of complete immunity; to be let alone." *Wallace v. Ford, 1972*

On the other hand, the right to govern one's personal appearance is not a fundamental constitutional right:

A public schoolteacher, while teaching, may not wear distinctly religious garb...*Finot v. Pasadena City Board of Education, 1967*

ON FREEDOM OF SPEECH

On the one hand, free speech is protected by the Constitution, including the right to use the word "God" in a derogatory or vulgar manner. Recall from *Cohen v. California, 1971,* that the Court declared it was a sign of our society's strength to permit the air to be filled with profanity. Recall also from *Grove v. Mead, 1985,* that the Court defended the right of the school to use a textbook describing Jesus as a "poor white trash God" and "a...white s.o.b." With such language permitted, it would appear that nearly any expression or word is constitutionally protected.

Although there is protection for free speech, and although the word "God," when hyphenated with any other profanity is protected by the Court, such constitutional protection does not include the right to use the word "God" in a respectful manner:

To include reference to God...in State Board of Education minimum standards relating to operation of schools would violate establishment clause of First Amendment. *The State of Ohio v. Whisner, 1976*

Furthermore, it is improper to provide opportunity for the expression of respect for God:

> During the regular school day...no themes will be assigned on such topics as "Why I believe...in religious devotions."
> *Reed v. van Hoven, 1965*

Not only is it improper for school officials and students to use the word "God" in a respectful manner, recall from *DeSpain v. DeKalb, 1967,* that it is also improper for students to think about God.

It is constitutional to express contempt for God, but unconstitutional to express respect for Him.

ON FREE EXERCISE

On the one hand, free exercise of religion cannot be interfered with unless its exercise creates a paramount danger to the public:

> The scales are always weighed in favor of free exercise of religion, and the state's interest must be compelling, it must be substantial, and the danger must be clear and present and so grave as to endanger paramount public interests before the state can interfere with the free exercise of religion. *Swann v. Pack, 1975*

However, on the other hand, the "period for the free exercise of religion" with students voluntarily meeting together before school for prayer was evidently a clear and present danger to the community, because it was prohibited by the Court in *State Board of Educ. v. Board of Educ. of Netcong, 1970.*

ON THE OWNERSHIP OF CHILDREN

On the one hand, children are not wards of the state:

> The fundamental theory of liberty upon which all governments in this Union repose excludes any general power of the state to standardize its children...The child is not the mere creature of the state...*Pierce v. Society of Sisters; Reed v. van Hoven, 1965*

On the other hand, children are wards of the state:

> ...the courts for many years have held: Children are the wards of the State...*State Board of Educ. v. Board of Educ. of Netcong, 1970*

ON PROTECTION OF CHILDREN

On the one hand, the Court intervened in *State Board of Educ. v. Board of Educ. of Netcong, 1970,* to protect children from voluntary prayer. On the other hand, the Court would not intervene in *Erznoznik v. City of Jacksonville, 1975,* to protect children from public lewdness and nudity. Apparently the Court considers prayer harmful to children but not promiscuous public nudity.

ON LONGSTANDING PRACTICES

On the one hand, the Court pointed out in *Walz v. Tax Commission, 1970,* that the fact that tax exemptions for churches had existed 200 years had a strong effect on declaring them constitutional:

> ...in resolving questions of interpretation "a page of history is worth a volume of logic." *New York Trust Co. v. Eisner.* The more longstanding and widely accepted a practice, the greater its impact upon constitutional interpretation...

On the other hand, as pointed out by a dissenting Justice in the same case, school prayer had existed for 340 years and that had no effect in protecting it from being declared unconstitutional.

CONCLUSION

Notice the pattern that has emerged in many of these double standards? The general public may hear the prayers of the Congressional Chaplain, students may not. The general public may view the Ten Commandments, students may not. The general public may view nativity scenes, students may not. Why does the Court so zealously prohibit religious activity from students? It is not mere coincidence that so many of the Court's double standards involve students; as Abraham Lincoln stated:

> The philosophy of the schoolroom in one generation will be the philosophy of government in the next. 1

~12~
Toward A New Constitution?

Every government in history, both before and since the creation of our own Constitution, has been the product of a specific political theory. Each government has its own philosophy that, in its own eyes, justifies its existence and manner of conducting business. In short, people have distinct reasons for establishing governments as they do. Our Founders were no exception. The Constitution and Declaration of Independence were well-devised plans for government, declaring a specific political and governing philosophy.

There has never been a shortage of philosophies on which to base a government; numerous and widely differing types have long abounded. From the records of Ben Franklin's speech at the Constitutional Convention, it is evident that our wise Founders researched many of these different philosophies in their quest for the one they felt would yield a prosperous, successful government. How can we determine which philosophy they finally selected?

> One way is to read what they wrote, and check the sources they cited...Two professors, Donald S. Lutz and Charles S. Hyneman, have reviewed an estimated 15,000 items, and closely read 2,200 books, pamphlets, newspaper articles, and monographs with explicitly political content printed between 1760 and 1805...From these items, Lutz and Hyneman identified [the philosophers quoted most frequently by our Founders]...Baron Charles Montesquieu...followed closely by Sir William Blackstone...and John Locke... [1]

What did Montesquieu, Blackstone, and Locke think, believe, and articulate that caused them to be the three most quoted men in America's founding era?

The Baron Montesquieu of France (Charles Louis Joseph de Secondat, 1689-1755) lived in France and taught in French universities. His writing, *The Spirit of Laws (1748)*, greatly influenced our own Constitution. He believed that certain unchanging laws underlie all things:

> ...society, notwithstanding all its revolutions, must repose on principles that do not change...[2]

It was man's responsibility to discover and apply these laws. What did Montesquieu believe to be the source of these unchanging principles?

> The Christian religion, which ordains that men should love each other, would, without doubt, have every nation blest with the best civil, the best political laws; because these, next to this religion, are the greatest good that men can give and receive...3

Montesquieu believed that Christianity fostered good laws and good government. His philosophy of governing was Biblically based and many of his concepts were adopted by the Founders. For example, the Founders incorporated Montesquieu's belief that powers of government should be distinct and separate so that power could check power. The separation of powers doctrine had been based on two Biblical concepts. First, Isaiah 33:22 identified the three branches of government--legislative, executive, and judicial. Second, the Bible taught that man was not in himself naturally good. When left unchecked, he tended toward moral and civil degradation. Because of this, man must have some type of outside safeguards and checks placed on him. Separation of powers was, as were most of the Founder's political innovations, a Biblically based idea.

While Montesquieu provided the separation of powers, Blackstone contributed the superstructure for the natural law philosophy utilized by the Founders. Blackstone, the second most frequently quoted man by our Founders, was an English judge, professor, and author. His *Commentaries on the Laws of England (1765-69)* were the basis of legal education in America. Evidence that he was widely accepted by Americans was provided by Edmund Burke in remarks delivered before Parliament:

> I hear that they have sold nearly as many of Blackstone's *Commentaries* in America as in England. 4

James Madison, our own Constitution's chief architect, heartily endorsed Blackstone:

> I very cheerfully express my approbation of the proposed edition of Blackstone's *Commentaries*...5

Blackstone influenced many great founding Americans:

> It was from Blackstone that most Americans, including John Marshall, acquired their knowledge of natural law... Blackstone remained the standard manual of law until the publication of the *Commentaries on American Law (1826-1830)* of Chancellor James Kent of New York. 6

Blackstone, like Montesquieu, was very explicit concerning the source of good laws and good government:

> Man, considered as a creature, must necessarily be subject to the laws of his Creator, for he is entirely a dependent being...And, consequently, as man depends absolutely upon his Maker for everything, it is necessary that he should in all points conform to his Maker's will. This will of his Maker, is called the law of nature. 7

That phrase, the "law of nature," was a key term identifying the natural law philosophy and was a very revealing term in our founding documents. This natural law, or law of nature, as it was sometimes called, was made up of two important elements--the *physical* laws of nature and the *revealed* or Divine law of the Scriptures:

> ...the revealed or divine law...found only in the Holy Scriptures...are found upon comparison to be really a part of the original law of nature...This law of nature...dictated by God Himself, is of course superior in obligation to any other ...no human laws are of any validity, if contrary to this...8

How important were these two elements of the law of nature?

> Upon these two foundations, the law of Nature and the law of Revelation, depend all human law; that is to say, no human laws should be suffered to contradict these. 9

According to natural law, civil laws could not be allowed to contradict either the physical laws of nature or the revealed laws of the Bible. In areas where there were neither natural nor Divine laws, men were free to determine their own laws. Blackstone provided examples of each occasion:

198 THE MYTH OF SEPARATION

To instance in the case of murder: this is expressly forbidden by the divine, and demonstrably by the natural law; and from these prohibitions arises the true unlawfulness of this crime...if any human law should allow or enjoin us to commit it, we, are bound to transgress that human law, or else we must offend both the natural and the divine. But with regard to matters that are...not commanded or forbidden by [the Scriptures]; such, for instance, as exporting of wool into foreign countries; here the...legislature [of men] has scope and opportunity to interpose and to make that action unlawful which before was not so. 10

John Locke, the third most cited man in early American political thought, was a British philosopher and author. He had been strongly influenced by the writings of Richard Hooker:

Hooker argued that where the Scripture is clear, Scripture alone must govern. Where Scripture is unclear...tradition may be employed to help interpret it; and where both Scripture and...tradition are unclear, or where new circumstances arise, reason may also be employed to apprehend God's truth. 11

John Locke, like Montesquieu, Blackstone, and Hooker, was a strong advocate of the natural law philosophy. Locke's writings, particularly his *Two Treatises of Government, 1690,* strongly influenced Jefferson. When Jefferson wrote the Declaration of Independence, he quoted directly from the phraseology of John Locke.

In addition to utilizing Locke's natural law beliefs, the Founders also adopted his theory of social compact:

...the idea that men in a state of nature realize their rights are insecure, and compact together to establish a government and cede to that government certain power so that government may use that power to secure the rest of their rights. 12

Under the social compact theory, the power that is given to the government is:

...only the power God and/or people delegate. This is the cornerstone of limited government. It finds expression in the Tenth Amendment to the Constitution and in the Declaration of Independence which states that governments exist to secure human rights and "derive their just powers from the consent of the governed." 13

Natural law, social compact, limited government, the consent of the governed--Locke's concepts were incorporated throughout the government established by our Founders. Locke had relied heavily on the Bible when developing his political views:

> In his first treatise on government he cited the Bible eighty times...Twenty-two biblical citations appear in his second treatise...His basic doctrines of parental authority, private property, and social compact were based on the historical existence of Adam and Noah. 14

Notice some of Locke's statements on laws and government:

> Thus the Law of Nature stands as an eternal rule to all men, legislators as well as others. The rules that they make for other men's actions, must...be conformable to the Law of Nature, i.e. to the will of God...no human sanction can be good, or valid against it. 15

> ...so the laws human must be made according to the general Laws of Nature, and without contradiction to any positive Law of Scripture, otherwise they are ill made. 16

In addition to these three men, there were others whose philosophies the Founders found quite agreeable to their own. Alexander Hamilton, another influential Constitutional thinker, made this recommendation:

> Apply yourself, without delay, to the study of the law of nature. I would recommend to your perusal Grotius, Pufendorf, Locke, Montesquieu...17

Grotius and Pufendorf, like Locke and Montesquieu, maintained natural law as the basis of their philosophies:

> Hugo Grotius (1583-1645), [was a] famous Dutch lawyer, theologian, statesman...In his writings on law and government Grotius attempted to apply Christian principles to

politics. He emphasized, perhaps more clearly than any other writer, that "What God has shown to be his will that is law." 18

Samuel de Pufendorf (1632-1694), held diplomatic posts in Germany and Sweden and was university professor, royal historian for Sweden...Pufendorf, influenced by Grotius, helped to establish the law of nature as the basis for international law. 19

Pufendorf was widely respected by many of the Founders:

Alexander Hamilton, Benjamin Franklin, James Wilson, Samuel Adams and other founding fathers paid tribute to Pufendorf, acknowledged his influence on their thinking, and recommended his writings to others. 20

The philosophers embraced by the Founders all had a common factor--their strong belief in the importance of natural law as the basis of any government established by men. Natural law formed the basis of our Founder's political theories and was incorporated as part of their new government:

George Mason, author of the Virginia's Bill of Rights in its Constitution, stated before the General Court of Virginia: "The laws of nature are the laws of God, whose authority can be superseded by no power on earth." It was in this context that the phrase, "the laws of nature and nature's God," was subsequently incorporated in the Declaration of Independence. 21

Just as the natural law belief is evident in the Declaration of Independence, it is also apparent in our Constitution:

...the Constitution is not a neutral document but presupposes a belief in a *transcendent, unchanging order,* and the cause behind that order: God. It is founded on the conviction that rights do not derive from government but from God. Indeed, governments are instituted to secure the inalienable rights endowed by the Creator. The Constitution in short, is not a positivistic document but presupposes and is deeply rooted in *theism.* This is only natural for the men who framed the Constitution were all theists--mostly Christians, some deists. 22

We were unquestionably a nation established on the natural law belief: God's laws as revealed through both nature and the Bible were the basis of government. This is even further established by re-examining the results of the research conducted by the political science professors cited earlier in this chapter. Recall that the three men most often quoted by the Founders were Montesquieu, Blackstone, and Locke. Yet, there was a source the Founders cited four times more often than Montesquieu, and sixteen times more often than either Blackstone or Locke. What was that source?

By far, the most often quoted source of [the Founders'] political ideas was the Bible. This accounts for over one-third of all their citations. The next most quoted source [Montesquieu] is not even cited one-fourth as frequently. Another 60% of all references can be attributed to authors which themselves derived their ideas from the Bible. Therefore, it can be said that 94% of the ideas in our Constitution are based either directly or indirectly on the Bible.

The Bible and Civil Liberty are inseparable. Even *Newsweek*, on December 26, 1982, acknowledged after a major analysis of the Bible's influence in America, that "Now historians are discovering that the Bible, perhaps even more than the Constitution is our Founding document." 23

The fact that the Founders quoted the Bible *four times* more often than any other source is an impressive testimony to its importance in our form of government!

The philosophies on which this nation was birthed and established remained the basis of governmental practices until the early 1900's, at which time an opposing philosophy began gaining strength among the nation's leading educators and judges. By the 1940's, strong signals began appearing in Supreme Court decisions which indicated that a philosophy known as legal positivism was being embraced. The widespread acceptance and application of legal positivism within the judiciary led to the repudiation and discarding of the natural law theories which had formed the foundation of our government. Replacing the foundation cannot be accomplished without causing substantial damage to what had been a healthy structure for over a century and a half.

The Court's current philosophy of legal positivism was derived from the philosophies of pragmatism and relativism. Pragmatism and relativism had been promoted by the American philosophers Charles

S. Pierce, William James, and John Dewey. Pierce advanced the basic tenets of relativism, James made them practical and understandable, and Dewey applied them to key areas of life. The central theme of their philosophy was:

> ...the belief that truth cannot be immutable, that there are no abiding, timeless truths or absolute moral norms, because reality is judged to be in a constant state of flux. "Truth"...is whatever "works" in a given situation. 24

The basic tenets of relativism are described in this encyclopedia excerpt:

> RELATIVISM. ...views are to be evaluated relative to the societies or cultures in which they appear and are not to be judged true or false, or good or bad, based on some overall criterion but are to be assessed within the context in which they occur. Thus, what is right or good or true to one person or group may not be considered so by others...there were no absolute standards..."Man is the measure of all things," and ...each man could be his own measure...cannibalism, incest, and other practices considered taboo are just variant kinds of behavior, to be appreciated as acceptable in some cultures and not in others...[relativism] urges suspension of judgment about right or wrong...25

Relativism originally was embraced only among a few individuals and in isolated groups. For example, the Supreme Court embraced and began to apply relativism at a time when the majority of Americans were still strong adherents to the natural law philosophy. As relativism became firmly entrenched in the Court's decisions and became the national judicial policy following the 1940's, it became possible to introduce this philosophy to other aspects of public affairs. Consequently, curriculum programs based on relativism were widely introduced into public schools during the 1970's. These courses were known under the generic title of "situation ethics," and later as "values clarification."

Since the Court had effectively removed the belief in any absolute values, students were taught that everything was relative. Nothing was, of itself, right or wrong but was determined by the "circumstances." "Dilemmas" were posed to the students who then had to decide the "right" course of action for the situation. The following "dilemma" is typical of those proposed to students under relativism:

> A young girl finds herself interned by an oppressive govern-
> ment in a prison where "unpleasant" things frequently
> happen. While confined, the girl discovers that there is a law
> which states that anyone pregnant cannot be held in the
> prison. However, this girl is very "traditional" and holds "tradi-
> tional" views on marriage and pre-marital sexual relations.
> She now faces a "dilemma": she can seduce a guard, have
> sex with him regularly until she becomes pregnant, and then
> be released from prison, but only by violating the standards
> which she has been taught constitute right and wrong. She
> ends up seducing the guard and does eventually become
> pregnant. The question is now posed to the students: "Was
> what she did right or wrong?" The answer? Since what she
> did helped achieve her release from prison, it was not wrong
> (according to the philosophy of relativism).

Students (as well as all others exposed to relativism) are condi-
tioned to reject absolutes--that there is no law above man-made law.
Anything can, in the "proper" situation, be right (incest, cannibalism,
murder, adultery, lying, etc.). Right and wrong are determined only
by how something "turns out." Acts absolutely wrong under natural
law can be right under relativism, where the end *always* justifies the
means.

Those who embrace relativism (also called pragmatism) typically
hold the Founders and their beliefs in disdain, as evidenced by this
statement from John Dewey:

> The belief in political fixity, of the sanctity of some form of
> state consecrated by the efforts of our fathers and hallowed
> by tradition, is one of the stumbling blocks in the way of
> orderly and directed change...26

Many Justices agreed with Pierce, James, and Dewey, and
rejected the beliefs of the Founders. These Judges believed:

> ...the natural law and natural rights principles which [earlier
> Justices] had also been reading into the Constitution...were
> not applicable to a society that was in a constant state of flux
> and change. And therefore "progressive" members of the
> judiciary turned to...the *pragmatism* of John Dewey and the

legal positivism of such men as Oliver Wendell Holmes, Jr., Benjamin Cardozo, and Roscoe Pound...But in the process, the idea of transcendent rights would be discarded, and there would be no appeal from the edicts of the true law-giver--the Court. Government would become the sole source of rights. 27

Relativism, when expressed through the Courts, is called legal positivism and can be easily identified by its major tenets:

(1) There are no objective, God-given standards of law, or if there are, they are irrelevant to the modern legal system.

(2) Since God is not the author of law, the author of law must be man; it is law simply because the highest human authority, the state, has said it is law and is able to back it up.

(3) Since man and society evolve, law must evolve as well.

(4) Judges, through their decisions, guide the evolution of law.

(5) To study law, get at the original sources of law--the decisions of judges; hence most law schools today use the "case law" method of teaching law. 28

Justices Holmes (who served on the Court from 1902-1932) and Cardozo (from 1932-1938), and legal educator Roscoe Pound (active in the 1920's and '30's) helped pioneer the trail which enabled the Court to repudiate the philosophy of the Founders. Holmes, as did other relativists, rejected the beliefs of the Founders:

Everyone instinctively recognizes that in these days the justi-fication of a law for us cannot be found in the fact that our fathers always have followed it. It must be found in some help which the law brings toward reaching a social end...29

According to Holmes, decisions were not to be based upon natural law and fixed standards, but upon:

The felt necessities of the time, the prevalent moral and polit-ical theories...even the prejudices which judges share with their fellow men, [which] have had a good deal more to do than the syllogism in determining the rules by which men should be governed. 30

Justice Benjamin Cardozo was another strong relativist. As such, he too rejected any fixed standard that embraces right and wrong (natural law):

If there is any law which is back of the sovereignty of the state, and superior thereto, it is not law in such a sense as to concern the judge or lawyer, however much it concerns the statesman or moralist. [31]

According to Supreme Court Justice Cardozo, the Judge is not to "concern" himself with natural law. Many other Judges have followed in the footsteps of these "pioneers" in relativism as indicated by the following comment from Chief Justice Warren, who served on the Court from 1953-1969. Writing about the Constitution in *Trop v. Dulles,* Warren stated that the Constitution:

...must draw its meaning from the evolving standards of decency that mark the progress of a maturing society. [32]

Cardozo, in addition to his rejection of natural law, also advocated usurping the traditional separation of powers which made legislators the sole lawmakers:

I take judge-made law as one of the existing realities of life. [33]

The Court has eradicated the use of the philosophy on which our nation and its government was founded. It has disregarded the basis for the legal decisions made over the previous 150 years. The current Court has:

...liberated itself from what the Declaration of Independence called "the Laws of Nature and of Nature's God." [34]

How significant is it that the intent and basis of the Constitution and Declaration of Independence has been discarded?

If a judge can interpret the Constitution or laws to mean something obviously not intended by the original makers-- then the nation's Constitution and laws are meaningless. [35]

As Chief Justice Charles Evan Hughes said:

...the Constitution is what the judges say it is. [36]

~13~
Even A Child...

There are two different and distinct philosophies under which the Constitution has now been interpreted--the first being natural and Divine law (adhering to original intent), the second being legal relativism and positivism. The primary difference in these two types of philosophies has been articulated by two Supreme Court Justices, one from each school of thought:

> Justice Felix Frankfurter...declared [in *Wallace v. Jaffree, 1984]* "What governs is the Constitution, and not what we have written about it." In contrast was a statement by New York Governor Charles Evans Hughes, later named Chief Justice: "We are under a Constitution, but the Constitution is what the judges say it is." 1

These two different legal philosophies are reflected in the degree plans of law schools--some emphasize the study of constitutional law and some the study of case law. The focus of constitutional law is the study of the Constitution itself, while the focus of case law is the study of the opinions of Justices that have been expressed in different cases. In case law, since the original intent is not the guide, it is possible to obtain a law degree without ever having read the Constitution. The primary difference in these two systems of study is summed up by the United States Attorney General in a speech given before the American Bar Association in 1985:

> ...under the old system the question was *how* to read the Constitution; under the new approach, the question is *whether* to read the Constitution...2

There are avid proponents of each system, but does it really make a difference which one is followed? Does the current Courts' rejection of Divine and natural law really have any effect on our lifestyles? That question can be answered by an ancient proverb:

> Even a child is known by his doings, whether his work...be right. Proverbs 20:11

Simply check the results that have come from each philosophy--

see if there is any difference. As actions speak louder than words, the measured outworkings of each philosophy will speak far louder than any words of conjecture or debate as to which one is better.

Although many of the Justices had already individually rejected Divine law standards, it was not until 1962-63 that the collective outworking of their individual philosophies was manifested in their rulings. In *Abington v. Schempp* in 1963, the Court made its first open and absolute repudiation of the Bible and of its teachings (the heart of Divine and natural law) in public affairs. That year marked the beginning of scores of cases overturning long-standing practices stemming from Divine law. Those decisions have caused marked changes in the philosophical approaches toward dealing with morality, education, families, and society.

Indicators from diverse areas during the years of rulings under Divine law standards will be compared with the same indicators for the years of decisions under legal positivism standards. It can be visually determined if there is a measurable difference based on which philosophy is being applied. The statistics for the years under each judicial philosophy were obtained primarily from cabinet level departments of the federal government and have been compiled into individual charts representing several diverse areas. These charts (only a few of the many published in an earlier work by this author: *America: To Pray or Not To Pray?)* accentuate the year in which the Court openly rejected Divine law in applying their decisions. The charts demonstrate the stark results of that rejection.

Birth Rates For Unwed Women
15-19 Yrs. Of Age

Births Per 1,000 Unwed Women

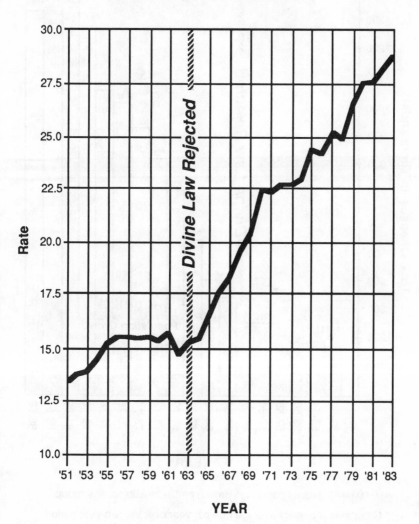

YEAR

Basic data from Department of Health and Human Services,
Statistical Abstracts of the United States.

Violent Crime:
Number Of Offenses

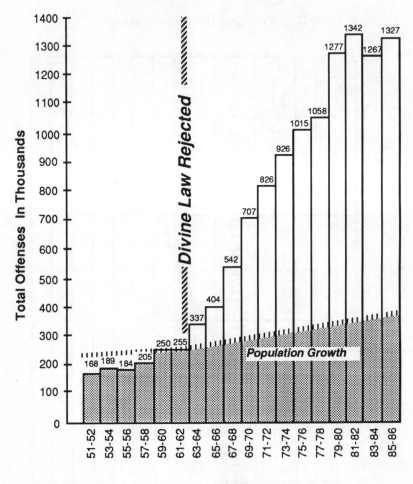

IIIIIIIIIII Indicates population growth profile for subject age group.

* Groupings represent average rate per year over the two-year period.

Basic data from the Department of Commerce, Census Bureau, and
Statistical Abstracts of the United States.

Sexually Transmitted Diseases
Gonorrhea: Age Group 15-19

Cases Per 100,000 Total Population

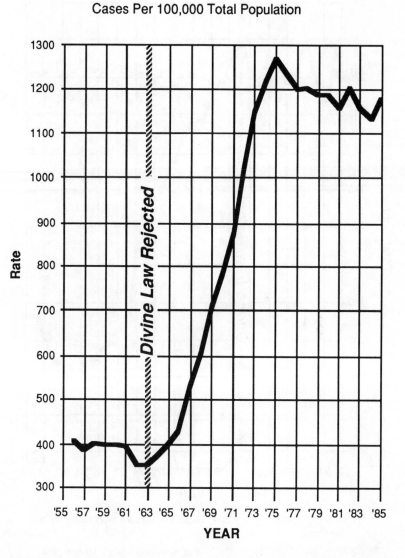

Basic data from the Center for Disease Control, Department of Health and Human Resources

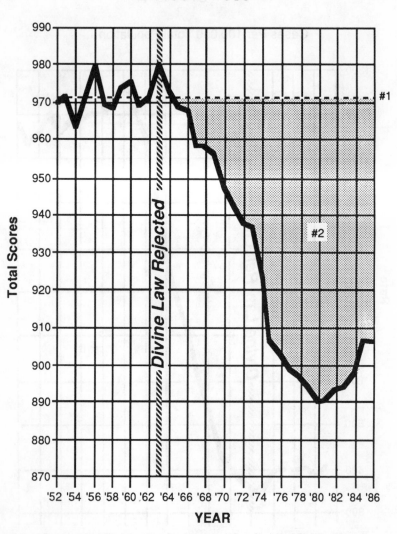

SAT Total Scores
1951 - 1986

#1 - Average achievement level when Divine Law was included in education

#2 - Amount of reduced academic achievement since Divine Law was excluded from education

Basic data from the College Entrance Exam Board.

Pregnancies To Unwed Women
Under 15 Years of Age

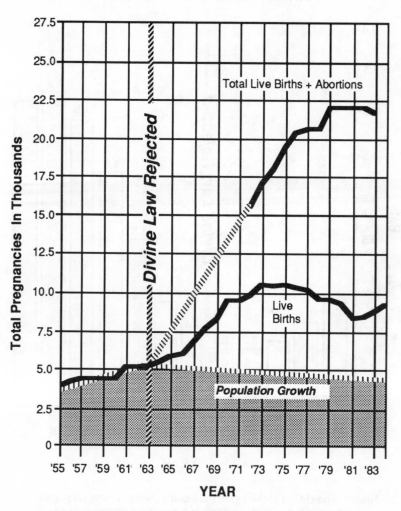

IIIIIIIIIII Indicates population growth profile for subject age group.

ʌʌʌʌʌʌʌʌʌ Indicates extrapolated data.

Basic data from Department of Health and Human Services, the Center for Disease Control, the Department of Commerce, Census Bureau, and *Statistical Abstracts of the United States.*

Divorce Rates

Divorces Per 1,000 Total Population

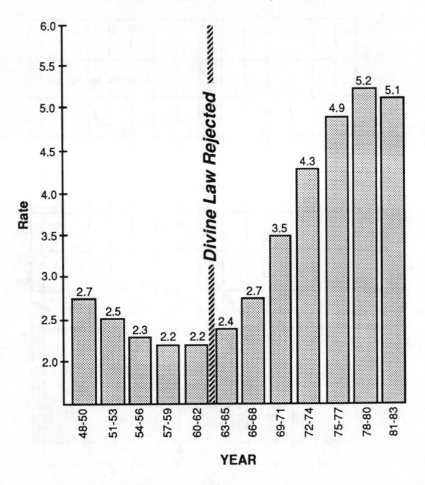

Notes: "The U.S. is at the top of the world's divorce charts on marital breakups." *U.S. News and World Report,* June 8, 1987, pgs. 68-69.

"The number of divorces tripled each year between 1962 and 1981." *Time,* July 13, 1987, pg. 21.

Basic data from the Department of Health and Human Services,
Monthly Vital Statistics Report, Sept. 25, 1986.

National Cases Of Sexually Transmitted Diseases--All Ages

Includes: Gonorrhea, Syphilis, Chancroid, Granuloma Inguinale, Lymphogranuloma Venereum, and AIDS

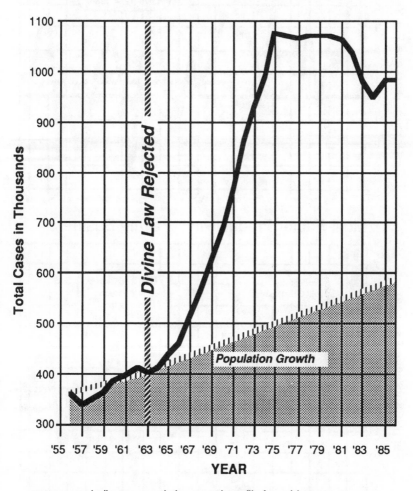

IIIIIIIIIII Indicates population growth profile for subject age group.

Basic data from Department of Health and Human Services, the Center for Disease Control, and the Deparment of Commerce, Census Bureau.

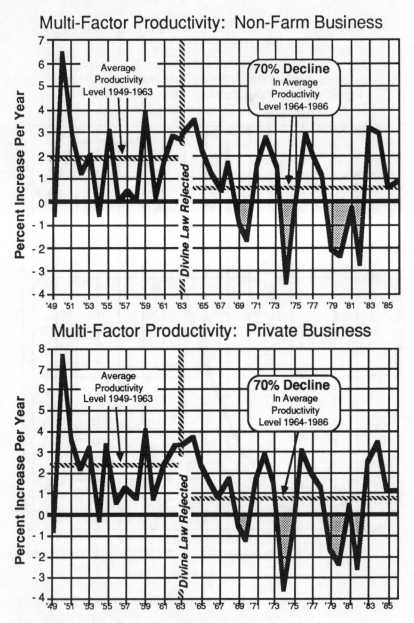

Basic data from *News: United States Department of Labor,*
Bureau of Labor Statistics, October 13, 1987.

These are but a few examples of the many dramatic reversals that have occurred in the nation since 1962-1963. As a result of the reversals, the United States is now number one in the *world* in violent crime, divorce, and illegal drug use; number one in the western world in teenage pregnancies; and number one in the industrial world in illiteracy. We have always been a world leader; however, since 1962-63, we have begun to lead the world in many of the wrong categories. The philosophies of relativism and positivism have not produced national stability and prosperity, but their opposites! By rejecting Divine Law, the Supreme Court has rejected the base that produced the stability our nation previously experienced.

In the early state constitutions, politicians were required to express their belief in future punishments and rewards. By so doing, they were personally accepting responsibility for the effects of their actions, decisions, and laws. They knew that their actions would have consequence, either good or bad, and that they would answer for them, either in this life or the next.

Just as politicians were individually accountable while in office, there was also a national accountability. However, a nation, unlike an individual, does not have an afterlife in which to answer for its actions. The only way a nation can be recompensed for its actions, whether good or bad, is during its present existence. A statement articulating that fact was made by George Mason, a Virginia delegate at the Constitutional Convention:

> ...As nations cannot be rewarded or punished in the next world, they must be in this. By an inevitable chain of causes and effects, Providence punishes national sins by national calamities. [3]

Ben Franklin expressed the same sentiment at the same Convention when he declared:

> I have lived, Sir, a long time, and the longer I live, the more convincing proofs I see of this truth--that God governs in the affairs of men...We have been assured, Sir, in the Sacred Writings, that "except the Lord build the house, they labor in vain that build it." I firmly believe this; and I also believe that without His concurring aid, we shall succeed in this political building no better than the builders of Babel: We shall be divided by our little partial local interests; our projects will be confounded; and we ourselves shall become a reproach...[4]

THE MYTH OF SEPARATION

The previous charts tend to validate what was predicted by Mason, Franklin, and many other Founders. Since rejecting His concurring aid, the nation has experienced an inevitable chain of causes and effects. The rejection of Divine law has had national and individual repercussions.

When the contemporary Courts rejected Divine law-natural law, they not only used poor judgment, they acted illegally. They rejected the standard of "the laws of nature and of nature's God" that had been established in the Declaration of Independence. Many people erroneously consider the Constitution to be a higher document than the Declaration. However, under our form of government, the Constitution is *not* superior to the Declaration of Independence. A violation of the Declaration is as serious as a breech of the Constitution:

> The role of the Declaration of Independence in American law is often misconstrued. Some believe the Declaration is simply a statement of ideas that has no legal force whatsoever today. Nothing could be further from the truth. The Declaration has been repeatedly cited by U.S. Supreme Court as part of the fundamental law of the United States of America [at least 10 cases].
>
> The *United States Code Annotated* includes the Declaration of Independence under the heading "The Organic Laws of the United States of America" along with the Articles of Confederation, the Constitution, and the Northwest Ordinance. Enabling acts frequently require states to adhere to the principles of the Declaration; in the Enabling Act of June 16, 1906, Congress authorized Oklahoma Territory to take steps to become a state. Section 3 provides that the Oklahoma Constitution "shall not be repugnant to the Constitution of the United States and the principles of the Declaration of Independence." 5

The Declaration of Independence, and thus "the laws of nature and of nature's God," holds an important legal position in our form of government:

> The Declaration of the United States is our Charter. It is the legal document that made us a nation like all the other nations of the world. It doesn't tell us how we are going to run our country--that is what our Constitution does. In a corporation, the Charter is higher than the By-laws and the By-laws

must be interpreted to be in agreement with the Charter. Therefore, the Constitution of the United States must be in agreement with the Declaration of the United States (more commonly known as the Declaration of Independence). The most important statement in our Declaration is that we want to operate under the laws of God.

Why is all of this so important? Because today, when the courts are deciding what the Constitution means, they should remember our Charter--the Declaration of the United States. The Constitution doesn't specifically mention God, but then it doesn't have to because the Declaration is a higher document.

The Declaration says that we are a nation under God's laws. Therefore, all other laws of our country should be consistent with the law of God or they violate our national charter. 6

The Constitution does not contain explicit value declarations of right and wrong. It does not need to. It was derived from a document that had already announced which value system would be used in the nation: "the laws of nature and of nature's God."

The United States Constitution is not a source of funda-
mental values. It is an instrument whereby fundamental values can be protected...But the Constitution itself cannot give that content. In the early days, no one supposed that it would. There was a sufficiently clear value-consensus among Americans...there was little doubt as to the funda-mental nature of good and evil, of virtue and vice...Today, if there is disagreement or ignorance--as increasingly there is--fundamental values cannot be found in the Constitution. They simply are not there. 7

Contemporary Americans simply do not realize how profound the statement "the laws of nature and of nature's God" actually is. It encompasses an entire legal and political system; the phrase was commonly used and well-understood at the time of the founding. Now, however, the majority of those in today's legal profession would be hard-pressed to offer an acceptable definition of Divine or natural law; it is missing in current legal training! It is important to under-stand natural law:

...the American Republic was founded upon the natural law...From natural law flow basic human rights, such as the right to life, liberty, and property, which are ultimately derived from God and which are antecedent to all government. Natural law was thus perceived by the Founders to be unchanging because it was grounded in the constancy of human nature...8

...natural law-natural rights was...a body of moral law superior to human law...each department of the government would be composed of men imbued with natural law-natural rights principles. 9

The Constitution cannot be correctly applied without the use of the natural law principles defined in the Declaration. This was well understood at the time of our founding, and it was for this reason that President John Adams declared:

Our Constitution was made only for a moral and religious people. It is wholly inadequate to the government of any other. 10

The two documents must be used together to understand either one individually:

The Declaration of Independence...stated clearly the purpose of the government of this nation, which was to preserve and protect certain God-given rights for every citizen...eleven years later...the Constitution of the United States...stated the plan by which government would carry out its purpose.

The Declaration of Independence and the Constitution must be seen as one. Each is incomplete without the other. This nation stands strong and free today, two hundred years later, because one foot stands on the Declaration of Independence; the other, on the Constitution. Remove either document and the nation will not stand at all. 11

The beliefs and convictions upon which the Founders formed this nation are essential to our form of government and to the continued existence of this nation. In order for something to perform to its maximum potential, it must be used in accordance with the guidelines of its makers. The same is true for this nation:

It is said that James Russell Lowell was asked by the French historian Francois Guizot, "How long will the American republic endure?" He sagely replied, "As long as the ideas of the men who founded it continue dominant." 12

~14~
...Government of the People,
By the People, For the People...

Not only did the Founders clearly define the system of values on which the government was established, they also specified the proper function of each of its three branches. For their design to perform as intended, each of the three branches must confine itself to the responsibilities assigned it. Not only has the contemporary Court rejected the Founders' philosophy, it has rejected many of the restrictions they placed on the judiciary.

The primary reason that the Court succeeds in its massacre of the Constitution is that most individuals have never read the Constitution for themselves. In current education, little exposure is given to the content of the Constitution or of the Declaration of Independence. The instruction received by students emphasizes what others have said about the Constitution, not what the Constitution itself says. Such a practice instills in the students any prejudices that exist in a commentator's personal interpretation (or misinterpretation) of the Constitution. The Constitution is perhaps the single most important document of our entire government--certainly it is one of the two most important documents. It is not particularly long and should be read by *every* individual.

There are many things in the Constitution that indicate what our Founders intended as the correct relation between the branches of the government. Following the preamble, Article I describes the Congress, Article II the Presidency, and Article III the Judiciary. As in many documents, the Constitution lists the most significant items first, progressing to those of lesser import; in this case moving from the Legislative to the Judiciary.

The amount of detail provided about each branch also reflects its relative importance. In the Constitution, the Legislature (Article I) received 255 lines of print while the Presidency (Article II) required only 114 lines. The Judiciary (Article III) merited a mere 44 lines!

The fact that Congress was presented first and that 255 of the 413 lines describing the responsibilities of the three branches (over 60 percent) were dedicated to Congress indicates that our Founders felt it to be the most important aspect of the new government. The emphasis on Congress in the Constitution is obvious to those who read it:

I have read and reread the Constitution. It doesn't take many readings to see that the responsibilities of Congress are most carefully and specifically stated. They should be. Congress makes the laws. The president executed the laws, and the courts interpret them; but Congress is the branch given responsibility to make them in the first place. [1]

The Founders never intended nor imagined that the Court would become as powerful as it has today. It currently wields power greater than that of the Congress or the President. It strikes down their acts and determines which of them will survive and which will be condemned to oblivion. If Congress does not introduce "proper" legislation, the Court decrees its own policies (prison reform, educational reform, business policies, etc.)--policies made without any input from the people or their representatives.

The Founders would be astounded by today's Supreme Court as indicated both by the meager discussion of the judicial branch in Article III of the Constitution and by the history of the early Court:

Indeed, the designers of the National Capitol neglected to provide even a chamber for the Court, and the Court's first home when the government was transferred to Washington was in "a humble apartment in the basement beneath the Senate Chamber." [2]

An idle passerby might wander in and find two or three onlookers and a court clerk and several men who had given up trying to find work and felt grateful for a warm place to sit on a cold day...one could not tell he had entered the highest courtroom in the land. [3]

Even those who were part of the Court realized that it was never destined for great power, as reflected in the comments of the nation's first Chief Justice, who had been appointed by George Washington:

When John Jay refused to resume the chief justiceship in 1801, he told President Adams that he had no faith the Court could acquire enough "energy, weight, and dignity" to play a salient part in the nation's affairs. [4]

And John Jay was one of the men influential in the construction of our government and in the division of its powers! This same sentiment had been expressed by the philosophers from which the Founders most frequently quoted, in this instance, Montesquieu:

> Of the three powers above mentioned [executive, legislative, judiciary], the judiciary is in some measure next to nothing...5

Things are certainly different now! The role of judges was well known and understood during our founding, as documented both by the Court practices and by the writings of that day. The Constitution did not specifically delineate all the prohibitions on the Court's power--it did not need to:

> Following the ancient traditions of biblical and common law, the framers assumed that judges would know their limits. The judges are asked to judge, no more. They hear all sides in disputes about the law under the Constitution of the United States. They discover and decide the meaning of the laws. They apply the laws. They judge between the parties who disagree about the laws. But they do not *make* laws... And those judicial judgments are not laws but only opinions about the law...6

Blackstone, another favorite of the Founders, described what constituted improper judicial conduct:

> If [the legislature] will positively enact a thing to be done, the judges are not at liberty to reject it, for that were to set the judicial power above that of the legislature, which would be subversive of all government. 7

Like Montesquieu and Blackstone, the Founders were very clear about the proper role of the judiciary. For example, James Madison opposed the assertion that the Courts should have the final say on laws. He contended that allowing the Courts the position of:

> ...refusing or not refusing to execute a law, to stamp it with its final character...makes the judiciary department paramount in fact to the legislature, which was never intended and can never be proper. 8

Thomas Jefferson expressed similar sentiments in a letter:

> You seem to consider the judges as the ultimate arbiters of all Constitutional questions: a very dangerous doctrine indeed, and one which would place us under the despotism of an oligarchy. The Constitution has erected no such single tribunal...It has more wisely made all the departments co-equal and co-sovereign within themselves. 9

Alexander Hamilton, writing in *Federalist 81* of *The Federalist Papers,* confirmed that under the Constitutional plan, the Court was *not* being given the power to strike down laws:

> In the first place, there is not a syllable in the plan under consideration which directly empowers the national courts to construe the laws according to the spirit of the Constitution...

Congress, not the Courts, was to judge laws against the spirit of the Constitution. Congress was to build its laws on the intent of the Constitution, and the Courts were to interpret the laws according to the intent of Congress.

Records from the Constitutional Convention provide additional information on how the Founders viewed the judiciary's role. During the Constitutional debates, a plan for a Council of Revision was considered. This council was to be composed of members from the executive and judicial branches and would rule on the constitutionality of proposed legislation *before* it became law. However, the decision of this council would not be binding; it could be overridden by the legislature. Even though limited to an *advisory* capacity, delegate Elbridge Gerry of Massachusetts argued that:

> It [the Council of Revision] was making statesmen of the judges, and setting them up as guardians of the rights of the people, as the guardians of their rights and interests. It was making the [judges into] legislators, *which ought never to be done..."* 10

As the debates at the Convention continued, and the role of each branch was defined, the Court was delegated very limited spheres of jurisdiction and could only rule on restricted types of cases. However, delegate William Johnson of Connecticut wanted to increase the Court's power, so he moved:

..."to extend the judicial power to all cases in law and equity arising under the Constitution." However, James Madison: "Doubted whether it was not going too far, to extend the jurisdiction of the court...The right of expounding the Constitution in cases not of this nature ought not to be given to that department." 11

The Council of Revision was *not* approved. When the final draft of the Constitution was ratified, the right for the judiciary to impose its opinion of constitutionality on the other branches was not found:

Read Article III, looking for the line or phrase that gives the Supreme Court power to make laws or to discard laws that the Congress or state and local legislatures have made. You will not find it. 12

Luther Martin, one of Maryland's delegates to the Convention, explained why the roles had been defined as they were:

A knowledge of mankind and of legislative affairs cannot be presumed to belong in a higher degree to the judges than to the legislature...It is necessary that the supreme judiciary should have the confidence of the people. This will soon be lost if they are employed in the task of remonstrating against popular measures of the legislature. 13

Even the judicial branch understood that it was not the focus of power. The center and source of power was the people--and the legislature was the branch closest to the people. The judiciary expressed their keen understanding of their own role in *Commonwealth v. Kneeland, 1846:*

The Court, therefore, from its respect for the legislature, the immediate representation of that sovereign power whose will created and can at pleasure change the constitution itself, will ever strive to sustain and not annul its expressed determination...and whenever the people become dissatisfied with its operation, they have only to will its abrogation or modification and let their voice be heard through the legitimate channel, and it will be done. But until they wish it, *let no branch of the government, and least of all the judiciary, undertake to interfere with it.* (emphasis added)

The Courts accepted their proper role in the government, and in this case, 60 years after its ratification, they were still adhering to the intent of the Constitution. The Founders never intended the judiciary to be the chief branch, as emphasized through their writings identifying the most important branch. In *Federalist 51*, James Madison said:

> In republican government, the legislative authority necessarily predominates.

John Locke had similarly stated:

> ...the first and fundamental positive law of all commonwealths is the establishing of the legislative power...[14]

In *Federalist 49*, Madison explained why the legislative branch was the most important in a republican form of government:

> The members of the legislative department are numerous. They are distributed and dwell among the people at large. Their connections of blood, of friendship, and of acquaintance embrace a great proportion of the most influential part of the society...they are more immediately the confidential guardians of the rights and liberties of the people.

Since the legislature is closest to the people, it most accurately reflects their will. If changes and reforms were to occur, it was to be through the legislature, not the Courts. But if Congress is the predominant branch, what is the check or balance on Congress? Congressman John Randolph of Roanoke stated:

> ...the proper restraint of Congress lay not with the Supreme Court, but with the people themselves, who at the ballot box "could apply the Constitutional corrective. That is the one, true check; every other is at variance with the principle that a free people are capable of self-government." [15]

The check on Congress is the people, not the Supreme Court. If any branch was to review the others, it would be the legislative, not the judicial. As Montesquieu, in *The Spirit of Laws*, had written:

> ...and as these [three branches] have need of a regulating power to moderate them, the part of the legislative body...is

extremely proper for this purpose...it has a right and ought to
have the means of examining in what manner its laws have
been executed...16

Logic demands that those making the laws hold a more important
position than those interpreting them:

> It is of the very essence of law in a republican form of govern-
> ment that the legislative power has primacy over the judicial,
> the power to make laws is antecedent to the power to inter-
> pret them. The judicial power, passive in nature, is attendant
> upon legislative initiative. To invert this order would be a
> subversion of republican government. 17

It was important to the success of this form of government that
each branch not encroach into the designated responsibilities of the
others. George Washington warned them to:

> ...confine themselves within their respective constitutional
> spheres, avoiding in the exercise of the powers of one
> department to encroach upon another. The spirit of
> encroachment tends to consolidate the powers of all the
> departments in one, and this to create...a real despotism...
> Let there be no change by usurpation...it is the customary
> weapon by which free governments are destroyed. 18

James Madison issued a similar caution:

> The preservation of a free government requires not merely
> that the metes and bounds which separate each department
> of power be invariably maintained...The rulers who are guilty
> of such an encroachment, exceed the commission from
> which they derive their authority, and are tyrants. The
> people who submit to it are governed by laws made neither
> by themselves nor by an authority derived from them, and
> are slaves. 19

The warnings of Washington and Madison echoed Montesquieu's:

> Were the power of judging joined with the legislative, the life
> and liberty of the subject would be exposed to arbitrary
> control, for the judge would then be the legislator.

There would be an end of everything, were...the same body...to exercise those three powers, that of enacting laws, that of executing the public resolutions, and of trying the causes of individuals...[20]

Our national charter and by-laws (the Declaration and Constitution) use phrases such as: "...government of the people, by the people, and for the people..."; "...the consent of the governed..."; etc. It is no secret that our Founders intended the power of this government to reside solely in the hands of the people. Congressman Robert K. Dornan, in a statement from his book *Judicial Supremacy,* accurately summarized the beliefs of the Founders when he stated:

The representatives are chosen by the people, act in place of the people for the people's welfare, are accountable to the people, and have superior resources with which to determine and provide for the welfare of the people. The aloofness and unaccountability of the judicial branch creates around it an atmosphere in which it is all too easy for the judiciary to substitute its own idea of the general welfare for that of the people...Furthermore, the resources available to the judiciary for determining the general welfare are in no way superior to those of the national legislature. [21]

Laws are to reflect the general public consensus, not the desires of a few individuals, or of a small group such as the Court. Samuel Adams summarized the basic tenet of a republic:

..."laws they are not, which the public approbation hath not made so." This seems to be the language of nature and common sense; for if the public are bound to yield obedience to laws to which they cannot give their approbation, they are slaves to those who make such laws and enforce them...[22]

229

~15~
Judicial Supremacy--
The Three Percent Majority

Although we are accustomed to hearing that we are a democracy, such is actually not the case. The form of government entrusted to us by our Founders was a republic, not a democracy; there is a definite difference between the two. A democracy conducts business by direct majority vote only. When an issue is to be decided, the entire population votes on it and the majority wins and rules. A democracy is a series of referendum votes. A republic differs in that the general population conducts business by directly electing representatives who then vote on issues. Although a majority vote of the representatives will determine a policy, in a republic, the minority view will have some influence in the majority decision. Compromises are worked out whereby the majority rules with consideration given to minority rights. Under our form of government, there is direct vote of the people on the selection of their chief executive and of their representatives--for this we might be termed a democratic republic, but we are not a democracy.

Not only is a republic the highest form of human government, it also requires the greatest amount of care and maintenance. If a republic is neglected, it can deteriorate into one of several inferior forms of government: a democracy, an anarchy, an oligarchy, or a dictatorship. As mentioned above, a democracy is government conducted by direct vote and popular referendum. In an anarchy, every person is his own final authority--each individual determines his own rules. An oligarchy is a government run by a small council or group of elite individuals. A dictatorship is rule by a single individual.

In a republic or a democracy, numbers are important. When the majority has expressed itself on an issue, that expression is significant and it becomes the policy. Since oligarchies and dictatorships are based on minority rule, numbers are not important. Policies are enacted by a small group or by a single individual, even if contrary to the will of the majority of the population.

In our government, our documents make it clear that we are established in such a manner that numbers *are* important. Our government is to function with the consent of the governed, and the percentages given in the Constitution define what constitutes "the consent of the governed": a majority vote, and on occasion, a two-thirds or three-fourths vote. At no time is a nationwide policy to be enacted by a minority group over the objection of the majority.

In a republic, discounting a unanimous vote, there will be a majority and a minority on every issue. The minority has the right to attempt to persuade the majority to its point of view, or to persuade them to include portions of the minority views in their decisions. However, the minority is not the equivalent of the majority and is never to exercise strength over the majority.

This was the original plan, but it has now changed, particularly in domestic areas. In some fundamental ways that seriously distort Constitutional checks and balances, our nation is no longer a republic, or even a democratic republic--it has become an oligarchy. A council of nine individuals is able to make final, irreversible determinations on what will and will not become domestic policy in the land. A simple majority of those nine (a mere five votes) can overturn any law of the land, even though it has been legitimately enacted by the people through their elected representatives. Despite being composed of unelected officials not answerable to the people, this council of nine, the Supreme Court, has become the most powerful ruling body in the nation.

In a republic, the group whose policies are becoming the law of the land is the majority. However, in many areas, with the willing assistance of the Court, the minority view and belief has become the "majority" view--the law of the land. An example is the removal of school prayer. The Court's own records reveal that only 3 percent of the nation had no religious ties of any type--no belief in God. The Supreme Court aligned itself with the 3 percent and declared that, in opposition to the beliefs of the 97 percent, the acknowledgment of God and non-denominational prayer to Him would be prohibited in schools. That decision was enacted by the three percent "majority"! The percentages given by the Court in the *Abington* case in 1963 have shown little change, as confirmed by the numbers provided in 1986:

> A recent Gallup Poll shows that 95% of the American public reports a belief in God (a figure that has remained unchanged since 1944 when Gallup first asked the question). In a typical month, over 50% of Americans go to a religious service. 1

> Fifty million Americans claim to have had a life-changing experience centering on Jesus Christ. More than 100 million

adults belong to a church or synagogue. Forty million go to church weekly, and seventeen million Americans go to church more than once a week. [2]

The following numbers were provided, and then ignored, by the Court in *Board of Educ. v. Board of Educ. of Netcong, 1970:*

...public opinion polls, such as the Gallup, Harris, and Good Housekeeping polls, one of which...shows that 82% of the public favors prayer in public schools.

Well over 90 percent of the nation continues to believe in God, and over 80 percent of both students and citizens want prayer returned to schools. A Gallup poll published in *Emerging Trends* in March 1985, showed that 87 percent of Americans pray to God, down only 3 percent from the 90 percent mark in 1948. Such percentages would meet the requirement of a majority, a two-thirds, or even a three-fourths vote. Yet the public, despite extensive effort, has been absolutely powerless to overturn the decisions of the minority. Virtually every state has, in a constitutional manner and through the people's elected representatives, approved a law to return voluntary prayer to schools. The nine-member unelected Supreme Court continues to block all efforts to acknowledge God or to pray in public.

It is obvious that the 80 plus percent is *not* in power; the unelected judges are in power. Their form of rulership is identified by the term "judicial supremacy":

According to the doctrine of judicial supremacy, the judiciary has the sole right to place an authoritative interpretation on the Constitution, an interpretation that is, moreover, binding on the executive and legislative branches of the government. The only recourse for those who disagree with the Supreme Court is the formal amendment procedures of Article V of the Constitution. Thus, a Supreme Court decision has acquired the same status as a fixed provision of the Constitution itself!...The one respect in which a Supreme Court decision differs from a fixed provision is that it has acquired that status not through the endorsement of a clear national consensus (three-fourths of the states), as required by Article V, but through the certification of a mere five-man majority! Moreover, if the interpretation of the Constitution of one coordinate department is final and binding upon the other coordinate departments, then obviously this department is no longer "coordinate," but "supreme." Thus, the Supreme Court has in fact become the supreme branch of a supposedly republican form of government. 3

The Court portrays itself as supreme and allows no discussion of or recourse from its decisions. In *Wallace v. Jaffree (1984),* the Court issued a stiff rebuke to any lower Court who might attempt to "read" the Constitution for itself:

Federal district courts and circuit courts are bound to adhere to the controlling decisions of the supreme Court...a precedent of this Court must be followed by the lower federal courts no matter how misguided the judges of those courts may think it to be...only this Court may overrule one of its precedents...

A similar warning was also delivered in *Board of Educ. v. Board of Educ. of Netcong (1970):*

...[A] Trial Court cannot claim right to independent interpretation of United States Constitution, and is obliged to apply law as last pronounced by superior judicial authority...

The Court has appointed itself as the sole custodian of the Constitution. As Chief Justice Charles Evan Hughes said:

...the Constitution is what the judges say it is. 4

Such statements reveal an underlying contempt that the judiciary holds for the legislature, the presidency, and especially the people. The Court believes it is the only one able to "understand" the Constitution. That belief, and the statements proceeding from it, are ludicrous:

The spectacle of even *one* unelected judge...successfully thwarting the will of a majority of the duly elected representatives of an entire nation, representatives who have sworn to uphold the Constitution, reveals the very essence of judicial supremacy...It is government by judiciary in place of government of, by, and for the people. 5

When Thomas Jefferson observed and commented on what some judges were attempting to do during his term of office, he accurately described what has now happened in America:

> [They] have retired into the judiciary as a stronghold...and from that battery, all the works of Republicanism are to be beaten down and erased...[6]

The Court has gradually usurped more and more power, moving further and further away from its proper role. Jefferson had foreseen this tendency on the part of the judiciary:

> The germ of dissolution of our Federal government is in...the federal judiciary; an irresponsible body working like gravity by night and by day, gaining a little today and a little tomorrow, and advancing its noiseless step like a thief, over the field of jurisdiction, until all shall be usurped from the states, and the judges as the ultimate arbiters of all constitutional questions is a very dangerous doctrine indeed, and one which would place us under the despotism of an oligarchy...The Constitution has erected no such tribunal. [7]

With the position the Court now holds, it wields incredible power:

> ...at one bold stroke the federal judiciary is able to by-pass the legislative process...and by judicial fiat and without the necessity of compromise impose its own values on an entire nation. [8]

In its first eighty years, acting in accord with Constitutional intent, the Supreme Court had declared only two laws unconstitutional, and its decisions had not been binding on the other branches. In recent years the Court has declared hundreds of laws unconstitutional and imposed its decisions upon legislatures and the presidency:

> Today, the Court no longer limits itself to settling disputes between parties; it strikes down laws in all fifty states, issues restraining orders, and the like that usurps both legislative and executive powers. The Warren Court that struck down prayer and Bible reading in 1962 did not have any judges with any prior judicial experience. [9]

The Court has moved far beyond its designated role of decision making about laws and into actual legislation and policy making, previously the sole responsibility of elected representatives:

> ...judicial usurpation of legislative power has become so common and so complete that the Supreme Court has become our most powerful...instrument of government in terms of determining the nature and quality of American life. Questions literally of life and death (abortion and capital punishment), of public morality (control of pornography, prayer in the schools, and government aid to religious schools), and of public safety (criminal procedure and street demonstrations) are all, now, in the hands of judges under the guise of questions of constitutional law. The fact that the Constitution says nothing of, say, abortion, and indeed, explicitly and repeatedly recognizes the capital punishment the Court has come close to prohibiting, has made no difference.
>
> The result is that the central truth of constitutional law today is that it has nothing to do with the Constitution... constitutional law has become a fraud, a cover for a system of government by the majority vote of a nine-person committee of lawyers, unelected and holding office for life. 10

The following is a graphic example of the type of case now routinely handled by the Courts--a case having nothing at all to do with any law or any violation of a law. The Court's ruling in this case is merely a social engineering decision; the type of decision that is appropriately to be handled by the legitimate policy makers--the legislature:

> The case started when a group of radical activists, mostly white, sued the school system on behalf of a group of black families. They claimed that the poor academic progress of the blacks was due to the fact that their native language was black English while standard English was used in the schools. The solution was for teachers to be trained to use and respect black English...To those on the scene the proposed position seemed frivolous. For example, there was no evidence that black children spoke black English exclusively, or that they couldn't understand standard English. After all, these black children watched television

daily and talked easily with their white classmates. Those who really knew these children reported "that black English is a variant dialect that can be turned on and off depending on the circumstances, in much the same way that many middle class Southern children learn to speak both standard English and 'country.'"...However, a federal judge decided to hear the case. To the community's astonishment, he decided that black English was a factor in these children's poor performance. The remedy ordered was to require teachers to attend lectures on black English. Subsequent tests showed that this remedial program for teachers made no difference in the children's performance.

What should trouble us most about this case is the ease with which a judge has intruded himself into the heart of the educator's domain, into what is to be taught, how it is to be taught, and how teachers are to be trained to teach it. What qualifies the judge to do so? What qualifies him to pronounce on the linguistics of English dialects? What qualifies him to pronounce on the causes of scholastic achievement, and the means needed to enhance it? The answer is-nothing at all...11

The Supreme Court amends and changes the meaning of the Constitution at will to reflect its own view:

The problem is that...where the Supreme Court's interpretation of the Constitution is considered final and binding upon all other authorities, the philosophical predilections of the Justices become, in effect, part of the Constitution. This allows the Supreme Court to act as somewhat of a continuous constitutional convention, continually amending the written document by interpretation, so that the Constitution means whatever five members of the Supreme Court decide it should mean. 12

As Jefferson so aptly described it:

The Constitution...is a mere thing of wax in the hands of the judiciary, which they may twist and shape into any form they please...13

The following piercing statements concerning the Court are worthy of contemplation and reflection:

> The President may slip without the state suffering, for his duties are limited. Congress may slip without the Union perishing...But if ever the Supreme Court came to be composed of rash or corrupt men, the confederation would be threatened...[14]

> When the ultra-liberals lose elections, they fight all the more desperately for control of our third branch, the courts. Why? Because the courts control the constitution and the constitution is the "trump card" in politics. That's why this war is crucial. Now, there are only two sides really in this struggle. Either the constitution controls the judges, or the judges rewrite the constitution. [15]

> ...government of, by, and for the people has become government of and by judges and lawyers for the people. [16]

> How long can public respect for the Court, on which its power ultimately depends, survive if the people become aware that the tribunal which condemns the acts of others as unconstitutional is itself acting unconstitutionally? [17]

~16~
When Three Percent Was A Minority

The Court has worked diligently to achieve the power it now possesses. It refuses to allow itself to be called into question by anyone, as evidenced by the remarks of Justice Felix Frankfurter in *American Federation of Labor v. American Sash and Door Co., (1949)*:

> Our right to pass on the validity of legislation is now too much part of our constitutional system to be brought into question. [1]

Yet the Court's power must be called into question! We must reclaim from the Courts the right to be a republic, returning the oligarchy of judges to its proper position--the least of three co-sovereign branches. The people of the nation, not its Courts, must control its destiny. Any national reforms that occur must be guided by the people, not by the social engineering of an elite few.

The Court is now so far from its origins that an observation offered by Alexis de Tocqueville in the 1830's seems foreign to current thinking. In contrasting America's Courts with those in France, he admired the American system, where the power was properly with the people, not with the Courts. De Tocqueville observed that the French Courts did not have the Constitutional restraints the American Courts did. As a result:

> ...in France the courts could disobey the laws on the ground that they found them unconstitutional...power would really be in their hands, as they alone would have the right to interpret a constitution...In that way they would take the nation's place and be the dominant power in society... [2]

Notice how the French Courts gained their power: by claiming the sole right to interpret the constitution, they could then make their own opinions on the laws binding on others. Throughout our own early history, American Courts periodically attempted to do the same thing. Whenever that occurred, the Founders quickly rose up and dramatically forced the Court back to its proper constitutional function. The example delivered to us of how our Founders responded to the Court's attempts to encroach on the other branches is worthy of emulation today.

The first occasion in which the Supreme Court attempted to flex and enlarge its judicial "muscle" was during the presidency of Thomas Jefferson. In the final days of the presidency of John Adams, just before Jefferson took office, Adams made several federalist appointments of justices of the peace to positions in the District of Columbia. Jefferson, an anti-federalist, had been voted to office over the federalist candidate. He felt his election was a clear mandate that the people did not want the federalist philosophy further extended or strengthened.

When Jefferson became President, several appointments from Adams had not yet been delivered. Jefferson ordered them stopped. William Marbury, one of the thwarted appointees, sued James Madison, Jefferson's Secretary of State, to receive the appointment he felt was rightfully his. That suit, *Marbury v. Madison,* went before the Supreme Court.

The Court, speaking through the Chief Justice, ruled against Jefferson's administration and ordered Madison to award the appointment. The Court had not only ruled and delivered its opinion, it was now *ordering* the executive branch to submit to its decision. This was an overt action by the Court to gain more power by attempting to force its own opinion on another branch of government. What would be the response?

Madison, the defendant in the case, was neither a constitutional neophyte nor a "lightweight." As Chief Architect of the Constitution, he was intimately acquainted with the proper role for each of the three branches. As shown by his statements, he was neither impressed with nor intimidated by the Court's order:

> [Some contend] that wherever [the Constitution's] meaning is doubtful, you must leave it to take its course, until the judiciary is called upon to declare its meaning...but I beg to know upon what principle it can be contended that any one department draws from the Constitution greater powers than another...I do not see that any one of these independent departments has more right than another to declare their sentiments on that point. 3

The attempt by the Court to impose its view on the other branches either overlooked or ignored a basic principle: President Jefferson and Secretary of State James Madison had both taken an oath to uphold the Constitution, as did the Supreme Court Justices. The

Court's attempt to force its view upon the President and Secretary of State (both of whom were obviously well-versed in Constitutional understanding) implied:

> ...only the judges *really* understand [the Constitution] and truly uphold it...lesser mortals must allegedly defer to the "enlightened" views of a few, and this in a republican form of government! In a word, the Justices avow themselves to be superior in mental and moral faculties to their colleagues in the other supposedly coordinate branches of the government...! 4

Jefferson felt that each branch had the ability, and indeed, the sworn responsibility, to interpret the Constitution for itself. If this were not true, America could never be called a true republic with three co-equal and co-sovereign branches. Consequently, Jefferson completely ignored the Court's decision in *Marbury v. Madison.* This presidential act was *not* greeted by outrage from the public, Congress, or even the Court. Jefferson's action was normal under this form of government.

Shortly after this incident, in a letter to Mrs. John Adams, Jefferson expounded his belief on the power and position of the judiciary:

> Nothing in the Constitution has given them a right to decide for the Executive more than the Executive to decide for them. The opinion which gives the judges the right to decide what laws are unconstitutional and what are not...for the Legislature and the Executive...would make the judiciary a despotic branch. 5

This was not the only incident in which Jefferson refused to become a servant of the Court; although commanded by the Court to appear at the Aaron Burr conspiracy trial, he refused.

Jefferson and Madison have provided a valuable precedent for handling the Court's attempts to gain more power: flatly refuse to allow them to assume a position not rightfully theirs. If the other two branches submit to the Court's decisions as binding and final, there remains no checks and balances over the power of the Court!

> Jefferson saw quite clearly that any acquiescence to assertions of judicial supremacy would result in the Court becoming the final judge of its own authority. 6

The need to keep the Court's power in check was widely understood by the Founders. In fact, many of them did more than merely
ignore the Court when it began to declare the acts of Congress
unconstitutional. On the floor of the Senate, William Giles of Virginia
declared:

> ...if the judges of the Supreme Court should dare...to declare
> the acts of Congress unconstitutional...it was the undoubted
> right of the House to impeach them, and of the Senate to
> remove them...7

Although alien to current thinking, in early America, it was custo-
mary for the legislature to reverse the judiciary, not vice versa:

> In 1787, judicial interpretation of the law was often not final
> even in the decision of cases, it being common practice for
> the legislature...to reverse decisions of the ordinary courts,
> to order cases re-tried or appeals granted...8

This was logical since it was a government of the people--the
people's representatives could change the decisions of government
to reflect the people's will. However, even Congress was not
supreme over the nation--its check and balance was the people
themselves. If the people felt their representatives were acting in an
improper manner, they would replace them. As John Randolph of
Roanoke had stated in Congress:

> ...the proper restraint of Congress lay not with the Supreme
> Court, but with the people themselves, who at the ballot box
> "could apply the Constitutional corrective." 9

This policy toward the Court was practiced for decades following
Jefferson, Madison, and other Founders. For example, when
Andrew Jackson was President, the Court ruled in the *Cherokee
Indian* cases (1831-1832) that the President was to take certain
actions. As Presidents before him, Jackson refused to be ordered
about by the Court. In reply to the Court's decision, Jackson
declared:

> [The Chief Justice] has made his decision; now let him
> enforce it! 10

That declaration indicated Jackson's strong beliefs about three *distinct* branches of government. His explanation of his beliefs sharply mirrored those of the Founders before him:

> Each public officer who takes an oath to support the Constitution swears that he will support it as he understands it, and not as it is understood by others...The opinion of the judges has no more authority over the Congress than the opinion of Congress has over the judges, and on that point the President is independent of both. The authority of the Supreme Court must not, therefore, be permitted to control the Congress or the Executive...11

Madison had made a similar statement:

> Nothing has yet been offered to invalidate the doctrine that the meaning of the Constitution may as well be ascertained by the legislature as by the judicial authority. 12

Abraham Lincoln was another President who acted "unconstitutionally." In the infamous *Dred Scott* case of 1857, the Court denied the personhood of blacks, declaring them to be only property and not "persons" eligible to receive any rights. Lincoln, like his predecessors, ignored the Court's ruling. In the Emancipation Proclamation, in which he declared freedom for the slaves, he was ignoring the ruling of the Court in the *Dred Scott* case--in the Court's opinion, he was acting "unconstitutionally." Had Lincoln allowed the Court's ruling to be binding on the executive branch, and had he not been guided by his own understanding of the Constitution, he could not have declared freedom for slaves. Lincoln expressed his keen understanding of the roles of each branch in his first inaugural address:

> I do not forget the position, assumed by some, that constitutional questions are to be decided by the Supreme Court...At the same time, the candid citizen must confess that if the policy of the government, upon vital questions affecting the whole people, is to be irrevocably fixed by decisions of the Supreme Court, the instant they are made...the people will have ceased to be their own rulers, having...resigned their government into the hands of that eminent tribunal. 13

The *Dred Scott* decree had not only denied citizenship to slaves, it also protected slavery and permitted it to be extended into other free territories. Congress openly rejected the Court's "constitutional" decree when, on June 19, 1862, it *prohibited* the extension of slavery into the free territories. 14

The cure for judicial supremacy, based on the examples and writings of our nation's heroes, is simply to refuse to allow the Courts to rule the nation. A foreign observer of this nation today would undoubtedly conclude that the President and Congress had taken oaths, not to uphold the Constitution, but to uphold the Court's *opinion* of the Constitution. By allowing the Court to preempt the President and Congress, those branches are required to relinquish the responsibilities for which they were elected:

> ...Congress and the President are vested not only with the *power* but with the *duty* to read the Constitution for themselves...they are entitled to consult the opinions of the Court...[but] they are *not* entitled to abdicate their own official function of independent judgment...15 (emphasis added)

A notable speech delivered by Charles Hodge of Princeton, during a celebration of the nation's centennial in 1876, presents a convincing argument that this constitutional republic should truly continue to reflect the foundation upon which it was built:

> The proposition that the United States of America [is] a Christian...nation is...the statement of a fact. That fact is not simply that the great majority of the people are Christians ...the organic life, the institutions, laws, and an official action of the government, whether that action be legislative, judicial, or executive, is...in accordance with the principles of...Christianity.
>
> ...If a man goes to China, he expects to find the government administered according to the religion of the country. If he goes to Turkey, he expects to find the Koran supreme and regulating all public action. If he goes to a [Christian] country, he has no right to complain, should he find the Bible in the ascendancy and exerting its benign influence not only on the people, but also on the government.
>
> ...In the process of time thousands have come among us, who are [not] Christians. Some are...Jews, some infidels, and some atheists. All are welcomed; all are admitted to

equal rights and privileges.   All are allowed to acquire
property, and to vote in every election...All are allowed to
worship as they please, or not to worship at all...No man is
molested for his religion or for his want of religion.   No man is
required to profess any form of faith, or to join any religious
association. More than this cannot reasonably be demanded.
More, however, is demanded. The infidel demands that the
government should be conducted on the principle that
Christianity is false. The atheist demands that it should be
conducted on the assumption that there is no God...The sufficient answer to all this is that it cannot possibly be done. [16]

Despite the fact that "it cannot possibly be done," it has been
done--not by the people, but by the Courts! Government is now
conducted on the assumption that "Christianity is false" and that
"there is no God." It should never have happened:

...judicial supremacy was never intended because it was not
a republican remedy...The indictment against judicial supremacy is that it is unconstitutional. The bitter irony is that the
Justices acting in the name of the constitution are often
acting unconstitutionally.

We therefore exhort the members of Congress and the
Executive branch to return to the meaning of the Constitution
that was intended by the framers and so ably expounded by
such great men as Madison, Jefferson, Jackson, and
Lincoln.   Two of the grandest and most resplendent
monuments in our capital are dedicated to Thomas Jefferson
and Abraham Lincoln, yet we do not heed their words
regarding the meaning of the Constitution. [17]

~17~
The Potential Downfall of the Republic

Just as the Founders had strong beliefs on what constituted a good government, they also held equally strong beliefs about what would cause its downfall. Their warnings are numerous and convey the same message: the stability of this government is based on the morality of its citizens, and the morality of its citizens is based on religion--when the importance of religion is diminished, so is the effectiveness of government. Notice their overwhelming consensus on this belief--religion and morality are essential to good government:

> Of all the dispositions and habits which lead to political prosperity, religion and morality are indispensable supports. In vain would that man claim the tribute of patriotism, who should labor to subvert these great pillars...The mere politician...ought to respect and cherish them...Whatever may be conceded to the influence of refined education...reason and experience both forbid us to expect that national morality can prevail in exclusion of religious principle. *George Washington* 1

> Statesmen...may plan and speculate for liberty, but it is religion and morality alone which can establish the principles upon which freedom can securely stand. The only foundation of a free constitution is pure virtue. *John Adams* 2

> The principles of all genuine liberty, and of wise laws and administrations are to be drawn from the Bible and sustained by its authority. The man therefore who weakens or destroys the divine authority of that book may be accessory to all the public disorders which society is doomed to suffer. *Noah Webster* 3

> The only assurance of our nation's safety is to lay our foundation in morality and religion. *Abraham Lincoln* 4

> God grant that in America true religion and civil liberty may be inseparable, and the unjust attempts to destroy the one, may in the end tend to the support and establishment of both. *John Witherspoon* 5

> We have staked the whole future of American civilization, not upon the power of government, far from it. We have staked

the future of all of our political institutions...upon the capacity of each and all of us to govern ourselves, to control ourselves, to sustain ourselves according to the Ten Commandments of God. *James Madison* 6

The state must rest upon the basis of religion, and it must preserve this basis, or itself must fall. But the support which religion gives to the state will obviously cease the moment religion loses its hold upon the popular mind. *B. F. Morris* 7

Religion is the only solid basis of good morals; therefore education should teach the precepts of religion, and the duties of man toward God. *Gouverneur Morris* 8

Neither the wisest constitution nor the wisest laws will secure the liberty and happiness of a people whose manners are universally corrupt. *Samuel Adams* 9

Religion is considered as the guardian of [morals], and [morals] are regarded as the guarantee of the laws and pledge for the maintenance of freedom itself. *Alexis de Tocqueville* 10

...where there is no religion, there is no morality...with the loss of religion...the ultimate foundation of confidence is blown up, and the security of life, liberty and property buried in ruins. *Timothy Dwight* 11

Republican government loses half its value where the moral and social duties are...negligently practiced. To exterminate our popular vices is a work of far more importance to the character and happiness of our citizens, than any other improvements in our system of education. *Noah Webster* 12

...true religion affords to government its surest support. *George Washington* 13

A general dissolution of principles and manners will more surely overthrow the liberties of America than the whole force of the common enemy. While the people are virtuous they cannot be subdued; but when once they lose their virtue they will be ready to surrender their liberties to the first external or internal invader... *Samuel Adams* 14

Only a virtuous people are capable of freedom. As nations become corrupt and vicious, they have more need of masters. *Benjamin Franklin* 15

We have no government armed with power capable of contending with human passions unbridled by morality and religion...Our Constitution was made only for a moral and religious people. It is wholly inadequate to the government of any other. *John Adams* 16

At what point then, is the approach of danger to be expected? If it ever reaches us, it must spring up among us, it cannot come from abroad. If destruction is our lot, we must ourselves be its author and finisher; as a nation of free men, we must live through all time or die by suicide. *Abraham Lincoln* 17

[This] form of government...is productive of every thing which is great and excellent among men. But its principles are as easily destroyed as human nature is corrupted...private and public virtue is the only foundation of republics. *John Adams* 18

...the cultivation of the religious sentiment represses licentiousness...inspires respect for law and order, and gives strength to the whole social fabric... *Daniel Webster* 19

What follows from this? That he is the best friend to American liberty, who is most sincere and active in promoting true and undefiled religion, and who sets himself with the greatest firmness to bear down on profanity and immorality of every kind. Whoever is an avowed enemy of God, I scruple not to call him an enemy to his country. *John Witherspoon* 20

...the happiness of a people and the good order and preservation of civil government essentially depend upon piety, religion and morality... *United States Supreme Court, 1892*

...religion and morality...are the foundations of all governments. Without these restraints no free government could long exist. *Pennsylvania Supreme Court, 1824*

...offenses against religion and morality...strike at the root of moral obligation, and weaken the security of the social ties....This [First Amendment] declaration...never meant to withdraw religion...and with it the best sanctions of moral and social obligation from all consideration and notice of the law... *Supreme Court of New York, 1811*

...Religion, morality, and knowledge being necessary to good government, the preservation of liberty, and the happiness of mankind... *United States Supreme Court, 1892*

The destruction of morality renders the power of the government invalid... *Pennsylvania Supreme Court, 1815*

Governments like clocks, go from the motion men give them; and as governments are made and moved by men, so by them they are ruined too. Wherefore governments rather depend upon men, than men upon governments...Let men be good, and the government cannot be bad... *William Penn* 21

In vain are schools, academies, and universities instituted, if loose principles and licentious habits are impressed upon children in their earliest years...the vices and examples of the parents cannot be concealed from the children. How is it possible that children can have any just sense of the sacred obligations of morality or religion if, from their earliest infancy, they learn that their mothers live in habitual Infidelity to their fathers, and their fathers in as constant infidelity to their mothers? *John Adams* 22

It yet remains a problem to be solved in human affairs whether any free government can be permanent where the public worship of God, and the support of religion, constitute no part of the policy or duty of the state in any assignable shape. *Supreme Court Justice Joseph Story* 23

It is impossible to rightly govern the world without God and the Bible. *George Washington* 24

The moral principles and precepts contained in the Scriptures ought to form the basis of all our civil constitutions and laws. All the miseries and evils which men suffer from vice, crime, ambition, injustice, oppression, slavery, and war, proceed from their despising or neglecting the precepts contained in the Bible. *Noah Webster* 25

Suppose a nation in some distant region, should take the Bible for their only law book, and every member should regulate his conduct by the precepts there exhibited...What a Eutopa, What a Paradise would this region be! *John Adams* 26

A patriot without religion...is as great a paradox as an honest man without the fear of God...The Scriptures tell us righteousness exalteth a Nation. *Abigail Adams* 27

The foundations of our society and our government rest so much on the teachings of the Bible that it would be difficult to support them if faith in these teachings would cease to be practically universal in our country. *President Calvin Coolidge* 28

Without God there is not virtue because there is no prompting of the conscience...without God there is a coarsening of the society; without God democracy will not and cannot long endure...If we ever forget that we are One Nation Under God, then we will be a Nation gone under. *President Ronald Reagan* 29

...without an humble imitation of the characteristics of the Divine Author of our blessed religion...we can never hope to be a happy nation. *George Washington* 30

Moral habits...cannot safely be trusted on any other foundation than religious principle, nor any government be secure which is not supported by moral habits...Whatever makes men good Christians, makes them good citizens. *Daniel Webster* 31

He who shall introduce into public affairs the principles of... Christianity will change the face of the world. *Benjamin Franklin* 32

To the kindly influence of Christianity we owe that degree of civil freedom, and political and social happiness which mankind now enjoys. In proportion as the genuine effects of Christianity are diminished in any nation...in the same proportion will the people of that nation recede from the blessings of genuine freedom...Whenever the pillars of Christianity shall be overthrown, our present republican forms of government, and all the blessings which flow from them, must fall with them. *Jedediah Morse* 33

The purest principles of morality are to be taught. Where are they found? Whoever searches for them must go to the source from which a Christian man derives his faith--the Bible. *United States Supreme Court, 1844*

...and the morality of the country is deeply engrafted on Christianity. *Pennsylvania Supreme Court, 1824*

...the morality of the country is deeply engrafted upon Christianity, and not upon the doctrines or worship of [other religions]...[in] people whose manners are refined and whose morals have been elevated and inspired with a more enlarged benevolence [it is] by means of the Christian religion. *Supreme Court of New York, 1811*

...the morality of the country is deeply engrafted upon Christianity, and not upon the doctrines or worship of [other religions]. *United States Supreme Court, 1892*

...Christianity has reference to the principles of right and wrong...it is the foundation of those morals and manners upon which our society is formed; it is their basis. Remove this and they would fall...[morality] has grown upon the basis of Christianity. *Supreme Court of South Carolina, 1846*

...What constitutes the standard of good morals? Is it not Christianity? There certainly is none other. Say that it cannot be appealed to, and...what would be good morals? The day of moral virtue in which we live would, in an instant, if that standard were abolished, lapse into the dark and murky night of...immorality. *Supreme Court of South Carolina, 1846*

...a malicious intention...to vilify the Christian religion and the scriptures...would prove a nursery of vice, a school of preparation to qualify young men for the gallows, and young women for the brothel, and there is not a skeptic of decent manners and good morals who would not consider such...a common nuisance and disgrace... *Pennsylvania Supreme Court, 1824*

...for that whatever strikes at the root of Christianity tends manifestly to the dissolution of civil government...because it tends to corrupt the morals of the people, and to destroy good order. *Supreme Court of New York, 1811*

...religion...must be considered as the foundation on which the whole structure rests...In this age there can be no substitute for Christianity...the great conservative element on which we must rely for the purity and permanence of free institutions. *Senate Judiciary Committee, 1853*

...the Christian religion is the most important and one of the first things in which all children, under a free government, ought to be instructed...No truth is more evident...than that the Christian religion must be the basis of any government intended to secure the rights and privileges of a free people. *Noah Webster* 34

No free government now exists in the world, unless where Christianity is acknowledged and is the religion of the country. Christianity is part of the common law...Its foundations are broad and strong, and deep...it is the purest system of morality...and only stable support of all human laws. *Pennsylvania Supreme Court, 1824*

...the great vital and conservative element in our system is the belief of our people in the pure doctrines and divine truths of the gospel of Jesus Christ... *Senate Judiciary Committee, 1853*

Our Founders believed intensely that religion, specifically Christianity, produced morality, and that government could not survive without morality. On this basis, they certainly would neither create nor tolerate legislation diminishing Christianity's effect. To do so would ensure the demise of good government, and no intelligent government would intentionally commit suicide by destroying its very foundation!

There has been a strong campaign conducted in this nation to desensitize the citizenry to the importance of religion in government. But this government cannot stand without morality, and morality does not exist apart from religious principles. Morality, which comes from religion, must be publicly encouraged and supported for the sake of the future of this nation which we love and respect.

Advocates of natural law believe, as did the Founders, that there are fixed standards for right and wrong. Proponents of relativism believe that the only thing absolutely wrong is having fixed standards of right and wrong. Those who resent restraints and discipline proclaim, "You can't legislate morality!" That is not true. Relativists fail to realize that morality is *always* legislated--it is simply a matter of *whose* morality is being legislated:

> "Morality"...pits right against wrong. To "legislate" means to make a law...What law has ever been enacted by any government in the history of mankind that has not named something wrong and its opposite right? 35

Even those who argue against the legislation of morality cling to their own standards of morality. The debate, therefore, is not really over legislating morality--it is over which standards should be used to legislate it:

> What today's critics are saying is, "We don't want God to have anything to do with today's morality. We want to determine what is right and wrong without God."
> ...It is no accident that America has moved from George Washington's "it is impossible to rightly govern the world without God and the Bible," to today's humanistic view that insists "you can't legislate morality."...What is happening is that America has become the battleground between the world's two oldest religions. The first religion to appear in the history of mankind worships God. The second worships man. In America, the first is expressed primarily by Christianity. The second by humanism.
> Check out the latest law enacted or the most recent Supreme Court decision. God was either recognized as the Creator or ignored; man was either recognized as the created or deified.
> ...it is not a question of whether morality can or should be legislated. It is a question of which religious guidelines will

undergird the legislation: religious guidelines that deify God, or religious guidelines that deify man? [36]

For the Founders, the only standards of morality that could withstand the scrutiny applied under the "laws of nature and of nature's God" were Christian principles. Excluding any religious reasons for including Christianity in government, there are pragmatic rewards for basing civil laws on Christianity. Consider murder as an example. Civil law prohibits murder apart from any religious principle. How can Christianity contribute anything more? Christianity, unlike purely civil statutes, attempts to deal with murder before it occurs, while it is still only a thought:

> You have heard that it was said..."Do not murder,"...But I tell you that anyone who is angry with his brother will be subject to judgment. *Matthew 5:22-23*

Civil laws can only address externalized crimes, but Christianity can address and help prevent crimes while they are still internalized. In the case of murder, Christianity can deal with it before it occurs; the civil laws can do nothing until after the fact. The government cannot deal with the heart, which is the actual source of violence, crime, drug abuse, etc. Without the influence of religion, government utilizes extensive manpower and expends massive sums attempting to restrain behavior which is the external manifestation of internal sins. The moral teachings of Christianity provide a basis for civil stability which allows a government to perform its primary function: serving, not restraining.

To deal effectively with internal sin is to prevent external crime. Hate is not a crime, it is a sin; yet it often leads to a crime (assault, murder, perjury, slander, etc.). To covet is not a crime, it is a sin; yet it often leads to a crime (theft, burglary, embezzlement, etc.). It was because of Christianity's vital contributions to good government that the Founders emphasized its importance:

> A Christian society is capable of having its individuals self-govern themselves under God...A Christian society asks its citizens to deal with their heart condition. A [non-Christian] society is turbulent and riotous because there isn't any prescription or medicine for the sinful inward man. [37]

Thomas Jefferson, in explaining why the teachings of Christianity were so valuable, stated:

The precepts of philosophy, and of the Hebrew code, laid hold of actions only. [Jesus] pushed his scrutinies into the heart of man, erected his tribunal in the region of his thoughts. [38]

Man must either be controlled by the internal restraints provided through religion, or he will be controlled by the threat of force and punishment from a civil authority. As Robert C. Winthrop stated in 1852:

Men, in a word, must necessarily be controlled either by a power within them, or by a power without them; either by the Word of God, or by the strong arm of man; either by the Bible or by the bayonet. [39]

Noah Webster had similarly stated:

...there are two powers only which are sufficient to control men and secure the rights of individuals and a peaceable administration; these are the combined force of religion and law, and the force or fear of the bayonet. [40]

The argument of whether religion is necessary to society and government is not new. The same dispute occurred between two prominent men in the founding era. The first asserted:

The legitimate powers of government extend only to such acts as are injurious to others. But it does me no injury for my neighbor to say there are twenty gods, or no God. It neither picks my pocket nor breaks my leg. [41]

William Linn, an outspoken critic of this philosophy, responded with a statement that summarized the convictions of the majority of the Founders and that has since been confirmed in this country by experience:

Let my neighbor once persuade himself that there is no God, and he will soon pick my pocket, and break not only my leg but my neck. If there be no God, there is no law, no future account; government then is the ordinance of man only, and we cannot be subject for conscience sake. 42

In a nation such as ours (a democratic republic), it is imperative that religion and morality be maintained, encouraged, and promoted:

...freedom belongs only to people who are morally responsible. It is not possible for a people to be corrupt and conniving liars, cheaters, and thieves, stealing from one another, and still remain free. To have a good country we have to build a nation of good people.

If we as a nation do not soon return our official public policy to the Christian consensus of our Founding Fathers and the Biblical principles of law that have provided the freedoms we've enjoyed for over two hundred years, it is just a matter of time before we lose those freedoms. 43

It **does** make a difference which standards of morality are applied! The real danger lies in believing that one set of standards is just as good as another--that ethics are merely subject to the "eye of the beholder." When that belief is embraced, any motivation to restore former standards becomes paralyzed. As Puritan Nathaniel Ward stated:

Nothing is easier to tolerate when you do not seriously believe that differences matter. 44

The decision by the Courts to reject God, the Bible, and natural law was not purely a philosophical decision, it was actually a religious one:

Behind every system of law there is a god. To find the god in any system, look for the source of law in that system. If the source of law is the individual, then the individual is the god of that system...If our source of law is the court, then the court is our god. If there is no higher law beyond man, then man is his own god...When you choose your authority, you choose your god, and where you look for your law, there is your god. 45

The Biblical book of Proverbs proclaims what our Founders had asserted concerning morality: it is vital to the success and prosperity of either a nation or an individual. The first nine chapters of Proverbs present the rewards of attaining wisdom: security, stability, no fear of disaster, abundance, the promise of Providential assistance, etc. Those nine chapters contain 254 individual verses. Of these, 76 verses (30 percent) directly address morality. Nearly one-third of the Biblical requirements for obtaining the long-term benefits needed, desired, and hoped for by the people of this nation involves maintaining morality: individual and national morality!

~18~
The Solution

It required decades for the Supreme Court to dispose of natural law, install relativism, discard God from public affairs, and redistribute governmental powers between the branches. Consequently, correcting what has happened in and to America will not necessarily be accomplished through a singular act. Although the Court's "achievements" seem to be diverse and unrelated, they do have a common denominator: if the public had not acquiesced to judicial supremacy, none of these travesties could have occurred. Had the public been educated about the proper role of the Supreme Court, the Court could never have forced the view of 3 percent upon the 97 percent.

Since the deterioration occurred through a breakdown in our thinking and beliefs concerning the Court, the solution must focus on correcting those thoughts and beliefs. As attitudes on what will not be tolerated by the Court are changed, actions will change correspondingly. Therefore, the solution involves three steps: removing wrong information from the mind, replacing it with correct information, then acting on the new information. This book satisfies only the second step: the input of new, correct information. The other two steps (discarding the wrong information and acting on the new) must be accomplished by the reader. This final chapter offers some comments and suggestions on changing thoughts and actions.

Recall that most of the original state constitutions included a stipulation that each member of government must verbalize a belief in future punishments and rewards. This requirement was beneficial to government and to the people, for it forced each public official to recognize and acknowledge that one day he would answer for his actions while in office. Furthermore, through this declaration, he was accepting responsibility for any long-term consequences of his decisions and actions, either for good or for bad. Warnings concerning this subject, like the following one from Noah Webster, helped keep the nation's leaders cognizant of their personal accountability to God:

> The principles of all genuine liberty, and of wise laws and administrations are to be drawn from the Bible and sustained by its authority. *The man therefore who weakens or destroys the divine authority of that book may be accessory to all the public disorders which society is doomed to suffer.* 1
> (emphasis added)

Unfortunately, our political leaders are no longer required to face or accept personal responsibility for the long-term consequences of their actions. Contemporary politicians tend to look no further than 2, 4, or 6 years into the future, depending on their term of office. Consequently, their short-term decisions (taken to help ensure re-election) frequently jeopardize long-term prosperity.

In recent decades, the pattern has been to spend, and to spend liberally. Every special interest group had its pet projects; rather than anger a "valuable" group of constituents, legislators appropriated money without consideration of any future impact beyond re-election. As a result, these spending habits, which seemed "good" then, have now created such a millstone of debt around the neck of the nation that the short-term benefits do not justify the long-term damage.

It is a natural law principle that short-term and long-term objectives generally oppose rather than complement each other. Whether in business, agriculture, religion, etc., the attainment of immediate, short-term success frequently compromises and endangers long-term success. For example, financial investments with immediate short-term benefits rarely provide long-term security. Conversely, investments that yield excellent long-term results typically provide low returns in the short-term. In agriculture, tree-harvesting is conducted on the same principle. To harvest all the trees in an area produces a good short-term profit, but seriously jeopardizes future yields. Maintaining a continuing long-term supply of lumber requires a well-conceived plan with great short-term restraint.

As a nation, we must again return to a consideration of the future when making current decisions. The decisions made by our leaders *do* have potentially serious repercussions. As George Mason, a statesman from Virginia, explained it:

> As nations cannot be rewarded or punished in the next world, they must be in this. By an inevitable chain of causes and effects, Providence punishes national sins by national calamities. 2

If God does repay, then the stands we allow our government to make will eventually affect every individual in the nation, either beneficially or detrimentally. Puritan leader John Winthrop, author of *A Model of Christian Charity,* also issued a solemn warning of the consequences that arise from a nation's actions toward God:

...if we shall deal falsely with our God in this work we have
undertaken and so cause him to withdraw his present help
from us, we shall be made a story and a byword through the
world...3

Lincoln, too, stressed the importance of a nation's relationship
toward God:

It is the duty of nations...to own their dependence upon the
overruling power of God and to recognize the sublime truth
announced in the Holy Scriptures and proven by all history,
that those nations only are blessed whose God is the Lord. 4

Because Lincoln fully understood this principle, he attempted to
conduct the nation's affairs in such a way as to receive God's aid and
favor rather than His opposition. Confirming his position, Lincoln
once declared concerning the government's actions in the Civil War:

Sir, my concern is not whether God is on our side; my great
concern is to be on God's side. 5

Collectively, this nation's leaders have allowed the Supreme Court
to reject the standards delivered to us by our Fathers. We must learn
to view our government's actions from God's viewpoint, as the
Founders did:

Man's law is important, but it must reflect God's law to be
truly valid...What a gift our forefathers have given us. By
their example we learn that it is our right and duty as citizens
to judge the laws and the lawmakers of this nation by the
laws of God in the created order and in God's Word, and
then to act. 6

It is imperative that this nation's institutions return to the principles
expressed through the Bible:

It is impossible to enslave mentally or socially a Bible-
reading people. The principles of the Bible are the ground-
work of human freedom. *Horace Greely* 7

...but for the Book we could not know right from wrong. All
the things desirable to man are contained in it. *Abraham
Lincoln* 8

The basis of our Bill of Rights comes from the teachings we get from Exodus and St. Matthew, from Isaiah and St. Paul. I don't think we emphasize that enough these days. If we don't have a proper fundamental moral background, we will finally end up with a...government which does not believe in rights for anybody except the State! *President Truman* 9

From a purely pragmatic viewpoint, the inclusion of religious principles within government has had tangible social and civil benefits:

Both Old and New Testament standards create a law of the heart. Whether one lives life by the Ten Commandments of the Old Testament or the fruit of God's Spirit in the New, the law of the heart helps regulate your response to the laws of this nation. Imagine how different the world would be without these biblically based constraints. Imagine what might happen to this nation without them. 10

In this nation, religion in public affairs has proven its benefits for so long and has produced such a history of international respect and national stability as to demand its continued inclusion in civil affairs. When considering the benefit that religion has provided to this nation, a thought offered by Montaigne is worthy of contemplation:

If I did not follow the straight road for the sake of its straightness, I should follow it having found by experience that, all things considered, it is the happiest and the most convenient. 11

Religious arguments aside, it makes good sense to return to the philosophy that produced nationwide moral, emotional, and social stability. As President Woodrow Wilson so astutely observed:

A nation which does not remember what it was yesterday, does not know what it is today, nor what it is trying to do. We are trying to do a futile thing if we do not know where we came from or what we have been about...The Bible...is the one supreme source of revelation of the meaning of life, the nature of God and...nature and needs of men. It is the only guide of life which really leads the spirit in the way of peace and salvation. 12

We must not only remember our roots and former values, we must also rekindle the understanding of the government our Founders delivered to us. We were conceived and born a republic; never a democracy nor an oligarchy. It is by neglect and abdication of personal responsibilities that a republic deteriorates into an oligarchy. To return to being a true republic, we must individually accept the responsibility of citizenship and become involved, giving time and effort into rebuilding the nation.

If we do not return our government to its roots, we will have placed ourselves under a new constitution. The old one will be gone, and the new one will become whatever the Court says it is:

If a judge can interpret the Constitution or laws to mean something obviously not intended by the original makers-- then the nation's Constitution and laws are meaningless. 13

We must not allow our foundations to be destroyed by the Court! In the words of a rhetorical question posed in Psalms 11:3:

If the foundations be destroyed, what can the righteous do?

In early biblical manuscripts, "foundations" were defined as the "political and moral supports." Indeed, if our "political and moral supports" are destroyed by the Courts, what can people do? If the foundation is gone, what upholds the structure? We must protect our foundation! To preserve that foundation, we should follow the advice given in Isaiah 1:26:

...restore our judges as at the first, and our counsellors as at the beginning...

In order for us to be a nation of morality and godliness, our judges and political counselors must return to the values and respect for God that their predecessors held. Appointing judges who interpret and administer law by the natural law principles of their predecessors is something recommended in Ezra 7:25:

...appoint magistrates and judges...which know the laws of God...

Our national policy must not be one of the denial of God, nor of apathy toward Him. It should, as it formerly did, "press on to acknowledge God" (Hosea 6:3, NIV), recognizing that the nation who

262 THE MYTH OF SEPARATION

acknowledges Him will be honored, and the nation who disregards Him will be dishonored (1 Samuel 2:30, Luke 9:26). Nations, like individuals, will be recompensed for the actions and stands they take under the watchful eye of God. Taking the right, or wrong, stand does have an effect:

Righteousness exalts a nation, but sin is a reproach to any people. *Proverbs 14:34*

When the righteous are in authority, the people rejoice; when the wicked rule, the people mourn. *Proverbs 29:2*

Happy is the nation whose God is the Lord. *Psalms 144:15*

Although at times it appears that there is an unstoppable tide rising toward the complete eradication of God in public affairs, that movement has been initiated and maintained by a very small minority of the nation. For this reason, there remains hope--a strong hope. All that is needed to restore what has been lost in this republic is for the majority to rise up and take its proper place. Alexis de Tocqueville accurately described the dilemma which this country now faces:

...the Christian nations of our day present an alarming spectacle; the movement which carries them along is already too strong to be halted, but it is not yet so swift that we must despair of directing it; our fate is in our hands, but soon it may pass beyond control. 14

Our fate *is* still in our hands; however, unless we act, it will soon pass completely beyond our control. As Edmund Burke stated:

All that is necessary for evil to triumph is for good men to do nothing. 15

Ironically, we can find solace in the fact that our current condition has been caused through our own neglect:

If our nation's problems were the result of some conspiracy of men, then the solution would be beyond the reach of most of us, and thus fatalism, apathy and despair would prevail.

However, since...the real problem began with our neglect, then the power for change is also within [our] grasp...If we accept our responsibility and do our duty, we have grounds for hope. 16

This encouragement should inspire our thinking and turn our thoughts in the right direction. Simply changing the way we think *will* make a difference. As Harvard Professor Raoul Berger explained it:

How long can public respect for the Court, on which its power ultimately depends, survive if the people become aware that the tribunal which condemns the acts of others as unconstitutional is itself acting unconstitutionally? 17

We must become indignant over and reject the Court's unprecedented attempts to rule the nation and to impose its own political and religious philosophies on the people. As Jefferson insisted, we must:

...carry ourselves back to the time when the Constitution was adopted, recollect the spirit manifested in the debates, and instead of trying what meaning may be squeezed out of the text, or invented against it conform to the probable one in which it was passed. 18

But we must not stop with merely changing our thoughts--there are definite actions we should take. Although the first action to take is relatively simple, it is very profound: read the Constitution. As described by one attorney:

I spent three years getting my law degree at Yale Law School. From the moment I enrolled, I was assigned huge, leather-bound editions of legal cases to study and discuss. I read what lawyers and judges, professors and historians said about the Constitution. But never once was I assigned the task of reading the Constitution itself...
Over the last decade, however, I have become a student of the Constitution, searching each line for its meaning and intent. Studying the Constitution is like studying the Bible. It is amazing how much more you will learn when you quit studying about it and pick it up to read it for yourself. 19

If we will personally examine the Constitution, we can judge the actions and statements of our government against the blueprint for that government (a copy of the Constitution is provided in Appendix A). The second action focuses on waging a strong fight for sound education. Not only must we change the way we think about the nation's actions, we must also change the way we think about the nation's schools. For too long we have backed off into complacency and non-involvement, not aggressively resisting and preventing the efforts of others who implement policies that destroy long-term educational success and stability. We must *not* give up the schools; we must stand and fight for them! As Abraham Lincoln indicated, schools *are* the future:

> The philosophy of the school room in one generation will be the philosophy of government in the next. [20]

Martin Luther expressed even more forcefully the impact schools can have on a nation by explaining what would happen if educational systems moved away from the Scriptures:

> I am much afraid that schools will prove to be the great gates of hell unless they diligently labor in explaining the Holy Scriptures, engraving them in the hearts of youth. [21]

Noah Webster, one of the early nation's foremost educators, perceptively described not only the importance of a good educational system, but its essential ingredients:

> ...the education of youth should be watched with the most scrupulous attention. Education...forms the moral characters of men, and morals are the basis of government. Education should therefore be the first care of...political regulations; for it is much easier to introduce and establish an effectual system for preserving morals, than to correct by penal statutes the ill effects of a bad system...The goodness of a heart is of infinitely more consequence to society than an elegance of manners...The education of youth...lays the foundations on which both law and gospel rest for success. [22]

Morality must again become an emphasis in education, and morality is obtained only through religious principles. The education of youth is now on the wrong foundation, as evidenced by the lack of morality produced in students by current education. Education has abandoned the religious principles that create morality and no longer even provides support for the law, as evidenced by the 544 percent increase in violent crime that has occurred since 1963, when the Court barred God and religious principles from education.

The educational philosophy that previously yielded a highly successful and internationally respected educational system has been overthrown by a revolution--a Court-initiated revolution. No longer does this nation officially recognize the principles that brought it to the summit of the educational world. Action must be taken to *un-*reform education and return it to the successful and proud position it held when God and religious principles were part of its curriculum.

The third area in which action must be taken is described by Charles Finney, a famous and respected preacher from the early 1800's:

> The Church must take right ground in regard to politics...The time has come that Christians must vote for honest men, and take consistent ground in politics or the Lord will curse them...God cannot sustain this free and blessed country, which we love and pray for, unless the Church will take right ground. Politics are a part of a religion in such a country as this, and Christians must do their duty to the country as a part of their duty to God...He will bless or curse this nation, according to the course [Christians] take [in politics]. 23

Noah Webster delivered a similar warning to young people to impress on them the importance of the responsibilities of citizenship:

> When you become entitled to exercise the right of voting for public officers, let it be impressed on your mind that God commands you to choose for rulers just men who will rule in the fear of God. *The preservation of a republican government depends on the faithful discharge of this duty;* if the citizens neglect their duty and place unprincipled men in office, the government will soon be corrupted; laws will be made not for the public good so much as for selfish or local purposes; corrupt or incompetent men will be appointed to execute the laws; the public revenues will be squandered on unworthy men; and the rights of the citizens will be violated

or disregarded. If a republican government fails to secure public prosperity and happiness, it must be because the citizens neglect the divine commands, and elect bad men to make and administer the laws. 24 (emphasis added)

President James Garfield, celebrating the centennial of the Declaration of Independence, delivered a similar admonition:

Now, more than ever before, the people are responsible for the character of their Congress. If that body be ignorant, reckless, and corrupt, it is because the people tolerate ignorance, recklessness, and corruption. If it be intelligent, brave, and pure, it is because the people demand these high qualities to represent them in the national legislature...if the next centennial does not find us a great nation...it will be because those who represent the enterprise, the culture, and the morality of the nation do not aid in controlling the political forces...25

Elections are a matter of vital importance; we must actively participate in them! We *can* make a difference if we will get involved. Proof of this came in 1986 in five separate U.S. Senate races. The five candidates who stood for returning God to public affairs were narrowly defeated by a collective total of only 57,000 votes, an average of less than 12,000 votes per state. Yet, in those five states, there were over 5 million Christians who did not even vote! If only 1 of 1,000 who did not vote had voted for the candidate supporting God in public affairs, those five candidates would have been elected! Liberals didn't defeat those candidates; inactive Christians did!

Consider the impact those five might have had. Two years earlier, in 1984, an attempt to pass a Constitutional Amendment restoring prayer to schools failed in the Senate by 11 votes. Had they been elected, five votes against the amendment would have been replaced with five votes supporting its passage. Those five men would have created a ten-vote swing! Only one more vote would be required to submit the amendment proposal to the states!

It seems ironic that Constitutional Amendments are being proposed to return the Constitution to what it already says. Although the passage of the Constitutional Amendment to restore God to schools would have been a victory, the best solution is not in amending the Constitution, but in:

> ...changing the men in office. But this will never occur as
> long as less than 5% of godly Americans are involved in
> party politics on the local level. [26]

In elections, the candidate's party affiliation should not be the deciding factor. Investigate the position of each individual candidate apart from his party. There are good and bad candidates in each party. Important votes are wasted if they are cast for a poor candidate solely because they were cast in support of a party.

The fourth area in which action can be taken relates to improving the composition of the Courts. Elected officials recommend and confirm the appointment of federal judges. Therefore, we must make them accountable at the ballot box for the type of judges they appoint. Our politicians and representatives must work to maintain a republic and must not capitulate to an oligarchy! We must require our politicians to appoint constitutional judges, not relativists. This has become imperative because, for politically active minorities whose philosophical viewpoint opposes that of the majority, the judiciary is now the primary battlefield:

> When the ultra-liberals lose elections, they fight all the more
> desperately for control of our third branch, the courts. Why?
> Because the courts control the constitution and the constitu-
> tion is the "trump card" in politics. That's why this war is
> crucial. Now, there are only two sides really in this struggle.
> Either the constitution controls the judges, or the judges
> rewrite the constitution. [27]

When investigating a candidate prior to an election, be sure to investigate his views on the Courts. Specifically, ask him his feelings on judicial policy-making, judicial legislation, and judicial supremacy. Ask him his views on natural and Divine laws vs. relativism. If a candidate is willing to submit to judicial supremacy, then any selections or recommendations he might make for judicial appointments would strengthen the power of the Courts. However, if the candidate opposes Court rulership, then it is likely he would select and recommend justices who would also oppose judicial supremacy. We *do* have some control over the judiciary through the candidates we elect to office.

Remember, ultimately, in every issue, the enemy is not "them"; the enemy is "inactivity." When 82 percent of the nation wants voluntary prayer returned to schools, and all efforts have been unsuccessful, it is because much of the 82 percent has been inactive. The one thing preventing this nation from returning to its former principles of greatness is widespread inactivity. We must get involved so we can recover our roots!

It is said that James Russell Lowell was asked by the French historian Francois Guizot, "How long will the American republic endure?" He sagely replied, "As long as the ideas of the men who founded it continue dominant." 28

While complacency rules, wrong principles and policies will abound. Only when the majority begins to act like a majority will this nation return to its former greatness, both internally and externally. Let's get involved!

Our Founding Fathers did their part. They gave us a Constitution for the ages. Now it is up to us do everything we can to keep it. 29

Appendix A

The Constitution of the United States of America

Preamble to the Constitution of the United States

We the people of the United States, in order to form a more perfect Union, establish justice, insure domestic tranquility, provide for the common defence, promote the general welfare, and secure the blessings of liberty to ourselves and our posterity, do ordain and establish this Constitution for the United States of America.

ARTICLE I

Section 1. All legislative powers herein granted shall be vested in a Congress of the United States, which shall consist of a Senate and House of Representatives.

Section 2. The House of Representatives shall be composed of members chosen every second year by the people of the several States, and the electors in each State shall have the qualifications requisite for electors of the most numerous branch of the State legislature.

No person shall be a Representative who shall not have attained to the age of twenty-five years, and been seven years a citizen of the United States, and who shall not, when elected, be an inhabitant of that State in which he shall be chosen.

∞ [Representatives and direct taxes shall be apportioned among the several States which may be included within this Union, according to their respective numbers, which shall be determined by adding to the whole number of free persons, including those bound to service for a term of years, and excluding Indians not taxed, three fifths of all other persons.] The actual enumeration shall be made within three years after the first meeting of the Congress of the United States, and within every subsequent term of ten years, in such manner as they shall by law direct.   The number of Representatives shall not exceed one for every thirty thousand, but each State shall have at least one Representative; and until such enumeration shall be made, the State of New Hampshire shall be entitled to choose three, Massachusetts eight, Rhode Island and

Providence Plantations one, Connecticut five, New York six; New Jersey four, Pennsylvania eight, Delaware one, Maryland six, Virginia ten, North Carolina five, South Carolina five, and Georgia three.

∞ (The preceding portion in brackets is amended by the Fourteenth Amendment, Section 2).

Section 3. The Senate, of the United States shall be composed of two Senators from each State, chosen by the legislature thereof, for six years; and each Senator shall have one vote.

Immediately after they shall be assembled in consequence of the first election, they shall be divided as equally as may be into three classes. The seats of the Senators of the first class shall be vacated at the expiration of the second year, of the second class at the expiration of the fourth year, and of the third class at the expiration of the sixth year, so that one-third may be chosen every second year; and if vacancies happen by resignation, or otherwise, during the recess of the legislature of any State, the Executive thereof may make temporary appointments until the next meeting of the legislature, which shall then fill such vacancies.

No person shall be a Senator who shall not have attained to the age of thirty years, and been nine years a citizen of the United States, and who shall not, when elected, be an inhabitant of that State for which he shall be chosen.

The Vice-President of the United States shall be President of the Senate, but shall have no vote, unless they be equally divided.

The Senate shall choose their other officers, and also a President pro tempore, in the absence of the Vice-President, or when he shall exercise the office of President of the United States

The Senate shall have the sole power to try all impeachments. When sitting for that purpose, they shall be on oath or affirmation. When the President of the United States is tried, the Chief Justice shall preside: And no person shall be convicted without the concurrence of two thirds of the members present.

Judgment in cases of impeachment shall not extend further than to removal from office, and disqualification to hold and enjoy any office of honor, trust or profit under the United States: but the party convicted shall nevertheless be liable and subject to indictment, trial, judgment and punishment, according to Law.

Section 4. The times, places and manner of holding elections for Senators and Representatives, shall be prescribed in each State by the legislature thereof; but the Congress may at any time by law make or alter such regulations, except as to the places of choosing Senators.

The Congress shall assemble at least once in every year, and such meeting shall be on the first Monday in December, unless they shall by law appoint a different day.

Section 5. Each House shall be the judge of the elections, returns and qualifications of its own members, and a majority of each shall constitute a quorum to do business; but a smaller number may adjourn from day to day, and may be authorized to compel the attendance of absent members, in such manner, and under such penalties as each House may provide.

Each House may determine the rules of its proceedings, punish its members for disorderly behavior, and, with the concurrence of two thirds, expel a member.

Each House shall keep a Journal of its proceedings, and from time to time publish the same, excepting such parts as may in their judgment require secrecy; and the yeas and nays of the members of either House on any question shall, at the desire of one fifth of those present, be entered on the Journal.

Neither House, during the session of Congress, shall, without the consent of the other, adjourn for more than three days, nor to any other place than that in which the two Houses shall be sitting.

Section 6. The Senators and Representatives shall receive a compensation for their services, to be ascertained by law, and paid out of the Treasury of the United States. They shall in all cases, except treason, felony and breach of the peace, be privileged from arrest during their attendance at the session of their respective Houses, and in going to and returning from the same; and for any speech or debate in either House, they shall not be questioned in any other place.

No Senator or Representative shall, during the time for which he was elected, be appointed to any civil office under the authority of the United States, which shall have been created, or the emoluments whereof shall have been increased during such time; and no person holding any office under the United States, shall be a member of either House during his continuance in office.

Section 7. All bills for raising revenue shall originate in the House of Representatives; but the Senate may propose or concur with amendments as on other bills.

Every bill which shall have passed the House of Representatives and the Senate, shall, before it becomes a law, be presented to the President of the United States; If he approve he shall sign it, but if not he shall return it, with his objections to that House in which it shall have originated, who shall enter the objections at large on their Journal, and proceed to reconsider it. If after such reconsideration two thirds of that House shall agree to pass the bill, it shall be sent, together with the objections, to the other House, by which it shall likewise be reconsidered, and if approved by two thirds of that House, it shall become a law. But in all such cases the votes of both Houses shall be determined by yeas and nays, and the names of the persons voting for and against the bill shall be entered on the journal of each House respectively. If any bill shall not be returned by the President within ten days (Sundays excepted) after it shall have been presented to him, the same shall be a law, in like manner as if he had signed it, unless the Congress by their adjournment prevent its return, in which case it shall not be a law.

Every order, resolution, or vote to which the concurrence of the Senate and House of Representatives may be necessary (except on a question of adjournment) shall be presented to the President of the United States; and before the same shall take effect, shall be approved by him, or being disapproved by him, shall be repassed by two thirds of the Senate and House of Representatives, according to the rules and limitations prescribed in the case of a bill.

Section 8.   The Congress shall have power to lay and collect taxes, duties, imposts and excises, to pay the debts and provide for the common defense and general welfare of the United States; but all duties, imposts and excises shall be uniform throughout the United States;

To borrow money on the credit of the United States;

To regulate commerce with foreign nations, and among the several States, and with the Indian tribes;

To establish an uniform rule of naturalization, and uniform laws on the subject of bankruptcies throughout the United States;

To coin money, regulate the value thereof, and of foreign coin, and fix the standard of weights and measures;

To provide for the punishment of counterfeiting the securities and current coin of the United States;

To establish post offices and post roads;

To promote the progress of science and useful arts, by securing for limited times to authors and inventors the exclusive rights to their respective writings and discoveries;

To constitute tribunals inferior to the Supreme Court;

To define and punish piracies and felonies committed on the high seas, and offences against the law of nations;

To declare war, grant letters of marque and reprisal, and make rules concerning captures on land and water;

To raise and support armies, but no appropriation of money to that use shall be for a longer term than two years;

To provide and maintain a Navy;

To make rules for the government and regulation of the land and naval Forces;

To provide for calling forth the militia to execute the laws of the Union, suppress insurrections and repel invasions;

To provide for organizing, arming, and disciplining, the militia, and for governing such part of them as may be employed in the service of the United States, reserving to the States respectively, the appointment of the officers, and the authority of training the militia according to the discipline prescribed by Congress;

To exercise exclusive legislation in all cases whatsoever, over such district (not exceeding ten miles square) as may, by cession of particular States, and the acceptance of Congress, become the seat of the government of the United States, and to exercise like authority over all places purchased by the consent of the legislature of the State in which the same shall be, for the erection of forts, magazines, arsenals, dock-yards, and other needful buildings;--and

To make all laws which shall be necessary and proper for carrying into execution the foregoing powers, and all other powers vested by this Constitution in the government of the United States, or in any department or officer thereof.

Section 9. The migration or importation of such persons as any of the States now existing shall think proper to admit, shall not be prohibited by the Congress prior to the year one thousand eight hundred and eight, but a tax or duty may be imposed on such importation, not exceeding ten dollars for each person.

The privilege of the writ of Habeas Corpus shall not be suspended, unless when in cases of rebellion or invasion the public safety may require it.

No bill of attainder or ex post facto law shall be passed.

No capitation, or other direct, tax shall be laid, unless in proportion to the census or enumeration herein before directed to be taken.

No tax or duty shall be laid on articles exported from any State.

No preference shall be given by any regulation of commerce or revenue to the ports of one State over those of another: nor shall vessels bound to, or from, one State, be obliged to enter, clear, or pay duties in another.

No money shall be drawn from the Treasury, but in consequence of appropriations made by law; and a regular statement and account of the receipts and expenditures of all public money shall be published from time to time.

No title of nobility shall be granted by the United States: And no person holding any office of profit or trust under them, shall, without the consent of the Congress, accept of any present, emolument, office, or title, of any kind whatever, from any king, prince, or foreign State.

Section 10. No State shall enter into any treaty, alliance, or confederation; grant letters of marque and reprisal; coin money, emit bills of credit; make any thing but gold and silver coin a tender in payment of debts; pass any bill of attainder, ex post facto law, or law impairing the obligation of contracts, or grant any title of nobility.

No State shall, without the consent of the Congress, lay any imposts of duties on imports or exports, except what may be absolutely necessary for executing its inspection laws: and the net produce of all duties and imposts, laid by any State on imports or exports, shall be for the use of the Treasury of the United States; and all such laws shall be subject to the revision and control of the Congress.

No State shall, without the consent of Congress, lay any duty of tonnage, keep troops, or ships of war in time of peace, enter into any agreement or compact with another State, or with a foreign power, or engage in war, unless actually invaded, or in such imminent danger as will not admit of delay.

ARTICLE II

Section 1. The executive power shall be vested in a President of the United States of America. He shall hold his office during the term of four years, and, together with the Vice-President, chosen for the same term, be elected, as follows:

Each State shall appoint in such manner as the legislature thereof may direct, a number of electors, equal to the whole number of Senators and Representatives to which the State may be entitled in the Congress: but no Senator or Representative, or person holding an office of trust or profit under the United States, shall be appointed an elector.

∞ ["The electors shall meet in their respective States, and vote by ballot for two persons, of whom one at least shall not be an inhabitant of the same State with themselves. And they shall make a list of all the persons voted for, and of the number of votes for each; which list they shall sign and certify, and transmit sealed to the seat of the government of the United States, directed to the President of the Senate. The President of the Senate shall, in the presence of the Senate and House of Representatives, open all the certificates, and the votes shall then be counted. The person having the greatest number of votes shall be the President, if such number be a majority of the whole number of electors appointed; and if there be more than one who have such majority, and have an equal number of votes, then the House of Representatives shall immediately choose by ballot one of them for President; and if no person have a majority, then from the five highest on the list the said House shall in like manner choose the President. But in choosing the President, the votes shall be taken by States, the representation from each State having one vote; a quorum for this purpose shall consist of a member or members from two-thirds of the States, and a majority of all the States shall be necessary to a choice. In every case, after the choice of the President, the person having the greatest number of votes of the electors shall be the Vice-President. But if there should remain two or more who have equal votes, the Senate shall choose from them by ballot the Vice-President."]

∞ (The preceding section has been superseded by the Twelfth Amendment).

The Congress may determine the time of choosing the electors, and the day on which they shall give their votes; which day shall be the same throughout the United States.

No person except a natural born citizen, or a citizen of the United States, at the time of the adoption of this Constitution, shall be eligible to the office of President; neither shall any person be eligible to that office who shall not have attained to the age of thirty-five years, and been fourteen years a resident within the United States.

In case of the removal of the President from office, or of his death, resignation, or inability to discharge the powers and duties of the said office, the same shall devolve on the Vice-President, and the Congress may by law provide for the case of removal, death, resignation, or inability, both of the President and Vice-President, declaring what officer shall then act as President, and such officer shall act accordingly, until the disability be removed, or a President shall be elected.

The President shall, at stated times, receive for his services, a compensation, which shall neither be increased nor diminished during the period for which he shall have been elected, and he shall not receive within that period any other emolument from the United States, or any of them.

Before he enter on the execution of his office, he shall take the following oath or affirmation: -- "I do solemnly swear (or affirm) that I will faithfully execute the office of President of the United States, and will to the best of my ability, preserve, protect and defend the Constitution of the United States."

Section 2. The President shall be Commander in Chief of the Army and Navy of the United States, and of the militia of the several States, when called into the actual service of the United States; he may require the opinion, in writing, of the principal officer in each of the executive departments, upon any subject relating to the duties of their respective offices, and he shall have power to grant reprieves and pardons for offenses against the United States, except in cases of impeachment.

He shall have power, by and with the advice and consent of the Senate, to make treaties, provided two thirds of the Senators present concur; and he shall nominate, and by and with the advice and consent of the Senate, shall appoint Ambassadors, other public Ministers and Consuls, Judges of the Supreme Court, and all other Officers of the United States, whose appointments are not herein otherwise provided for, and which shall be established by law: but the Congress may by law vest the appointment of such inferior Officers, as they think proper, in the President alone, in the Courts of law, or in the heads of departments.

The President shall have power to fill up all vacancies that may happen during the recess of the Senate, by granting commissions which shall expire at the end of their next session.

Section 3. He shall from time to time give to the Congress information of the State of the Union, and recommend to their consideration such measures as he shall judge necessary and expedient; he may, on extraordinary occasions, convene both Houses, or either of them, and in case of disagreement between them, with respect to the time of adjournment, he may adjourn them to such time as he shall think proper; he shall receive Ambassadors and other public Ministers; he shall take care that the laws be faithfully executed, and shall commission all the officers of the United States.

Section 4. The President, Vice-President and all civil officers of the United States, shall be removed from office on impeachment for, and conviction of, treason, bribery, or other high crimes and misdemeanors.

ARTICLE III

Section 1. The judicial power of the United States, shall be vested in one Supreme Court, and in such inferior Courts as the Congress may from time to time ordain and establish. The Judges, both of the Supreme and inferior Courts, shall hold their offices during good behaviour, and shall, at stated times, receive for their services, a compensation, which shall not be diminished during their continuance in office.

Section 2. The judicial power shall extend to all cases, in law and equity, arising under this Constitution, the laws of the United States, and treaties made, or which shall be made, under their authority:--to all cases affecting Ambassadors, other public Ministers and Consuls;--to all cases of admiralty and maritime jurisdiction;--to controversies to which the United States shall be a party;--to controversies between two or more States;--between a State and citizens of another State;--between citizens of different States,--between citizens of the same State claiming lands under grants of different States, and between a State, or the citizens thereof, and foreign States, citizens or subjects.

In all cases affecting Ambassadors, other public Ministers and Consuls, and those in which a State shall be party, the Supreme Court shall have original jurisdiction. In all the other cases before mentioned, the Supreme Court shall have appellate jurisdiction, both as to law and fact, with such exceptions, and under such regulations as the Congress shall make.

The trial of all crimes, except in cases of impeachment, shall be by jury; and such trial shall be held in the State where the said crimes shall have been committed; but when not committed within any State, the trial shall be at such place or places as the Congress may by law have directed.

Section 3. Treason against the United States, shall consist only in levying war against them, or in adhering to their enemies, giving them aid and comfort. No person shall be convicted of treason unless on the testimony of two witnesses to the same overt act, or on confession in open court.

The Congress shall have power to declare the punishment of treason, but no attainder of treason shall work corruption of blood, or forfeiture except during the life of the person attainted.

ARTICLE IV

Section 1. Full faith and credit shall be given in each State to the public acts, records, and judicial proceedings of every other State.

And the Congress may by general laws prescribe the manner in which such acts, records and proceedings shall be proved, and the effect thereof.

Section 2. The citizens of each State shall be entitled to all privileges and immunities of citizens in the several States.

A person charged in any State with treason, felony, or other crime, who shall flee from justice, and be found in another state, shall on demand of the executive authority of the State from which he fled, be delivered up to be removed to the State having jurisdiction of the crime.

No person held to service or labour in one State, under the laws thereof, escaping into another, shall, in consequence of any law or regulation therein, be discharged from such service or labour, but shall be delivered up on claim of the party to whom such service or labour may be due.

Section 3. New States may be admitted by the Congress into this Union; but no new State shall be formed or erected within the jurisdiction of any other State; nor any State be formed by the junction of two or more States, or parts of States, without the consent of the legislatures of the States concerned as well as of the Congress.

The Congress shall have power to dispose of and make all needful rules and regulations respecting the territory or other property belonging to the United States; and nothing in this Constitution shall be so construed as to prejudice any claims of the United States, or of any particular State.

Section 4. The United States shall guarantee to every State in this Union a republican form of government, and shall protect each of them against invasion; and on application of the legislature, or of the Executive (when the legislature cannot be convened) against domestic violence.

ARTICLE V

The Congress, whenever two thirds of both Houses shall deem it necessary, shall propose amendments to this Constitution, or, on the application of the legislatures of two thirds of the several States, shall call a convention for proposing amendments, which, in either case, shall be valid to all intents and purposes, as part of this Constitution, when ratified by the legislatures of three fourths of the several States, or by conventions in three fourths thereof, as the one or the other mode of ratification may be proposed by the Congress; provided that no amendment which may be made prior to the year one thousand eight hundred and eight shall in any manner affect the first and fourth clauses in the ninth section of the first article; and that no State, without its consent, shall be deprived of its equal suffrage in the Senate.

ARTICLE VI

All debts contracted and engagements entered into, before the adoption of this Constitution, shall be as valid against the United States under this Constitution, as under the Confederation.

This Constitution, and the laws of the United States which shall be made in pursuance thereof; and all treaties made, or which shall be made, under the authority of the United States, shall be the supreme law of the land; and the judges in every State shall be bound thereby, any thing in the Constitution or laws of any State to the contrary notwithstanding.

The Senators and Representatives before mentioned, and the members of the several State legislatures, and all executive and judicial officers, both of the United States and of the several States, shall be bound by oath or affirmation, to support this Constitution; but no religious test shall ever be required as a qualification to any office or public trust under the United States.

ARTICLE VII

The ratification of the conventions of nine States, shall be sufficient for the establishment of this Constitution between the States so ratifying the same.

DONE in convention by the unanimous consent of the States present the seventeenth day of September in the Year of our Lord one thousand seven hundred and eighty seven, and of the independence of the United States of America the twelfth.

Amendments to the Constitution

AMENDMENT I

(First ten amendments adopted June 15, 1790)

Congress shall make no law respecting an establishment of religion, or prohibiting the free exercise thereof; or abridging the freedom of speech, or of the press; or the right of the people peaceably to assemble, and to petition the Government for a redress of grievances.

AMENDMENT II

A well regulated militia, being necessary to the security of a free State, the right of the people to keep and bear arms, shall not be infringed.

AMENDMENT III

No soldier shall, in time of peace be quartered in any house, without the consent of the owner, nor in time of war, but in a manner to be prescribed by law.

AMENDMENT IV

The right of the people to be secure in their persons, houses, papers, and effects, against unreasonable searches and seizures, shall not be violated, and no warrants shall issue, but upon probable cause, supported by oath or affirmation, and particularly describing the place to be searched, and the persons or things to be seized.

AMENDMENT V

No person shall be held to answer for a capital, or otherwise infamous crime, unless on a presentment or indictment of a grand jury, except in cases arising in the land or naval forces, or in the militia, when in actual service in time of war or public danger; nor shall any person be subject for the same offence to be twice put in jeopardy of life or limb; nor shall be compelled in any criminal case to be a witness against himself, nor be deprived of life, liberty, or property, without due process of law; nor shall private property be taken for public use, without just compensation.

AMENDMENT VI

In all criminal prosecutions, the accused shall enjoy the right to a speedy and public trial, by an impartial jury of the State and district wherein the crime shall have been committed, which district shall have been previously ascertained by law, and to be informed of the nature and cause of the accusation; to be confronted with the witnesses against him; to have compulsory process for obtaining witnesses in his favor, and to have the assistance of counsel for his defence.

AMENDMENT VII

In suits at common law, where the value in controversy shall exceed twenty dollars, the right of trial by jury shall be preserved, and no fact tried by a jury shall be otherwise re-examined in any Court of the United States, than according to the rules of the common law.

AMENDMENT VIII

Excessive bail shall not be required, nor excessive fines imposed, nor cruel and unusual punishments inflicted.

AMENDMENT IX

The enumeration in the Constitution, of certain rights, shall not be construed to deny or disparage others retained by the people.

AMENDMENT X

The powers not delegated to the United States by the Constitution, nor prohibited by it to the States, are reserved to the States respectively, or to the people.

AMENDMENT XI

(Adopted January 8, 1798)
The judicial power of the United States shall not be construed to extend to any suit in law or equity, commenced or prosecuted against one of the United States by citizens of another State, or by citizens or subjects of any foreign State.

AMENDMENT XII

(Adopted September 25, 1804)
The electors shall meet in their respective states, and vote by ballot for President and Vice-President, one of whom, at least, shall not be an inhabitant of the same state with themselves; they shall name in their ballots the person voted for as President, and in distinct ballots the person voted for as Vice-President, and they shall make distinct lists of all persons voted for as President, and of all persons voted for as Vice-President, and of the number of votes for each, which lists they shall sign and certify, and transmit sealed to the seat of the government of the United States, directed to the

President of the Senate;--the President of the Senate shall, in the presence of the Senate and House of Representatives, open all the certificates and the votes shall then be counted;--the person having the greatest number of votes for President, shall be the President, if such number be a majority of the whole number of electors appointed; and if no person have such majority, then from the persons having the highest numbers not exceeding three on the list of those voted for as President, the House of Representatives shall choose immediately, by ballot, the President. But in choosing the President, the votes shall be taken by states, the representation from each state having one vote; a quorum for this purpose shall consist of a member or members from two-thirds of the states, and a majority of all the states shall be necessary to a choice. And if the House of Representatives shall not choose a President whenever the right of choice shall devolve upon them, before the fourth day of March next following, then the Vice-President shall act as President, as in the case of the death or other constitutional disability of the President. The person having the greatest number of votes as Vice-President, shall be the Vice-President, if such number be a majority of the whole number of electors appointed, and if no person have a majority, then from the two highest numbers on the list, the Senate shall choose the Vice-President; a quorum for the purpose shall consist of two-thirds of the whole number of Senators, and a majority of the whole number shall be necessary to a choice. But no person constitutionally ineligible to the office of President shall be eligible to that of Vice-President of the United States.

AMENDMENT XIII

(Adopted December 18, 1865)

Section 1. Neither slavery nor involuntary servitude, except as a punishment for crime whereof the party shall have been duly convicted, shall exist within the United States, or any place subject to their jurisdiction.

Section 2. Congress shall have power to enforce this article by appropriate legislation.

AMENDMENT XIV

(Adopted July 21, 1868)

Section 1. All persons born or naturalized in the United States, and subject to the jurisdiction thereof, are citizens of the United States and of the State wherein they reside. No State shall make or enforce any law which shall abridge the privileges or immunities of citizens of the United States; nor shall any State deprive any person of life, liberty, or property, without due process of law; nor deny to any person within its jurisdiction the equal protection of the laws.

Section 2. Representatives shall be apportioned among the several States according to their respective numbers, counting the whole number of persons in each State, excluding Indians not taxed. But when the right to vote at any election for the choice of electors for President and Vice-President of the United States, Representatives in Congress, the Executive and Judicial officers of a State, or the members of the Legislature thereof, is denied to any of the male inhabitants of each State, being twenty-one years of age, and citizens of the United States, or in any way abridged, except for participation in rebellion, or other crime, the basis of representation therein shall be reduced in the proportion which the number of such male citizens shall bear to the whole number of male citizens twenty-one years of age in such State.

Section 3. No person shall be a Senator or Representative in Congress, or elector of President and Vice-President, or hold any office, civil or military, under the United States, or under any State, who, having previously taken an oath, as a member of Congress, or as an officer of the United States, or as a member of any State legislature, or as an executive or judicial officer of any State, to support the Constitution of the United States, shall have engaged in insurrection or rebellion against the same, or given aid or comfort to the enemies thereof. But Congress may by a vote of two-thirds of each House, remove such disability.

Section 4. The validity of the public debt of the United States, authorized by law, including debts incurred for payment of pensions and bounties for services in suppressing insurrection or rebellion, shall not be questioned. But neither the United States nor any State shall assume or pay any debt or obligation incurred in aid of insurrection or rebellion against the United States, or any claim for the loss or emancipation of any slave; but all such debts, obligations and claims shall be held illegal and void.

Section 5. The Congress shall have power to enforce, by appropriate legislation, the provisions of this article.

AMENDMENT XV

(Adopted March 30, 1870)

Section 1. The right of citizens of the United States to vote shall not be denied or abridged by the United States or by any State on account of race, color, or previous condition of servitude.

Section 2. The Congress shall have power to enforce this article by appropriate legislation.

AMENDMENT XVI

(Adopted February 25, 1913)

The Congress shall have power to lay and collect taxes on incomes, from whatever source derived, without apportionment among the several States, and without regard to any census or enumeration.

AMENDMENT XVII

(Adopted May 31, 1913.)

The Senate of the United States shall be composed of two Senators from each State, elected by the people thereof, for six years; and each Senator shall have one vote. The electors in each State shall have the qualifications requisite for electors of the most numerous branch of the State legislatures.

When vacancies happen in the representation of any State in the Senate, the executive authority of such State shall issue writs of election to fill such vacancies; *Provided,* That the legislature of any State may empower the executive thereof to make temporary appointments until the people fill the vacancies by election as the legislature may direct.

This amendment shall not be so construed as to affect the election or term of any Senator chosen before it becomes valid as a part of the Constitution.

AMENDMENT XVIII

(Adopted January 29, 1919)

Section 1. After one year from the ratification of this article the manufacture, sale, or transportation of intoxicating liquors within, the importation thereof into, or the exportation thereof from the United States and all territory subject to the jurisdiction thereof for beverage purposes is hereby prohibited.

Section 2. The Congress and the several States shall have concurrent power to enforce this article by appropriate legislation.

Section 3. This article shall be inoperative unless it shall have been ratified as an amendment to the Constitution by the legislatures of the several States, as provided in the Constitution, within seven years from the date of the submission hereof to the States by the Congress.

AMENDMENT XIX

(Adopted August 26, 1920)

The right of citizens of the United States to vote shall not be denied or abridged by the United States or by any State on account of sex.

Congress shall have power to enforce this article by appropriate legislation.

AMENDMENT XX

(Adopted January 23, 1933)

Section 1. The terms of the President and Vice-President shall end at noon on the 20th day of January, and the terms of Senators and Representatives at noon on the 3rd day of January, of the years in which such terms would have ended if this article had not been ratified; and the terms of their successors shall then begin.

Section 2. The Congress shall assemble at least once in every year, and such meeting shall begin at noon on the 3rd day of January, unless they shall by law appoint a different day.

Section 3. If, at the time fixed for the beginning of the term of the President, the President elect shall have died, the Vice-President elect shall become President. If a President shall not have been chosen before the time fixed for the beginning of his term, or if the President elect shall have failed to qualify, then the Vice-President elect shall act as President until a President shall have qualified; and the Congress may by law provide for the case wherein neither a President elect nor a Vice-President elect shall have qualified, declaring who shall then act as President, or the manner in which one who is to act shall be selected, and such person shall act accordingly until a President or Vice-President shall have qualified.

Section 4. The Congress may by law provide for the case of the death of any of the persons from whom the House of Representatives may choose a President whenever the right of choice shall have devolved upon them, and for the case of the death of any of the persons from whom the Senate may choose a Vice-President whenever the right of choice shall have devolved upon them.

Section 5. Sections 1 and 2 shall take effect on the 15th day of October following the ratification of this article (Oct., 1933).

Section 6. This article shall be inoperative unless it shall have been ratified as an amendment to the Constitution by the Legislatures of three-fourths of the several States within seven years from the date of its submission.

AMENDMENT XXI

(Adopted December 5, 1933)
Section 1. The eighteenth article of amendment to the Constitution of the United States is hereby repealed.
Section 2. The transportation or importation into any State, Territory, or Possession of the United States for delivery or use therein of intoxicating liquors, in violation of the laws thereof, is hereby prohibited.
Section 3. This article shall be inoperative unless it shall have been ratified as an amendment to the Constitution by conventions in the several States, as provided in the Constitution, within seven years from the date of the submission hereof to the States by the Congress.

AMENDMENT XXII

(Adopted February 27, 1951)
Section 1. No person shall be elected to the office of the President more than twice, and no person who has held the office of President, or acted as President, for more than two years of a term to which some other person was elected President shall be elected to the office of the President more than once. But this Article shall not apply to any person holding the office of President when this Article was proposed by the Congress, and shall not prevent any person who may be holding the office of President, or acting as President, during the term within which this Article becomes operative from holding the office of President or acting as President during the remainder of such term.
Section 2. This article shall be inoperative unless it shall have been ratified as an amendment to the Constitution by the Legislatures of three-fourths of the several States within seven years from the date of its submission to the States by the Congress.

AMENDMENT XXIII

(Adopted March 29, 1961)
Section 1. The District constituting the seat of Government of the United States shall appoint in such manner as the Congress may direct:
A number of electors of President and Vice-President equal to the whole number of Senators and Representatives in Congress to which the District would be entitled if it were a State, but in no event more than the least populous State; they shall be in addition to those

appointed by the States, but they shall be considered, for the purposes of the election of President and Vice-President, to be electors appointed by a State; and they shall meet in the District and perform such duties as provided by the twelfth article of amendment.

Section 2. The Congress shall have power to enforce this article by appropriate legislation.

Amendment XXIV

(Adopted January 233, 1964)

Section 1. The right of citizens of the United States to vote in any primary or other election for President or Vice-President, for electors for President or Vice-President, or for Senator or Representative in Congress, shall not be denied or abridged by the United States or any State by reason of failure to pay any poll tax or other tax.

Section 2. The Congress shall have power to enforce this article by appropriate legislation.

AMENDMENT XXV

(Adopted February 10, 1965)

Section 1. In case of the removal of the President from office or of his death or resignation, the Vice-President shall become President.

Section 2. Whenever there is a vacancy in the office of the Vice-President, the President shall nominate a Vice-President who shall take office upon confirmation by a majority vote of both houses of Congress.

Section 3. Whenever the President transmits to the President pro tempore of the Senate and the Speaker of the House of Representatives his written declaration that he is unable to discharge the powers and duties of his office, and until he transmits to them a written declaration to the contrary, such powers and duties shall be discharged by the Vice-President as Acting President.

Section 4. Whenever the Vice-President and a majority of either the principal officers of the executive departments or of such other body as Congress may by law provide, transmit to the President pro tempore of the Senate and the Speaker of the House of Representatives their written declaration that the President is unable to discharge the powers and duties of his office, the Vice-President shall immediately assume the powers and duties of the office as Acting President

Thereafter, when the President transmits to the President pro tempore of the Senate and the Speaker of the House of Representatives his written declaration that no inability exists, he shall resume the powers and duties of his office unless the Vice-President and a majority of either the principal officers of the executive department or of such other body as Congress may by law provide, transmit within four days to the President pro tempore of the Senate and the Speaker of the House of Representatives their written declaration that the President is unable to discharge the powers and duties of his office. Thereupon Congress shall decide the issue, assembling within forty-eight hours for that purpose if not in session. If the Congress, within twenty-one days after receipt of the latter written declaration, or, if Congress is not in session, within twenty-one days after Congress is required to assemble, determines by two-thirds vote of both houses that the President is unable to discharge the powers and duties of his office, the Vice-President shall continue to discharge the same as Acting President; otherwise, the President shall resume the powers and duties of his office.

AMENDMENT XXVI

(Adopted July 1, 1971)
Section 1. The right of citizens of the United States, who are 18 years of age or older, to vote shall not be denied or abridged by the United States or any state on account of age.
Section 2. The Congress shall have the power to enforce this article by appropriate legislation.

Footnotes

Chapter 1
The Way It Is

1. William Murray, "America Without God," *The New American,* June 20, 1988, pg. 19.
2. John Eidsmoe, *Christianity and the Constitution* (Michigan: Baker Book House, 1987), p. 406.
3. Tim LaHaye, *Faith of Our Founding Fathers* (Brentwood, Tennessee: Wolgemuth & Hyatt, Publishers, Inc., 1987), p. 27.
4. *The Washington Times,* December 12, 1988, "Parent silences teaching of carols," "School officials deny banning Bible..."
5. *IFA Newsletter,* February 1989, "Fifth Grader Sues for Right to Read Bible."
6. Robert Flood, *The Rebirth of America* (Philadelphia: The Arthur S. DeMoss Foundation, 1986), p. 12.
7. Stephen K. McDowell and Mark A. Beliles, *America's Providential History* (Virginia: Providence Press, 1988), p. 79.
8. Eidsmoe, p. 405.
9. Stephen K. McDowell and Mark A. Beliles, *The Spirit of the Constitution* (Charottesville, Virginia: Providence Press).
10. Paul C. Vitz, *Censorship: Evidence of Bias in Our Children's Textbooks* (Ann Arbor, Michigan: Servant Books, 1986), p. 1.
11. Ibid, p. 11.
12. Ibid, p. 79-80.
13. Ibid, p. 18-19.
14. McDowell and Beliles, *The Spirit of the Constitution.*
15. LaHaye, p. 15.

Chapter 2
The Way It Was--
The Building of the Constitution and
the First Amendment

1. M.E. Bradford, *A Worthy Company* (NH: Plymouth Rock Foundation, 1982), p. x.
2. Edwin S. Gaustad, *Faith of Our Fathers* (San Francisco: Harper & Row, 1987), p. 161. All the references to the states' constitutions are from this book and can also be found in *The Spirit of the Constitution* and *God and Government,* as well as being regularly quoted in early Supreme Court cases.
3. Bradford. All lists of the delegates and their denominational affiliations are taken from the table of contents.
4. Ibid, p. viii-ix.
5. Steve C. Dawson, *God's Providence in America's History* (California: Steve C. Dawson, 1988), p. 9:6.
6. All notes on the versions of the Amendmend used in this section are taken from Gaustad, p. 157-158, and some are cited by Gary DeMar, *God and Government: A Biblical and Historical Study* (Atlanta: American Vision Press, 1982), p. 171.
7. Noah Webster, *American Dictionary of the English Language, 1828* (San Francisco: Foundation for American Christian Education, 1967), definition of "religion."

8. B.F. Morris, *The Christian Life and Character of the Civil Institutions of the United States* (Philadelphia: George W. Childs, 1864), p. 318-329.
9. Stephen K. McDowell and Mark A. Beliles, *The Spirit of the Constitution* (Charottesville, Virginia: Providence Press).
10. Alexis de Tocqueville, *Democracy in America,* J.P. Mayer, ed., George Lawrence, trans. (Garden City, NY: Doubleday & Company, Inc. 1969), p. 293.
11. Ibid, p. 293.
12. Verna M. Hall, *The Christian History of the Constitution of the United States of America* (San Francisco: The Foundation for American Christian Education, 1966), p. 262A.
13. John Eidsmoe, *Christianity and the Constitution* (Michigan: Baker Book House, 1987), p. 325.
14. Stephen K. McDowell and Mark A. Beliles, *America's Providential History* (Virginia: Providence Press, 1988), p. 222.
15. Eidsmoe, p. 215-217.
16. Robert Flood, *The Rebirth of America* (Philadelphia: The Arthur S. DeMoss Foundation, 1986), p. 20. Quoted from *The Nature of the American System* by R. J. Rushdoony.

Chapter 3
The Origin of the Phrase
"Separation of Church and State"

1. John Eidsmoe, *Christianity and the Constitution* (Michigan: Baker Book House, 1987), p. 243.
2. Stephen K. McDowell and Mark A. Beliles, *The Spirit of the Constitution* (Charottesville, Virginia: Providence Press). Also cited in Eidsmoe p. 243-244.
3. Eidsmoe, p. 242-243.
4. Gary DeMar, *God and Government: A Biblical and Historical Study* (Atlanta: American Vision Press, 1982), p. 165. Quoted from J.M. O'Neill, *Religion and Education Under the Constitution,* pg. 4.
5. DeMar, pg. 163.
6. Tim LaHaye, *Faith of Our Founding Fathers* (Brentwood, Tennessee: Wolgemuth & Hyatt, Publishers, Inc., 1987), p. 3.

Chapter 4
The Court's Early Rulings

1. Robert K. Dornan and Csaba Vedlik, Jr., *Judicial Supremacy: The Supreme Court on Trial* (Massachusetts: Plymouth Rock Foundation, 1986), p. 10.
2. John Eidsmoe, *Christianity and the Constitution* (Michigan: Baker Book House, 1987), p. 57.
3. Ibid, p. 52.
4. Dr. Sterling Lacy, *Valley of Decision* (Texas: Dayspring Productions, 1988), p. 7-8.
5. Ibid, p. 6-7.
6. The information about the books *Planned Parenthood* recommends comes from a packet of informational materials dated January 15, 1987, and prepared by California Assemblyman Bill Bradley of the 76th District.
7. Stephen K. McDowell and Mark A. Beliles, *America's Providential History* (Virginia: Providence Press, 1988), p. 148.

8. Steve C. Dawson, *God's Providence in America's History* (Rancho Cordova, California: Steve C. Dawson, 1988), p. l:13, p. 10:5.
9. McDowell and Beliles, *America's Providential History*, p. 222.
10. Russ Walton, *Biblical Principles of Importance to Godly Christians* (New Hampshire: Plymouth Rock Foundation, 1984), p. 364. Also cited in Eidsmoe, p. 377, and McDowell and Beliles' *The Spirit of the Constitution.*
11. Verna M. Hall and Rosalie J. Slater, *The Bible and the Constitution of the United States of America* (San Francisco: The Foundation for American Christian Education, 1983), p. 38.
12. Peter Marshall and David Manuel, *From Sea to Shining Sea* (New Jersey: Fleming H. Revel Co., 1986), p. 204. Quoted from Albert J. Beveridge, *The Life of John Marshall* (Boston: Houghton Mifflin, 1919), p. 4:70-71.
13. Alexis de Tocqueville, *Democracy in America* (New York: Doubleday & Company, Inc., 1969), p. 18.
14. Ibid, p. 293.

Chapter 5
Other "Organic Utterances"

1. Stephen K. McDowell and Mark A. Beliles, *America's Providential History* (Virginia: Providence Press, 1988), p. 39.
2. Pat Robertson, *America's Dates With Destiny* (Nashville: Thomas Nelson Publishers, 1986), p. 29-30. Also cited in Russ Walton, *Biblical Principles of Importance to Godly Christians,* New Hampshire: Plymouth Rock Foundation, © 1984, p. 354, and McDowell and Beliles, *America's Providential History*, p. 54.
3. Walton, p. 354.
4. Robert Flood, *The Rebirth of America* (Philadelphia: The Arthur S. DeMoss Foundation, 1986), p. 31. Also cited in Walton, p. 354.
5. Robertson, p. 31. Also cited in McDowell and Beliles, *America's Providential History,* p. 76, and Stephen K. McDowell and Mark A. Beliles, *Principles for the Reformation of the Nations* (Charlottesville, Virginia: Providence Press, 1988), p. 42.
6. Walton, p. 354-355.
7. Peter Marshall and David Manuel, *From Sea to Shining Sea* (New Jersey: Fleming H. Revel Co., 1986), p. 23.
8. Verna M. Hall and Rosalie J. Slater, *The Bible and the Constitution of the United States of America* (San Francisco: The Foundation for American Christian Education, 1966), p. 15. Also cited in McDowell and Beliles, *Principles for the Reformation of the Nations* , p. 43.
9. Robertson, p. 31-32.
10. McDowell and Beliles, *America's Providential History,* p. 60.
11. Verna M. Hall, *The Christian History of the Constitution of the United States of America* (San Francisco: The Foundation for American Christian Education, 1966), p. 193. Also cited in Walton, p. 356.
12. McDowell and Beliles, *America's Providential History,* p. 54-55.
13. Ibid, p. 59. Also cited in Robertson, p. 32.
14. Ibid, p. 55.
15. Robertson, p. 32-33.
16. McDowell and Beliles, *America's Providential History,* p. 58. Also cited in Hall, *The Christian History of the Constitution,* p. 252.
17. Hall, *The Christian History of the Constitution,* p. 372.
18. Ibid, p. 253. Quoted from "Old South Leaflets," No. 8.

19. Ibid, p. 252-253. Also cited in Walton, p. 355.
20. McDowell and Beliles, *America's Providential History,* p. 59. Also cited in Walton, p. 355.
21. Walton, p. 356. Also cited in McDowell and Beliles, *America's Providential History,* p. 62.
22. Ibid, p. 356.
23. McDowell and Beliles, *America's Providential History,* p. 55.
24. Ibid, p. 60.
25. Ibid, p. 61. Also cited in McDowell and Beliles, *Principles for the Reformation,* p. 44.
26. Hall, *The Christian History of the Constitution,* p. 262A. Also cited in McDowell and Beliles, *America's Providential History,* p. 61, and *Principles for the Reformation of the Nations,* p. 44.
27. McDowell and Beliles, *America's Providential History,* p. 62. Also cited in McDowell and Beliles, *Principles for the Reformation,* p. 44.
28. Hall, *The Christian History of the Constitution,* p. 262A.
29. McDowell and Beliles, *America's Providential History,* p. 61.
30. Ibid.
31. Ibid. Also cited in Robertson, p. 47-48.
32. Steve C. Dawson, *God's Providence in America's History,* Rancho Cordova, California: Steve C. Dawson, © 1988, p. 8:5. Also cited in Robertson, p. 44; McDowell and Beliles' *America's Providential History,* p. 92; and Walton, p. 355.
33. McDowell and Beliles, *America's Providential History,* p. 91.
34. Ibid, p. 92. Also cited in Walton, p. 356.
35. Ibid. Also cited in Robertson, p. 45, and Walton, p. 356-357.
36. Ibid. Also cited in Robertson, p. 46.
37. Ibid, p. 93.
38. Robertson, p. 110. Quoted from *Basic Writings of George Washington,* ed. Saze Commins (New York: Random House, 1948), 356-57.
39. McDowell and Beliles, *America's Providential History,* p. 91.
40. Ibid, p. 100.
41. Hall, *The Christian History of the Constitution,* p. 367. Quoted from W.V. Wells' *Life of Samuel Adams,* 1865. Also cited in Walton, p. 357, and McDowell and Beliles, *America's Providential History,* p. 105.
42. McDowell and Beliles, *America's Providential History,* p. 148. Also cited in McDowell and Beliles, *The Spirit of the Constitution.*
43. Ibid, p. 148. Also cited in McDowell and Beliles' *The Spirit of the Constitution.*
44. John Eidsmoe, *Christianity and the Constitution* (Michigan: Baker Book House, 1987), p. 251.
45. Hall, *The Christian History of the Constitution,* p. 348. Quoted from Richard Frothingham's *The Rise of the Republic,* 1890.
46. Ibid, p. 343. Also cited in McDowell and Beliles, *America's Providential History,* p. 111.
47. Ibid. Also cited in McDowell and Beliles' *America's Providential History,* p. 111.
48. Ibid, p. 410. Quoted from "Warren-Adams Letters," Vol. 1, 1743-1777, Massachusetts Historical Society Collections--72.
49. Peter Marshall and David Manuel, *The Light and the Glory* (New Jersey: Fleming H. Revell Co., 1977), p. 323. Quoted from William J. Johnson, *George Washington, the Christian* (Nashville, Tenn: Abingdon Press, 1919), p. 112.
50. Ibid, p. 267. Quoted from George Bancroft, *Bancroft's History of the United*

States, Vol. VI, Third Edition (Boston: Charles C. Little & James Brown, 1838), p. 440-442.
    51. Hall and Slater, *Bible and the Constitution,* p. 31.
    52. Marshall and Manuel, *The Light and the Glory,* p. 268. Quoted from George Bancroft, *Bancroft's History of the United States,* Vol. VII, Third Edition (Boston: Charles C. Little & James Brown, 1838), p. 99.
    53. Hall and Slater, *Bible and the Constitution,* p. 31.
    54. Marshall and Manuel, *The Light and the Glory,* p. 267. Quoted from H. Niles, *Principles and Acts of the Revolution in America* (Baltimore, 1822), p. 198.
    55. Ibid. Quoted from Cushing Stout, *The New Heavens and the New Earth* (New York: Harper & Row, 1974), p. 59.
    56. McDowell and Beliles, *America's Providential History,* p. 122-123.
    57. Walton, p. 358.
    58. Robertson, p. 109.
    59. Walton, p. 359.
    60. McDowell and Beliles, *The Spirit of the Constitution.*
    61. Tim LaHaye, *Faith of Our Founding Fathers* (Tennessee: Wolgemuth & Hyatt, Publishers, Inc., 1987), p. 31.
    62. McDowell and Beliles, *America's Providential History,* p. 108.
    63. Ibid, p. 109.
    64. McDowell and Beliles, *The Spirit of the Constitution.*
    65. Walton, p. 357.
    66. McDowell and Beliles, *America's Providential History,* p. 123. Also cited in Walton, p. 358.
    67. Ibid.
    68. Walton, p. 359.
    69. Ibid. Also cited in LaHaye, p. 96, and McDowell and Beliles, *The Spirit of the Constitution.*
    70. Ibid.
    71. McDowell and Beliles, *America's Providential History,* p. 146.
    72. Ibid, p. 136. Quoted from *America,* Vol. III, issued by Veterans of Foreign Wars of the United States (Chicago, 1925), p. 284-285. Also cited in Marshall and Manuel, *The Light and the Glory,* p. 329 which was taken from Richard Wheeler, *Voices of 1776* (Greenwich: Fawcett Premier Book, 1972), p. 382.
    73. Ibid, p. 136-137, 146. Taken from the *Journals of Congress,* Vol. XVIII, p. 950-951.
    74. Ibid, p. 146. Also cited in McDowell and Beliles, *The Spirit of the Constitution.*
    75. Walton, p. 359. Also cited in Hall and Slater, *Bible and the Constitution,* p. 8.
    76. McDowell and Beliles, *The Spirit of the Constitution.*
    77. Tim LaHaye, p. 123-124. Quoted from *The Debates in the Federal Convention of 1787 Which Framed the Constitution of the United States of America, reported by James Madison* (New York: Oxford University Press, 1920), pp. 181-82, Gallard Hunt and James B. Scott, ed. Also cited in McDowell and Beliles, *America's Providential History,* p. 7, 142, and Marshall and Manuel, *Light and the Glory,* p. 343.
    78. McDowell and Beliles, *America's Providential History,* p. 142-143.
    79. Ibid, p. 143. Also cited in McDowell and Beliles' *The Spirit of the Constitution.*
    80. McDowell and Beliles, *The Spirit of the Constitution.*
    81. Ibid.
    82. Ibid.

83. Marshall and Manuel, *The Light and the Glory,* p. 343.

84. LaHaye, p. 71.

85. McDowell and Beliles, *The Spirit of the Constitution.* Quoted from B.F. Morris, *The Christian Life and Character of the Civil Institutions of the United States* (Philadelphia: George W. Childs, 1864), pg. 271-272.

86. Ibid.

87. Ibid. Also cited in Walton, p. 361.

88. Robertson, p. 111-112.

89. Eidsmoe, p. 124.

90. Lacy, p. 3.

91. Walton, p. 361.

92. McDowell and Beliles, *America's Providential History,* p. 145-146.

93. McDowell and Beliles, *The Spirit of the Constitution.* Quoted from the *Journals of Congress.*

94. Ibid.

95. Robertson, p. 112.

96. Hall, *The Christian History of the Constitution,* p. 411. Quoted from Benson J. Lossing's *Washington and the American Republic,* 1870. Also cited in McDowell and Beliles, *The Spirit of the Constitution;* LaHaye, p. 118; and McDowell and Beliles, *Principles for the Reformation of the Nations,* p. 54.

97. McDowell and Beliles, *America's Providential History,* p. 148. Also cited in McDowell and Beliles, *The Spirit of the Constitution.*

98. Ibid, p. 94.

99. Hall and Slater, *Bible and the Constitution,* p. 22. Also cited in McDowell and Beliles, *The Spirit of the Constitution.*

100. Marshall and Manuel, *The Light and the Glory,* p. 296.

101. Dawson, p. I:5

102. Eidsmoe, p. 313-314.

103. Ibid, p. 314.

104. Lacy, p. 3.

105. McDowell and Beliles, *America's Providential History,* p. 222.

106. Marshall and Manuel, *From Sea to Shining Sea,* p. 417, Footnote 26. Quoted from Morris, p. 153-154. Also cited in Eidsmoe, p. 170.

107. McDowell and Beliles, *America's Providential History,* p. 148.

108. Walton, p. 361. Also cited in McDowell and Beliles, *Principles for the Reformation of the Nations,* p. 54, and McDowell and Beliles, *The Spirit of the Constitution.*

109. Eidsmoe, p. 188. Quoted from Gouverneur Morris' *Notes on the Form of a Constitution for France,* probably the same general time as his *Observations on Government, Applicable to the Political State of France,* July 1789.

110. Eidsmoe, p. 324.

111. Ibid, p. 325.

112. Ibid, p. 273.

113. Robertson, p. 93-94. Quoted from John Adams, in *The Works of John Adams, Second President of the United States* collected by Charles Francis Adams (Boston: Little, Brown, 1854). Also cited in McDowell and Beliles, *Principles for the Reformation of the Nations,* p. 148; McDowell and Beliles, *The Spirit of the Constitution;* Eidsmoe, p. 273; and LaHaye p. 194.

114. Edwin S. Gaustad, *Faith of Our Fathers* (San Franscisco: Harper & Row, 1987), p. 92. Also cited in Walton, p. 357.

115. Eidsmoe, p. 277. Quoted from John Adams' diary entry for July 26, 1796.

116. Ibid, p. 293-294. Quoted from John Adams' diary entry for February 22, 1756.

117. Ibid, p. 294. Quoted from letter from John Adams to Benjamin Rush, August 28, 1811.

118. LaHaye, p. 90.

119. Hall, *The Christian History of the Constitution*, p. 411. Quoted from Benson J. Lossing's *Washington and the American Republic*, 1870. Also cited in McDowell and Beliles, *The Spirit of the Constitution;* LaHaye p. 118; and McDowell and Beliles, *Principles for the Reformation of the Nations*, p. 54.

120. Eidsmoe, p. 157.

121. Walton, p. 353, 363. Also cited in McDowell and Beliles, *Principles for the Reformation of the Nations*, p. 45, and Dawson, p. I:5.

122. McDowell and Beliles, *America's Providential History*, p. 163. Also cited in Walton, p. 363; Flood, p. 32; and McDowell and Beliles, *The Spirit of the Constitution*.

123. Flood, p. 33.

124. Noah Webster, *American Dictionary of the English Language, 1828* (San Franscisco: Foundation for American Christian Education, 1967), Preface, p. 12. Also cited in McDowell and Beliles, *America's Providential History*, p. 88.

125. Webster, p. 22.

126. Hall and Slater, *The Bible and the Constitution*, p. 28.

127. McDowell and Beliles, *Principles for the Reformation of the Nations*, Appendix. Quoted from Verna M. Hall, Comp., *Consider and Ponder*, p. 19-21, which was taken from *Preface to the Holy Bible containing the Old and New Testaments, in the Common Version*, with amendments of the language, by Noah Webster, LL.D. New Haven, 1833.

128. Dawson, p. 7:2. Also cited in McDowell and Beliles, *America's Providential History*, p. 207, and McDowell and Beliles, *The Spirit of the Constitution*.

129. McDowell and Beliles, *America's Providential History*, p. 90.

130. Walton, p. 363.

131. Hall,*The Christian History of the Constitution*, p. XIV. Also cited in McDowell and Beliles, *America's Providential History*, p. 94.

132. Eidsmoe, p. 188. Quoted from Gouverneur Morris' *Notes on the Form of a Constitution for France*, probably the same general time as his *Observations on Government, Applicable to the Political State of France*, July 1789.

133. McDowell and Beliles, *America's Providential History*, p. 152.

134. Ibid, p. 148.

135. Walton, p. 359. Also cited in Hall and Slater, *Bible and the Constitution*, p. 8.

136. Alexis de Tocqueville, *Democracy in America*, J.P. Mayer, ed., George Lawrence, trans. (Garden City, NY: Doubleday & Company, Inc. 1969), p. 295.

137. Lacy, p. 37. Quoted from *The New American*, September 29, 1986, p. 28.

138. Ibid.

139. de Tocqueville, p. 291.

140. Morris, p. 318-329.

141. Hall, *The Christian History of the Constitution*, p. 246. Quoted from Daniel Webster's "A Discourse delivered at Plymouth, on the 22 of December, 1820 by Daniel Webster," Vol. I, the *Works of Daniel Webster*, 1851.

142. Ibid, p. 248. Also cited in Walton, p. 362-363.

143. de Tocqueville, p. 295.

144. Ibid, p. 293.

145. Ibid, p. 292.
146. Ibid, p. 288.
147. Ibid, p. 292-293.
148. Ibid, p. 292.
149. DeMar, p. 110. Quoted from Morris, introduction by B. Sunderland on pg. 11.
150. Lacy, p. 8-9. Quoting from Emma Willard, 1843, quoted in *Teaching and Learning America's Christian History* (San Francisco, California: Foundation for American Christian Education, 1975), compiled by Verna M. Hall, p. xi.
151. McDowell and Beliles, *The Spirit of the Constitution.*
152. Associated Press, *Dallas Times Herald,* August 6, 1988, B-5.

Chapter 6
Protection from the Absurd

1. Pat Robertson, *America's Dates With Destiny* (Nashville: Thomas Nelson Publishers, 1986), p. 111-112.
2. B.F. Morris, *The Christian Life and Character of the Civil Institutions of the United States* (Philadelphia: George W. Childs, 1864), pg. 318-329.

Chapter 7
The Absurd Becomes Reality

1. John Eidsmoe, *Christianity and the Constitution* (Michigan: Baker Book House, 1987), p. 124.
2. Ibid, p. 294. Quoted from a letter from John Adams to Benjamin Rush, August 28, 1811.
3. Stephen K. McDowell and Mark A. Beliles, *America's Providential History* (Virginia: Providence Press, 1988), p. 148.
4. Verna M. Hall and Rosalie J. Slater, *The Bible and the Constitution of the United States of America* (San Francisco: The Foundation for American Christian Education, 1966), p. 22. Also cited in Stephen K. McDowell and Mark A. Beliles, *The Spirit of the Constitution* (Charottesville, Virginia: Providence Press).
5. Pat Robertson, *America's Dates With Destiny* (Nashville: Thomas Nelson Publishers, 1986), p. 93-94. Quoted from John Adams, in *The Works of John Adams, Second President of the United States* collected by Charles Francis Adams (Boston: Little, Brown, 1854).   Also cited in McDowell and Beliles, *Principles for the Reformation of the Nations,* p. 148; McDowell and Beliles, *The Spirit of the Constitution;* Eidsmoe, p. 273; and Tim LaHaye, *Faith of Our Founding Fathers* (Tennessee: Wolgemuth & Hyatt, Publishers, Inc., 1987), p. 194.
6. Eidsmoe, p. 396.
7. McDowell and Beliles, *America's Providential History,* p. 148.
8. Dr. Sterling Lacy, *Valley of Decision* (Texas: Dayspring Productions, 1988), p. 3.
9. Ibid.
10. Eidsmoe, p. 293-294. Quoted from John Adams' diary entry for February 22, 1756.
11. Russ Walton, *Biblical Principles of Importance to Godly Christians* (New Hampshire: Plymouth Rock Foundation, 1984), p. 359. Also cited in Hall and Slater, *Bible and the Constitution,* p. 8.

12. Robert Flood, *The Rebirth of America* (Philadelphia: The Arthur S. DeMoss Foundation, 1986), p. 33. Also cited in Walton, p. 354.
13. Walton, p. 353, p. 363. Also cited in Stephen K. McDowell and Mark A. Beliles, *Principles for the Reformation of the Nations* (Charlottesville, Virginia: Providence Press, 1988), p. 45, and Steve C. Dawson, *God's Providence in America's History* (Rancho Cordova, California: Steve C. Dawson, 1988), p. I:5.
14. Peter Marshall and David Manuel, *The Light and the Glory* (New Jersey: Fleming H. Revell Co., 1977), p. 370, Footnote 10.
15. B.F. Morris, *The Christian Life and Character of the Civil Institutions of the United States* (Philadelphia: George W. Childs, 1864), p. 318-329.
16. Ibid.
17. McDowell and Beliles, *America's Providential History*, p. 222.
18. Paul C. Vitz, *Censorship: Evidence of Bias in Our Children's Textbooks* (Ann Arbor, Michigan: Servant Books, 1986), p. 11.
19. Ibid, p. 49-55.
20. Walton, p. 361. Also cited in McDowell and Beliles, *Principles for the Reformation of the Nations*, p. 54, and McDowell and Beliles, *The Spirit of the Constitution*.
21. Dawson, p. I:5
22. McDowell and Beliles, *America's Providential History*, p. 94.
23. Robertson, p. 110. Quoted from *Basic Writings of George Washington*, ed. Saze Commins (New York: Random House, 1948), 356-57.
24. McDowell and Beliles, *America's Providential History*, p. 163. Also cited in Walton, p. 363; Flood, p. 32; and McDowell and Beliles, *The Spirit of the Constitution*.
25. Morris, p. 318-329.

Chapter 9
The Court's Defense of Its Position

1. Robert K. Dornan and Csaba (Jr.) Vedlik, *Judicial Supremacy: The Supreme Court on Trial* (Massachusetts: Plymouth Rock Foundation, 1986), p. 85.
2. Ibid, p. 35. Quoted from Samuel J. Konefsky, *John Marshall and Alexander Hamilton: Architects of the American Constitution* (New York: Macmillan, 1964), p. 51.
3. Pat Robertson, *America's Dates With Destiny* (Nashville: Thomas Nelson Publishers, 1986), p. 75.
4. Ibid.
5. Stephen K. McDowell and Mark A. Beliles, *The Spirit of the Constitution* (Charottesville, Virginia: Providence Press). Also cited in John Eidsmoe, *Christianity and the Constitution* (Michigan: Baker Book House, 1987), p. 243-244, and Stephen K. McDowell and Mark A. Beliles, *America's Providential History* (Virginia: Providence Press, 1988), p. 152.
6. Paul C. Vitz, *Censorship: Evidence of Bias in Our Children's Textbooks* (Ann Arbor, Michigan: Servant Books, 1986), p. 77.
7. McDowell and Beliles, *America's Providential History*, p. 152.
8. Ibid, p. 148.
9. Eidsmoe, p. 244.
10. McDowell and Beliles, *The Spirit of the Constitution*. Also cited in McDowell and Beliles, *America's Providential History*, p. 145-147; Russ Walton, *Biblical Principles of Importance to Godly Christians* (New Hampshire: Plymouth Rock Foundation, 1984), p. 362; and Eidsmoe, p. 124.

11. McDowell and Beliles, *America's Providential History,* p. 148.
12. Eidsmoe, p. 227. Quoted from "Notes on the State of Virginia," 1781, 1782, by Thomas Jefferson. Also cited in Robert Flood, *The Rebirth of America* (Philadelphia: The Arthur S. DeMoss Foundation, 1986), p. 24; Robertson, p. 65; Tim LaHaye, *Faith of Our Founding Fathers* (Brentwood, Tennessee: Wolgemuth & Hyatt, Publishers, Inc., 1987), p. 194; and Gary DeMar, *God and Government: A Biblical and Historical Study* (Atlanta: American Vision Press, 1982), p. 145.
13. McDowell and Beliles, *The Spirit of the Constitution.* Quoted from James Madison, "Memorial and Remonstrance of 1785." Also cited in McDowell and Beliles, *America's Providential History,* p. 148.
14. LaHaye, p. 127.
15. Dornan and Vedlik, p. 61-62. Quoted from Edward S. Corwin, *Court Over Constitution: A Study of Judicial Review as an Instrument of Popular Government,* Princeton, J.J.: Princeton University Press, 1914, p. 69-70.
16. Dornan and Vedlik, p. 62. Also cited in Robertson p. 99.
17. McDowell and Beliles, *America's Providential History,* p. 218.
18. Edwin S. Gaustad, *Faith of Our Fathers* (San Franscisco: Harper & Row, 1987), p. 143. Quoted from *A Memorial and Remonstrance,* by James Madison.
19. Robertson, p. 99.

Chapter 11
Double Standards

1. Stephen K. McDowell and Mark A. Beliles, *America's Providential History* (Virginia: Providence Press, 1988), p. 79.

Chapter 12
Toward a New Constitution

1. John Eidsmoe, *Christianity and the Constitution* (Michigan: Baker Book House, 1987), p. 51-52.
2. Verna M. Hall, *The Christian History of the Constitution of the United States of America* (San Francisco: The Foundation for American Christian Education, 1966), p. 138.
3. Eidsmoe, p. 55.
4. Hall, *The Christian History of the Constitution,* p. 130A.
5. Ibid.
6. Robert K. Dornan and Csaba (Jr.) Vedlik, *Judicial Supremacy: The Supreme Court on Trial* (Massachusetts: Plymouth Rock Foundation, 1986), p. 10.
7. Pat Robertson, *America's Dates With Destiny* (Nashville: Thomas Nelson Publishers, 1986), p. 66. Also cited in Hall, *The Christian History of the Constitution,* p. 141. Quoted from I.W. Blackstone, *Commentaries on the Laws of England* (39; reprint Chicago: University of Chicago, 1979).
8. Hall, *The Christian History of the Constitution,* p. 142-143. Quoted from excerpts from William Blackstone's "Commentaries"--1765, Jones Ed. 1915.
9. Robertson, p. 67. Quoted from I.W. Blackstone, *Commentaries on the Laws of England* (39; reprint Chicago: University of Chicago, 1979).
10. Hall, *The Christian History of the Constitution,* p. 143-144. Quoted from excerpts from William Blackstone's "Commentaries"--1765, Jones Ed. 1915.
11. Eidsmoe, p. 61.

12. Ibid, p. 62.
13. Ibid.
14. Ibid, p. 61.
15. Hall, *The Christian History of the Constitution,* p. 367. Quoted from John Locke, "Of Civil Government," page 94. Also cited in Robertson, p. 66.
16. Eidsmoe, p. 62.
17. Hall, *The Christian History of the Constitution,* p. 130A. Quoted from "The Farmer Refuted," 1775. Also cited in Eidsmoe, p. 65.
18. Eidsmoe, p. 62-63.
19. Ibid, p. 65.
20. Ibid, p. 66-67.
21. Russ Walton, *Biblical Principles of Importance to Godly Christians* (New Hampshire: Plymouth Rock Foundation, 1984), p. 358.
22. Dornan and Vedlik, p. 70-71.
23. Stephen K. McDowell and Mark A. Beliles, *America's Providential History* (Virginia: Providence Press, 1988), p. 156.
24. Dornan and Vedlik, p. 27.
25. The Encyclopedia of Religion, "Relativism," by Richard H. Popkin, Mircea Eliade, Editor in Chief, MacMillan Publishing Co., New York.
26. Dornan and Vedlik, p. 28. Quoted from John Dewey, *The Public and Its Problems* (New York: Henry Holt, 1938), p. 111.
27. Ibid, p. 26.
28. Eidsmoe, p. 394.
29. Dornan and Vedlik, p. 30. Quoted from Oliver Wendell Holmes, Jr., "The Law in Science--Science in Law," in *Collected Legal Papers,* p. 225.
30. Ibid, p. 29-30. Quoted from Oliver Wendell Holmes, Jr. *The Common Law* (Cambridge, Mass.: Harvard University Press, 1963), p. 5.
31. Ibid, p. 31. Quoted from Benjamin Cardozo, *The Growth of the Law* (New Haven: Yale University Press, 1924), p. 49.
32. Eidsmoe, p. 391.
33. Dornan and Vedlik, p. 32. Quoted from Benjamin Cardozo, *The Growth of the Law* (New Haven: Yale University Press, 1924), pp. 133-34.
34. Ibid, p. xi.
35. Gary DeMar, *God and Government: A Biblical and Historical Study,* Atlanta: American Vision Press, © 1982, pg. 141. Quoted from Lawrence Patton McDonald, *We Hold These Truths,* pg. 32.
36. McDowell and Beliles, *America's Providential History,* p. 218.

Chapter 13
Even a Child...

1. John Eidsmoe, *Christianity and the Constitution* (Michigan: Baker Book House, 1987), p. 397.
2. Ibid, p. 398.
3. Stephen K. McDowell and Mark A. Beliles, *America's Providential History* (Virginia: Providence Press, 1988), p. 190. .
4. Tim LaHaye, *Faith of Our Founding Fathers* (Brentwood, Tennessee: Wolgemuth & Hyatt, Publishers, Inc., 1987), p. 123-124. Quoted from *The Debates in the Federal Convention of 1787 Which Framed the Constitution of the United States of America, reported by James Madison,* New York: Oxford University Press, 1920, pp. 181-82, Gallard Hunt and James B. Scott, ed. Also cited in McDowell and Beliles' *America's Providential History,* p. 7, p. 142, and Peter Marshall and David Manuel, *The Light and the Glory* (New Jersey: Fleming H. Revell Co., 1977), p. 343.

300 THE MYTH OF SEPARATION

5. Eidsmoe, p. 360-361.
6. LaHaye, p. 41-42.
7. Gary DeMar, *God and Government: A Biblical and Historical Study* (Atlanta: American Vision Press, 1982), p. 140. Quoted from Harold O.J. Brown, *The Reconstruction of the Republic,* pg. 19.
8. Robert K. Dornan and Csaba (Jr.) Vedlik, *Judicial Supremacy: The Supreme Court on Trial* (Massachusetts: Plymouth Rock Foundation, 1986), p. 27.
9. Ibid, p. 70-71.
10. Pat Robertson, *America's Dates With Destiny* (Nashville: Thomas Nelson Publishers, 1986), p. 93-94. Quoted from John Adams, in *The Works of John Adams, Second President of the United States* collected by Charles Francis Adams, Boston: Little, Brown, 1854. Also cited in Stephen K. McDowell and Mark A Beliles, *Principles for the Reformation of the Nations* (Charlottesville, Virginia: Providence Press, 1988), p. 148; Stephen K. McDowell and Mark A. Beliles, *The Spirit of the Constitution,* Charottesville, Virginia: Providence Press; Eidsmoe, p. 273; and LaHaye p. 194.
11. Robertson, p. 88.
12. LaHaye, p. 48.

Chapter 14
Government of the People, By the People, and For the People...
...The Consent of the Governed...

1. Pat Robertson, *America's Dates With Destiny* (Nashville: Thomas Nelson Publishers, 1986), p. 97.
2. Robert K. Dornan and Csaba (Jr.) Vedlik, *Judicial Supremacy: The Supreme Court on Trial* (Massachusetts: Plymouth Rock Foundation, 1986), p. 15. Quoted from Albert J. Beveridge, *The Life of John Marshall,* 4 vols. (Boston: Houghton Mifflin, 1929), III:120.
3. Peter Marshall and David Manuel, *From Sea to Shining Sea* (New Jersey: Fleming H. Revel Co., 1986), p. 197-198.
4. Dornan and Vedlik, p. 15-16. Quoted from Robert G. McCloskey, *The American Supreme Court* (Chicago: University of Chicago Press, 1960), pg. 4.
5. Verna M. Hall, *The Christian History of the Constitution of the United States of America* (San Francisco: The Foundation for American Christian Education, 1966), p. 136. Quoted from excerpts from Montesquieu's "The Spirit of Law," as published by the Colonial Press, 1900.
6. Robertson, p. 98.
7. Dornan and Vedlik, p. 10.
8. Robertson, p. 99. Quoted from Gaillard Hunt, ed., *The Writings of James Madison,* 9 vols. (New York: G.P. Putnam's Sons, 1900-1910), V: 294.
9. Ibid, p. 99.
10. Dornan and Vedlik, p. 44. Quoted from Arthur Taylor Prescott, ed., *Drafting the Federal Constitution* (Baton Rough: Louisiana State University Press, 1941), July 21.
11. Ibid, p. 44. Quoted from Arthur Taylor Prescott, ed., *Drafting the Federal Constitution* (Baton Rough: Louisiana State University Press, 1941), August 27.
12. Robertson, p. 98.
13. Dornan and Vedlik, p. 49. Quoted from Arthur Taylor Prescott, ed., *Drafting the Federal Constitution* (Baton Rouge: Louisiana State University Press, 1941), July 21.
14. Hall, *The Christian History of the Constitution,* p. 368. Quoted from John Locke, "Of Civil Government," page 93.

15. Marshall and Manuel, *From Sea to Shining Sea*, 199-200. Quoted from Albert J. Beveridge, *The Life of John Marshall* (Boston: Houghton Mifflin, 1919), p. 85.
16. Hall,*The Christian History of the Constitution*, p. 136-137. Quoted from excerpts from Montesquieu's "The Spirit of Law," as published by the Colonial Press, 1900.
17. Dornan and Vedlik, p. 77.
18. Stephen K. McDowell and Mark A. Beliles, *America's Providential History* (Virginia: Providence Press, 1988), p. 189.
19. Edwin S. Gaustad, *Faith of Our Fathers*, San Franscisco: Harper & Row, © 1987, p. 143. Quoted from *A Memorial and Remonstrance*, by James Madison.
20. Hall,*The Christian History of the Constitution*, p. 135. Quoted from excerpts from Montesquieu's "The Spirit of Law," as published by the Colonial Press, 1900.
21. Dornan and Vedlik, p. 69.
22. Hall,*The Christian History of the Constitution*, p. 390. Quoted from Samuel Adams, Boston Gazette, Jan. 20, 1772.

Chapter 15
Judicial Supremacy--The Three Percent Majority

1. Paul C. Vitz, *Censorship: Evidence of Bias in Our Children's Textbooks* (Ann Arbor, Michigan: Servant Books, 1986), p. 87.
2. Robert K. Dornan and Csaba (Jr.) Vedlik, *Judicial Supremacy: The Supreme Court on Trial* (Massachusetts: Plymouth Rock Foundation, 1986), p. 74.
3. Ibid, p. 1-2.
4. Stephen K. McDowell and Mark A. Beliles, *America's Providential History* (Virginia: Providence Press, 1988), p. 218.
5. Dornan and Vedlik, p. 76.
6. Peter Marshall and David Manuel, *From Sea to Shining Sea* (New Jersey: Fleming H. Revel Co., 1986), p. 199. Quoted from Thomas Jefferson, *Writings of Thomas Jefferson*, ed. Andrew A. Lipscomb (Washington, D.C.: Thomas Jefferson Memorial Association, 1903), 10:302.
7. McDowell and Beliles, *America's Providential History*, p. 218.
8. Dornan and Vedlik, p. 4.
9. McDowell and Beliles, *America's Providential History*, p. 218.
10. John Eidsmoe, *Christianity and the Constitution* (Michigan: Baker Book House, 1987), p. 396.
11. Vitz, p. 85. Quoted from Joseph Adelson, "What Happened to the Schools," *Commentary* (March 1981), pp. 36-41.
12. Dornan and Vedlik, p. 3.
13. Ibid, p. 62.
14. Alexis de Tocqueville, *Democracy in America*, J.P. Mayer, ed., George Lawrence, trans. (Garden City, NY: Doubleday & Company, Inc. 1969), p. 151.
15. From an address by Judge Robert H. Bork, April 23, 1988.
16. Dornan and Vedlik, p. 21.
17. Ibid, p. 7.

Chapter 16
When Three Percent Was A Minority

1. Robert K. Dornan and Csaba (Jr.) Vedlik, *Judicial Supremacy: The Supreme Court on Trial* (Massachusetts: Plymouth Rock Foundation, 1986), p. 75.

2. Alexis de Tocqueville, *Democracy in America*, J.P. Mayer, ed., George Lawrence, trans. (Garden City, NY: Doubleday & Company, Inc. 1969), p. 101.
3. Dornan and Vedlik, p. 46. Quoted from Jonathan Elliot, ed., *The Debates in the Several State Conventions on the Adoption of the Federal Constitution,* 5 vols. (New York: Burt Franklin, 1888), IV:382.
4. Ibid, p. 60.
5. Ibid, p. 61-62. Quoted from Edward S. Corwin, *Court Over Constitution: A Study of Judicial Review as an Instrument of Popular Government* (Princeton, N.J.: Princeton University Press, 1914), p. 69-70.
6. Ibid, p. 61.
7. Peter Marshall and David Manuel, *From Sea to Shining Sea* (New Jersey: Fleming H. Revel Co., 1986), p. 201. Quoted from Albert J. Beveridge, *The Life of John Marshall* (Boston: Houghton Mifflin, 1919), p. 185.
8. Dornan and Vedlik, p. 11. Quoted from *The Doctrine of Judicial Review* (Princeton, N.J: Princeton University Press, 1914), pg. 13-14.
9. Marshall and Manuel, *From Sea to Shining Sea*, p. 199-200. Quoted from Albert J. Beveridge, *The Life of John Marshall* (Boston: Houghton Mifflin, 1919), p. 85.
10. Dornan and Vedlik, p. 65. Quoted from Samuel J. Konefsky, *John Marshall and Alexander Hamilton: Architects of the American Constitution* (New York: Macmillan, 1964), pp. 234-235.
11. Ibid, p. 65. Quoted from Edward S. Corwin, *Court Over Constitution: A Study of Judicial Review as an Instrument of Popular Government* (Princeton, N.J.: Princeton University Press, 1914), p. 71, and Charles Grove Haines, *The American Doctrine of Judicial Supremacy* (New York: Da Capo Press, 1973); originally printed by University of California Press, Berkeley, 1932, p. 234.
12. Ibid, p. 46. Quoted from Jonathan Elliot, ed., *The Debates in the Several State Conventions on the Adoption of the Federal Constitution,* 5 vols. (New York: Burt Franklin, 1888), IV:399.
13. Ibid, p. 65-66. Quoted from Charles Grove Haines, *The Conflict Over Judicial Powers in the United States to 1870* (New York: AMS Press, 1970), first printed in 1909 by Columbia University Press, p. 161-162.
14. Ibid, p. 66.
15. Ibid, p. 48. Quoted from Edward S. Corwin, "Curbing the Court," *The Annals of the American Academy of Political and Social Science* 185, May 1936, 51,55.
16. Stephen K. McDowell and Mark A. Beliles, *The Spirit of the Constitution,* Charottesville, Virginia: Providence Press. Also cited in Steve C. Dawson, *God's Providence in America's History,* Rancho Cordova, California: Steve C. Dawson, © 1988, p. 1:13.
17. Dornan and Vedlik, p. 76-77.

Chapter 17
The Potential Downfall of the Republic

1. Verna M. Hall, *The Christian History of the Constitution of the United States of America* (San Francisco: The Foundation for American Christian Education, 1966), p. 411. Also cited in Stephen K. McDowell and Mark A. Beliles, *America's Providential History* (Virginia: Providence Press, 1988), p. 148; Stephen K. McDowell and Mark A Beliles, *Principles for the Reformation of the Nations* (Charlottesville, Virginia: Providence Press, 1988), p. 54; Stephen K. McDowell and Mark A. Beliles, *The Spirit of the Constitution* (Charottesville, Virginia: Providence Press); Steve C. Dawson, *God's Providence in America's History* (Rancho Cordova, California: Steve C.

Dawson, 1988), p. 1:5; and Tim LaHaye, *Faith of Our Founding Fathers* (Brentwood, Tennessee: Wolgemuth & Hyatt, Publishers, Inc., 1987), p. 118--excerpted from Benson J. Lossing's *Washington and the American Republic,* 1870.
2.   Edwin S. Gaustad, *Faith of Our Fathers* (San Franscisco: Harper & Row, 1987), p. 92.   Also cited in Russ Walton, *Biblical Principles of Importance to Godly Christians* (New Hampshire: Plymouth Rock Foundation, 1984), p. 357.
3.   McDowell and Beliles, *Principles for the Reformation of the Nations,* Appendix. Quoted from Verna M. Hall, *Consider and Ponder,* p. 19-21.   Quoted from Preface to the *Holy Bible containing the Old and New Testaments, in the Common Version,* with Amendments of the Language, by Noah Webster, LL.D. New Haven, 1833.
4.   McDowell and Beliles, *America's Providential History,* p. 148.
5.   Verna M. Hall and Rosalie J. Slater, *The Bible and the Constitution of the United States of America* (San Franscisco: THe Foundation for American Christian Education, 1983), p. 22.
6.   Walton, p. 361.   Also cited in McDowell and Beliles, *Principles for the Reformation of the Nations,* p. 102; McDowell and Beliles, *The Spirit of the Constitution;* and McDowell and Beliles, *America's Providential History,* p. 221.
7.   McDowell and Beliles, *America's Providential History,* p. 94.
8.   John Eidsmoe, *Christianity and the Constitution* (Michigan: Baker Book House, 1987), p. 188.   Quoted from Gouverneur Morris' "Notes on the Form of a Constitution for France," probably the same general time as his "Observations on Government, Applicable to the Political State of France, " July 1789.
9.   LaHaye, p. 196.
10.   Alexis de Tocqueville, *Democracy in America,* J.P. Mayer, ed., George Lawrence, trans. (Garden City, NY: Doubleday & Company, Inc. 1969), p. 47.
11.   Peter Marshall and David Manuel, *The Light and the Glory* (New Jersey: Fleming H. Revell Co., 1977), p. 350. Quoted from Charles Roy Keller, *The Second Great Awakening in Connecticut,* New Haven: Yale University Press, © 1942, p. 36.
12.   Noah Webster, *American Dictionary of the English Language, 1828* (San Francisco: Foundation for American Christian Education, 1967), p. 10.
13.   Eidsmoe, p. 124.
14.   McDowell and Beliles, *The Spirit of the Constitution.*   Also cited in McDowell and Beliles, *Principles for the Reformation of the Nations,* p. 54, and McDowell and Beliles, *America's Providential History,* p. 148.
15.   LaHaye, p. 196.
16.   Pat Robertson, *America's Dates With Destiny* (Nashville: Thomas Nelson Publishers, 1986),   p. 93-94. Also cited in McDowell and Beliles, *Principles for the Reformation of the Nations,* p. 54; McDowell and Beliles, *The Spirit of the Constitution;* Dawson, p. 1:6; Eidsmoe, p. 272-273; and LaHaye, p. 194, p. 196. Quoted from John Adams, in *The Works of John Adams, Second President of the United States* collected by Charles Francis Adams (Boston: Little, Brown, 1854).
17.   Dawson, p. I-13, p. 10:5.
18.   Hall and Slater, *The Bible and the Constitution,* p. 17-18.
19.   Robert Flood, *The Rebirth of America,* Philadelphia: The Arthur S. DeMoss Foundation, © 1896, p. 21.
20.   Marshall and Manuel, *The Light and the Glory,* p. 296.
21.   McDowell and Beliles, *America's Providential History,* p. 62.
22.   Eidsmoe, p. 272.
23.   Hall and Slater, *The Bible and the Constitution,* p. 38.
24.   Dr. Sterling Lacy, *Valley of Decision* (Texas: Dayspring Productions, 1988), p. 3.

25. Flood, p. 33.

26. Eidsmoe, p. 293-294. Quoted from John Adams' Diary, February 22, 1756.

27. Hall, *The Christian History of the Constitution*, p. 410. Quoted from Abigail Adams to Mercy Warren, Braintree, November, 1775. Taken from "Warren-Adams Letters," Vol. 1, 1743-1777, Massachusetts Historical Society Collections--72.

28. Dawson, p. 12:3

29. McDowell and Beliles, *The Spirit of the Constitution*. Quoted from an Address by President Ronald Reagan, printed in *The Forerunner*, December 1984.

30. McDowell and Beliles, *America's Providential History*, p. 148.

31. Hall, *The Christian History of the Constitution*, p. 247. Quoted from excerpts from Daniel Webster's "A Discourse delivered at Plymouth, on the 22 of December, 1820 by Daniel Webster," Vol. I, the Works of Daniel Webster, 1851. Also cited in Flood, p. 29.

32. Marshall and Manuel, *The Light and the Glory*, p. 370, Footnote 10.

33. McDowell and Beliles, *America's Providential History,*, p. 207. Also cited in Dawson, p. 7-2.

34. McDowell and Beliles, *America's Providential History*, p. 88. Quoted from Noah Webster, *American Dictionary of the English Language, 1828*, Preface, p. 12.

35. Lacy, p. 7-8.

36. Ibid, p. 6-7.

37. Dawson, p. 5:4.

38. Eidsmoe, p. 230.

39. Dawson, p. 5:4.

40. McDowell and Beliles, *Principles for the Reformation of the Nations*, Appendix. Quoted from Preface to the *Holy Bible containing the Old and New Testaments, in the Common Version,* with Amendments of the Language, by Noah Webster, LL.D. New Haven, 1833.

41. Eidsmoe, p. 239.

42. Ibid.

43. LaHaye, p. 196.

44. Marshall and Manuel, *The Light and the Glory*, p. 350. Quoted from Cushing Stout, *The New Heavens and New Earth*, New York: Harper and Row, © 1974, p. 79.

45. Eidsmoe, p. 409.

Chapter 18
The Solution

1. Stephen K. McDowell and Mark A Beliles, *Principles for the Reformation of the Nations*, Charlottesville, Virginia: Providence Press, © 1988, Appendix. Quoted from Verna M. Hall, *Consider and Ponder*, p. 19-21. Quoted from Preface to the *Holy Bible containing the Old and New Testaments, in the Common Version,* with Amendments of the Language, by Noah Webster, LL.D. New Haven, 1833.

2. Stephen K. McDowell and Mark A. Beliles, *America's Providential History* (Virginia: Providence Press, 1988), p. 190.

3. McDowell and Beliles, *Principles for the Reformation of the Nations,* p. 43.

4. Robert Flood, *The Rebirth of America*, Philadelphia: The Arthur S. DeMoss Foundation, © 1896, p. 32.

5. Peter Marshall and David Manuel, *The Light and the Glory*, New Jersey: Fleming H. Revell Co., 1977, p. 295. Quoted from *The Encyclopedia of Religious*

Quotations, edited by Frank S. Mead, Westwood N.J.: Fleming H. Revell Company, © 1965, p. 265.

6. Pat Robertson, *America's Dates With Destiny,* Nashville: Thomas Nelson Publishers, 1986, p. 72.

7. Dr. Sterling Lacy, *Valley of Decision,* Texas: Dayspring Productions, 1988, p. 8.

8. Flood, p. 37.

9. Steve C. Dawson, *God's Providence in America's History,* Rancho Cordova, California: Steve C. Dawson, 1988, p. 13-1.

10. Robertson, p. 94-95.

11. Alexis de Tocqueville, *Democracy in America,* J.P. Mayer, ed., George Lawrence, trans. Garden City, NY: Doubleday & Company, Inc., 1969, p. 526.

12. Dawson, p. 11-7. Also cited in Flood, p. 12.

13. Gary DeMar, *God and Government: A Biblical and Historical Study,* Atlanta: American Vision Press, © 1982, p. 141. Quoted from Lawrence Patton McDonald, *We Hold These Truths,* pg. 32.

14. de Tocqueville, p. 12.

15. McDowell and Beliles, *America's Providential History,* p. 226.

16. Ibid, p. 206-207.

17. Robert K. Dornan and Csaba (Jr.) Vedlik, *Judicial Supremacy: The Supreme Court on Trial,* Massachusetts: Plymouth Rock Foundation, 1986, p. 7.

18. Ibid, p. 35. Quoted from Samuel J. Konefsky, *John Marshall and Alexander Hamilton: Architects of the American Constitution,* New York: Macmillan, 1964, p. 51.

19. Robertson, p. 95.

20. McDowell and Beliles, *America's Providential History,* p. 79.

21. Dawson, p. 11-8.

22. Tim LaHaye, *Faith of Our Founding Fathers,* Brentwood, Tennessee: Wolgemuth & Hyatt, Publishers, Inc., © 1987, p. 76-77.

23. McDowell and Beliles, *America's Providential History,* p. 225. Also cited in Robertson, p. 144, and Dawson, p. 10:2.

24. Verna M. Hall and Rosalie J. Slater, *The Bible and the Constitution of the United States of America,* San Franscisco: The Foundation for American Christian Education, 1983, p. 29. Also cited in McDowell and Beliles, *America's Providential History,* p. 221-222.

25. Dawson, p. I-8.

26. McDowell and Beliles, *America's Providential History,* p. 220.

27. From an address by Judge Robert H. Bork, April 23, 1988.

28. LaHaye, p. 48.

29. Ibid, p. 201.

Bibliography

American People's Encyclopedia. Chicago: The Spencer Press, Inc., 1953.

Barton, David. *America: To Pray or Not To Pray?* Aledo, Texas: Wallbuilder Press, 1988.

Barton, David. *What Happened In Education?* Aledo, Texas: Wallbuilder Press, 1988.

Bradford, M.E. *A Worthy Company*. Marlborough, NH: Plymouth Rock Foundation, 1982.

Century Edition of the American Digest, 1658 to 1896, St. Paul: West Publishing Co., 1902.

Collier's Encyclopedia. New York: P.F. Collier & Son, 1955.

Dawson, Steve C. *God's Providence in America's History*. Rancho Cordova, California: Steve C. Dawson, 1988.

DeMar, Gary. *God and Government: A Biblical and Historical Study*. Atlanta, Georgia: American Vision Press, 1982.

de Tocqueville, Alexis. *Democracy in America*. J.P. Mayer, ed., George Lawrence, trans. Garden City, NY: Doubleday & Company, Inc., 1969.

Dictionary of American Biography, edited by Dumas Malone, NY: Charles Scribner's Sons.

Dornan, Robert K. and Vedlik, Csaba (Jr.). *Judicial Supremacy: The Supreme Court on Trial*. Plymouth, Massachusetts: Plymouth Rock Foundation, 1986.

Eidsmore, John. *Christianity and the Constitution*. Grand Rapids, Mich.: Baker Book House, 1987.

Flood, Robert. *The Rebirth of America*. Philadelphia, Pennsylvania: The Arthur S. DeMoss Foundation, 1986.

Gaustad, Edwin S. *Faith of Our Fathers*. San Francisco: Harper & Row, 1987.

Hall, Verna M. *The Christian History of the Constitution of the United States of America*. San Francisco: The Foundation for American Christian Education, 1966.

Hall, Verna M. and Slater, Rosalie J. *The Bible and the Constitution of the United States of America*. San Francisco: The Foundation for American Christian Education, 1983.

Hamilton, Alexander and Madison, James and Jay, John. *The Federalist Papers*. New York: New American Library, 1961.

Lacy, Dr. Sterling. *Valley of Decision*. Texarkana, Texas: Dayspring Productions, 1988.

LaHaye, Tim. *Faith of Our Founding Fathers*. Brentwood, Tennessee: Wolgemuth & Hyatt, Publishers, Inc., 1987.

Marshall, Peter and Manuel, David. *From Sea to Shining Sea*. Old Tappan, New Jersey: Fleming H. Revell Co., 1986.

Marshall, Peter and Manuel, David. *The Light and the Glory*. Old Tappan, New Jersey: Fleming H. Revell Co., 1977.

308   THE MYTH OF SEPARATION

McDowell, Stephen K. and Beliles, Mark A.   *America's Providential History.* Charlottesville, Virginia: Providence Press, 1988.

McDowell, Stephen K. and Beliles, Mark A.   *Principles for the Reformation of the Nations.* Charlottesville, Virginia: Providence Press, 1988.

McDowell, Stephen K. and Beliles, Mark A. *The Spirit of the Constitution.* Charlottesville, Virginia: Providence Press.

Robertson, Pat. *America's Dates With Destiny.* Nashville: Thomas Nelson Publishers, 1986.

The World Book Encyclopedia. Chicago: World Book, Inc., 1987.

Vitz, Paul C. *Censorship: Evidence of Bias in Our Children's Textbooks.* Ann Arbor, Michigan: Servant Books, 1986.

Walton, Russ. *Biblical Principles of Importance to Godly Christians.* Marlborough, NH: Plymouth Rock Foundation, 1984.

Webster, Noah. *American Dictionary Of The English Language, 1828.* San Francisco, California: Foundation for American Christian Education, 1967.

Live Presentations to Motivate Your Group

The information in the book *The Myth of Separation* is now available to you at your church, school, civic group, political gathering, etc., in the form of a live slide-lecture presentation.

The presentation uses quotes from the Founding Fathers and from the early Courts to show that separation of church and state was neither designed nor desired by our Founders. It shows how important Christian princples are to the stability and prosperity of the nation, and emphasis, as did Benjamin Franklin, that "He who shall introduce the principles of primitive Christianity into public affairs will change the face of the world." It establishes the need for every individual to get involved in the recovery of our American heritage.

Similar presentations are also available on other topics related to our American heritage. You can make arrangements for one of our qualified speakers to address your group by calling or writing:

WallBuilders INC.

P.O. Box 397
Aledo, Texas 76008

817-441-6044

"You see the distress that we are in...come, let us build the walls that we may no longer be a reproach." Nehemiah 2:17

Educate Americans
About Our Foundations!

Give *Myth of Separation*

To Friends, Relatives, Neighbors,
Politicians, Civic Officials, Lawyers,
School Boards, Educators, and Parents!

Quantity Prices For *Myth of Separation*

1 copy: $7.95 each; 6 copies: $7.15 each; 11 copies: $6.40 each;
21 copies: $4,80 each; 101 copies: $4.40 each.

Other quantity and dealer rates available

• • •

Other Books by David Barton

AMERICA : TO PRAY OR NOT TO PRAY?   *$6.95*

A statistical look at what has happened since 39 million
students were ordered to stop praying in public schools.

WHAT HAPPENED IN EDUCATION?   *$2.95*

Statistical evidence that disproves several popular education
proposals for the decline in SAT scores. This is designed
especially for those in the educational community.

DID TELEVISION CAUSE
THE CHANGES IN YOUTH MORALITY?   *$2.95*

An examination to determine if TV caused the decline that
statistically began in 1963. The results are very enlightening
not only as to what happened in television, but when it
happened, and why.

Add 10% for shipping and handling, $1.00 minimun
Texas residents add 7.5% sales tax

WallBuilder Press
P.O. Box 397
Aledo, Texas 76008

Nehemiah 2:17: "You see the distress that
we are in...come, let us build the walls that
we may no longer be a reproach."

Cut Out and Mail
ORDER FORM
_____

Send me _____ copies of *The Myth of Separation* at _____ per copy.   Total: _____

Add 10% Postage & Handling, $1.00 minimum: _____

Texas residents add 7.5% sales tax: _____

Total enclosed (send check or money order): _____

Name _____

Address _____

City and State _____ Zip _____

WallBuilder Press
P.O. Box 397
Aledo, Texas 76008

Nehemiah 2:17: "You see the distress that we are in...come, let us build the walls that we may no longer be a reproach."